GREAT
EUROPEAN
CHEFS

GREAT EUROPEAN CHEFS

CAROLINE HOBHOUSE

PHOTOGRAPHY: MARTIN BRIGDALE

VNR VAN NOSTRAND REINHOLD
New York

CONVERSIONS OF WEIGHTS AND MEASURES

American Volume

1 pint = 2 cups = 16 fluid ounces
1 cup = 16 tablespoons = 8 fluid ounces
1 tablespoon = 3 teaspoons = ½ fluid ounce

Volume and Mass

1 liter = 1,000 grams = 1 kilogram = 34 fluid ounces
½ liter = 500 grams = 1 demiliter = 17 fluid ounces
¼ liter = 250 grams   8.5 fluid ounces
1 deciliter = 100 grams = 3.5 fluid ounces
1 centiliter = 10 grams = ½ fluid ounce = 2 teaspoons
1 milliliter = 1 gram
1 chopine (old measure) = about ½ pint = about 8 fluid ounces

British Volume

4 gills = 1 U.S. pint
1 pint = about 2½ U.S. cups = about 20 fluid ounces
1 cup = 20.8 U.S. tablespoons = about 10 fluid ounces
1 tablespoon = ⅘ U.S. tablespoon

Spoon and Wineglass Volumes

1 cuillere à bouche, a soupe = about 1 tablespoon = about ½ fluid ounce
1 cuillere à pot = about 1 small ladle = about 2 fluid ounces
1 cuillere à café = about about 1 level teaspoon
1 verre = 2 deciliters = about 7 fluid ounces
1 verre à Bordeaux = 1 deciliter = about 6 tablespoons = about 3 fluid ounces
1 verre à liqueur = 15 milliliters = about 1 tablespoon = about ½ fluid ounce
1 tasse à café = about 10 tablespoons = about 2½ fluid ounces

First published in Great Britain in 1990 by Pyramid Books,
an imprint of Reed International Books.

This edition published in the United States of America
by Van Nostrand Reinhold
115 Fifth Avenue, New York, New York 10003

Introductory Texts © Appleround Limited 1990
Design and Illustrations © Reed International Books Ltd., 1990

Library of Congress Cataloging-in-Publication Data
Hobhouse, Caroline.
    Great European chefs/Caroline Hobhouse.
        p.   cm.
    ISBN 0–442–30387–4:
1. Cookery, European.   2. Cooks–Europe– Biography   I. Title
    TX 723.5.A1H62   1990
    641.594–de20   90-35625
                                          CIP

Picture credits
Gianluigi Morini 164 bottom: Victoria Roque 179: Zefa Picture Library
(UK) Ltd 122-23, 210–211.

Produced by Mandarin Offset – printed in Hong Kong

CONTENTS

FOREWORD

CAROLINE HOBHOUSE

This is an account of eighteen outstanding restaurants in Europe, and of the remarkable men and women who have created them, nearly all of whom are chefs-patrons – either sole or part-owners of their enterprises. Not all have the highest ratings in the guides: they have been chosen for the individuality of their cuisine and for the personality of the chef. Some chefs are partly or entirely self-taught, the others have been through a grinding apprenticeship and promotion through the ranks to the point where they could strike out on their own, with the confidence to take the risks of independence. The self-teaching process can produce disaster as well as star status; long years in menial positions can lead to technical ability and utter mediocrity. Cooks of genius are born, not made.

Only eight of the restaurants are in major cities; the rest range from the comparatively remote, like Ballymaloe House, Les Prés d'Eugénie, and The Peat Inn, to those in small towns, like San Domenico and Schweizer Stuben. None are cheap, but all offer a standard of cooking and service which give more than value for money. Two restaurants from eastern Europe are included, in Budapest and Istanbul.

All the western European chefs in this book are cooking in the post-nouvelle cuisine era, retaining lightness and elegance of presentation, but eschewing the excesses of the movement. All are also working at a time when two important factors have tended to make cooking less regional and more uniform. The first is the development of rapid transportation, largely controlled by middlemen or factors, which allows, for instance, André Jaeger in land-locked Switzerland to offer absolutely fresh lobsters and langoustines from Brittany and even Maine, and ensures a year-round supply of vegetables which were previously seasonal or unobtainable locally but which now wing in from California, Israel or Kenya. Nearly every chef in this book is keenly aware of the need to make the most of their regional produce, whether it be Marc Meneau's seasonal local vegetables or David Wilson's Scottish pigeons, wild mushrooms and truffles. The second is the regulation of the agricultural and horticultural process by the EEC, and the growth of agribusiness at the expense of the small farmer whose expertise was devoted to quality rather than quantity.

Michel Guérard, for one, hopes for the voice of the consumer to be heard more loudly in Brussels and for a revival of interest in small-scale production of really good ingredients.

We are also in a period of polarization between convenience and excellence. On the one hand, there are mass-produced fast-food, frozen food or cook-chill dishes designed for the family in which no one has time to shop selectively and spend hours on preparation, or the restaurants aiming at acceptable low-cost meals; on the other are the luxury establishments where labour and running costs are enormous in proportion to the cost of the ingredients, and the bills are high enough to make a meal a special event for any but the rich or business client.

There is a remarkable *camaraderie* among great chefs. Most have been employed or served *stages* (short secondments for training) in other kitchens, and now exchange their own young cooks to widen their experience. They see each other regularly at meetings of the various chefs' associations, and consult each other about methods and suppliers. The mobility of upcoming young chefs is also greatly increased (together with the temptations and pressures emphasized by Roger Vergé) and a high proportion of the sous-chefs and chefs-de-partie in these restaurants has worked in at least one of the others.

In *Anna Karenina* Tolstoy wrote that 'Happy families are all alike, each unhappy family is unhappy in its own way'. The reverse is true of restaurants. Pretentious, inferior cooking and sloppy service are much the same and equally annoying anywhere, especially when combined with exorbitant prices. Good restaurants share professionalism and the passion for perfect ingredients, but excellence is born of individuality, imaginative innovation and perfect organization. A happy kitchen led by an inspired chef creates an almost telepathic communication between client and waiter, waiter and kitchen. There is a genuine feeling of teamwork, especially when a single dish may be the work of three or more cooks. It is no surprise to find that so many chefs and waiters are football-mad. As one young chef pointed out, football combines discipline and co-ordination with freedom of self-expression – something the best kitchens give their staff.

CAROLINE HOBHOUSE

FRANCE

MICHEL GUÉRARD

MARC MENEAU

DOMINIQUE NAHMIAS

ROGER VERGÉ

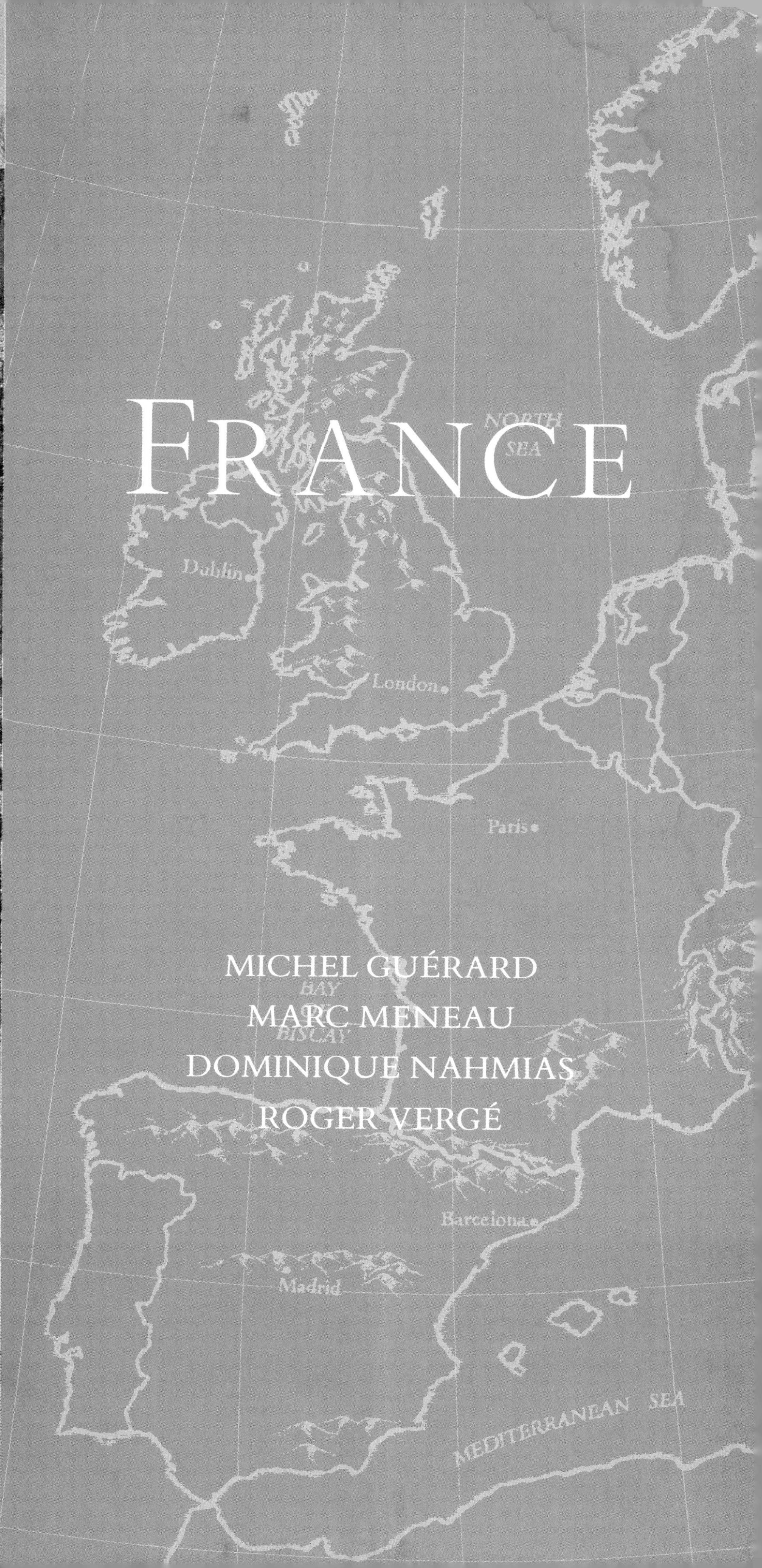

Michel Guérard

Les Prés d'Eugénie

Eugénie-les-Bains

Among the first things one sees of Eugénie-les-Bains is a road sign proclaiming it, quite truthfully, to be *'Ier Village-Minceur de France'*. It was here that Michel Guérard invented, out of boredom with the health-farm food served in his wife Christine Barthélémy's spa hotel, Cuisine Minceur: a low-calorie variation on the nouvelle cuisine for which he was already famous. It became a sensation overnight when it was taken up by the world's press and a surprised, but delighted, Michel Guérard found himself on the cover of *Time* magazine, operating a (then new-fangled) food-processor and crying (rather implausibly) 'Hold the butter!'. A very great deal of nonsense was written about this strictly specialist cuisine; many people confused it with nouvelle cuisine, and even more tried to practise it without either a correct understanding of its principles or the right ingredients. The results were disappointing, or worse. Most of the cooks were amateurs, but chefs and hoteliers who should have known better also climbed on the bandwagon. None of this was Michel Guérard's fault, and although the Minceur menu is still available (only) to the forty per cent of guests who visit Les Prés d'Eugénie for the cure, his reputation rests on his three-star restaurant there and on his magisterial book *Michel Guérard's Cuisine Gourmande*, first published in 1978. Now he is an elder statesman among chefs, no longer the controversial young man who could successfully impersonate the night-club singer Régine at the launch of his own book, or the practical joker who made a whole generation of chefs laugh. Rather, he is a man who has effortlessly maintained his supreme status for nearly a quarter of a century, and who shows no sign of resting on his laurels.

Born at Vétheuil in the Seine-et-Oise in 1933, he trained mainly as a *pâtissier* and worked in a number of kitchens, making friends along the way with other young chefs like Paul Bocuse, the Troisgros brothers and Jean Delaveyne. In 1965, he opened his own small restaurant in the unpromising Paris suburb of Asnières, serving food of such devastating freshness and originality that before long the Pot-au-Feu was the most fashionable place to eat in Paris. No doubt he would presently have been lured away to a luxury restaurant, but the Pot-au-Feu was closed abruptly for a road widening scheme, and in 1972 Michel married Christine Barthélémy, then running the most prestigious of her father's chain of spa hotels. In 1974 he created the restaurant Michel Guérard in her hotel Les Prés et les Sources d'Eugénie, at Eugénie-les-Bains, and since then they have spent the season from March to November in this remote and beautiful part of south-western France. Eugénie, like Asnières, is definitely not a place for a mere detour; in the *Guide Michelin* definition, it justifies the journey.

Les Prés d'Eugénie

Michel and Christine Guérard

Comparing notes before the lunch service

The exquisite decor is inspired by Christine Guérard and is slightly altered every year. Invariably sumptuous and beautiful, it is a subtle blend of modern and antique, with as many objects associated with the Empress Eugénie and her circle – like the family portrait here – as possible.

The main 'piano' or central cooking stove was designed by Christine Guérard. Her extraordinary eye for detail and fineness of taste is responsible for the gleaming brass Empire decoration on the shiny black enamel.

It was not until 1862, when the Empress Eugénie, wife of Napoleon III, discovered the cool and wooded Bahus valley in the Chalosse region of the Landes, that Eugénie-les-Bains was born. It became immensely fashionable and a village quickly sprang up round the hot springs. The white spa buildings and the hotel date in part from this period but have been embellished and modernized both by the Barthélémy family and by the Guérards. The spa interior is a miracle of white and coloured marble, and has two mineral springs – L'Impératrice and Marie-Christine – as well as its therapeutic mud baths. Endearingly, Michel Guérard claims to have the smoothest, most enticing mud in the world since calling in and acting on the advice of a team of Swiss chocolate technicians, as part of the reward for his international consultancy to the Nestlé group. White orchids and lilies are the only flowers, and the patients drift around in spotless robes to the distant sounds of running water and vigorous pummellings. Tactful organization keeps the medical activity of the spa – which takes in patients not just from the few Guérard rooms reserved for their use but also from the dozens of other hotels and guest houses which make up the village – well away from the hotel-restaurant itself.

There, the image is one of unashamed hedonism. Beautiful fabrics, antique furniture and paintings adorn the rooms and suites, all furnished in different colour schemes and equipped with every conceivable luxury. There are endless places to sit and laze in upholstered rattan chairs, or to work off lunch by swimming, playing tennis or even billiards. There are flowers everywhere, on the English chintzes, in huge vases and tiny table posies, and thriving in the gardens. Some romantics have

compared the atmosphere to that of the American South, but this is to do it an injustice. Eugénie is *unique en son genre*.

The taste is Christine's, and every year she changes this or that detail, buys new antiques, creates new perspectives, ensuring that no returning visitor will lack for fresh visual treats. It is a continual process, with some important piece of redecoration taking place during the winter. Even the main 'piano' or central cooking stove in the busy blue-and-white tiled kitchen was made to her own design and is a gleaming rectangle of black enamel and brass Empire decoration. There is a smaller version at the Château de Bachen which she and Michel restored and where they live with their two daughters Eléanore and Adeline.

All this is a reason for lingering for days or weeks at Eugénie, but it is only the frame for the magnificence of the food. If no expense has been spared in the surroundings, still less is spared in the kitchen. The finest produce of every kind flows in from a network of suppliers and is stored and prepared in spacious airy rooms. The eighteen kitchen staff – with among them a sprinkling of *stagiaires*, or cooks from other restaurants all over the world gaining experience – is large and dedicated, under the Luxembourgeois sous-chef Edgar Duhr who replaced Didier Oudill, Guérard's longtime deputy, when he left to start his own promising restaurant down the road in Grenade-sur-l'Adour.

Michel Guérard's cooking is already so well-known through his books, and through media coverage, that it hardly needs further description. Some of his dishes – like Le Homard Rôti et Fumé dans la Cheminée (lobster smoke-grilled over the open fire and served with the simplest of butter sauces), his parsleyed chicken, and truffle ravioli – are standard dishes on the menu, while others rotate with the season, and are supplemented each year by new dishes developed and tested during the previous autumn. The hallmarks are all still there: the lavish use of herbs from the beautifully tended herb garden, the attention paid to presentation, the love with which sauces are combined so that the main ingredient's own flavour shines through. A luncheon guest offered a Carpaccio of paper-thin duck breast '*en habit de fraîcheur*', surrounded by just-cooked vegetables decorated with herbs, followed by a small roast pigeon on a bed of cabbage with a 'millefeuille' of potatoes, and a slice of grilled salmon served with potatoes sautéed in truffle oil, can only look at the Corne d'Abondance with awe. And the service is perfect, both in the quality of the table settings and the unobtrusive efficiency of the waiters. When asked how he thinks cooking in France has developed since 1978 and how it will develop, Michel Guérard says that the Nouvelle Cuisine movement changed the face of French cooking completely, restoring it to its status as the best in the world, and that the stellar group of chefs led by Paul Bocuse – The 'Bande Bocuse' – has been a good act to follow for the young chefs of today. But they have to cope with far greater pressure of media attention and financial stress much earlier in their careers than was the case for chefs of the pre-Bocuse era – and they are not always prepared for it. Yet he is convinced that the best among them are using the principles and experience of the nouvelle cuisine as a springboard to new ways of working with food. He likens the art of cooking to that of the fashion designer, who has a product to sell which must constantly change if the paying customer is not to become bored, and thus

Christine Guérard and her daughters at the Château de Bachen

must sometimes look to the future for inspiration, sometimes to the traditional. 'It seems to me absolutely normal for a creator to look to the past – the kitchen is a timeless place. After all, much of the history of France can be discovered from its cookery books, and the competition between young chefs today is not unlike that of the eighteenth century, when great nobles encouraged their personal chefs to strive for more and more elaborate and subtle dishes with which to enhance their own prestige.'

Although he feels that in general the quality of produce and ingredients has risen and become more reliable, Michel Guérard regrets the disappearance of the small producers who, although they might not always maintain a consistent standard, could reach a perfection which will always be beyond the industrialized producers. 'Heaven send that one day we shall have a new breed of small farmer with the same skill as his forebears.' He also regrets that there has been no 'culinary lobby' in the EEC, and that decisions have been taken by technocrats – rules governing the pasteurization of cheeses and the marketing of poultry for example – who do not concern themselves with quality, but only with economics and rationalized marketing.

What he does not regret is the development of new food technology, in which he has taken a keen interest, advising the Nestlé group in particular, and working with both frozen and cook-chill foods. Many people, some inspired by jealousy, have accused him of abandoning his own high standards and degrading those of others. Michel Guérard's answer would be that society cannot stand still, and that to neglect the chance of improving the food choice and standards of ordinary people by stocking their supermarkets with prepared foods developed and cooked by skilled hands would be an opportunity missed. If working women cannot spend a day at the stove preparing a *daube*, or time on shopping for good ingredients, then they are better off cooking a high-quality frozen dish than resorting to fast-food snacks. Purists might not agree with him, but there are hundreds of busy people who do. And the genuine article, cooked by chefs of genius, will always be there.

A great deal has been written about the use of *sous-vide* – vacuum-packing – both for the storage and maturation of foods such as foie gras, fish and game, and as a means of pre-preparing

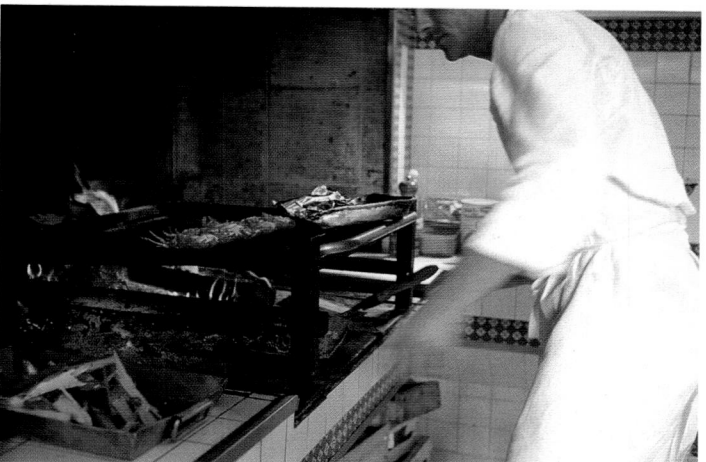
Grilling lobsters on the open hearth

meals for other, less skilled hands to finish. In this latter form it has revolutionized mass catering, producing safe approximations of good cooking at times and in premises where they would otherwise be impossibly difficult and expensive to produce from scratch. Michel Guérard's keen interest in new methods led him to investigate *sous-vide* at an early stage, but, unlike Dieter Müller and André Jaeger, he does not use it for the storage and ripening of fish, meat and game. In his own kitchens he uses it only rarely, and then as a means of efficient cooking at low temperatures – a modern equivalent of the pig's bladder used in the traditional cooking method '*en vessie*', where the ingredient is sealed in with all its flavourings and juices for a long period of time. He makes use of the most modern food processors, ice-cream makers, and hand-held liquidizers to add last-minute foaminess to sauces, but only where they are appropriate. Otherwise, traditional knives and whisks are used, and one of the most important features of his kitchen is the open wood fire over which salmon, lobsters and other fish are cooked on an open grill, with a specialist chef to turn and anoint them.

One day a few years back, Michel Guérard was thinking over his past career and his future. 'It was astonishing. I realized that here I was, a successful cook, and I had never learned to make either bread or wine. The bread was easy; wine was another matter.' In fact, wine and wine-making have become his great passion, and seven hectares round the Château de Bachen have been planted with vines. The first vintage of the 'Baron de Bachen' Tursan white wine will be ready in 1989, just in time for the bicentenary of the French Revolution. He and Christine have enrolled in the *cours d'oenologie* at the University of Bordeaux, and he has already transferred some of the lessons he has learned there about flavour and aroma to the creation of new dishes. He sees his future with his family – never having expected to have children, he now jokes that he is father and grandfather in one – combining his cooking with his wine-making. And he says with his quizzical smile and raised eyebrows, 'I'm not the kind of person to retire and simply go fishing all day: I have too much curiosity about the things of life and what makes them tick.'

The Château's 'miniature' range

La Salade de Homard et de Morue Douce au Confit de Courgettes

Lobster and Cod served with a Courgette 'Confit'

*2 lobsters of 600g (1 lb 5 oz) each, cooked for
8–10 minutes in court-bouillon
300g (10½ oz) cod, marinated in olive oil and
white wine with thyme, bay leaf, rosemary
and garlic
1 tablespoon olive oil
200g (7 oz) peeled and finely chopped onions
a small sprig of thyme
½ teaspoon sugar
3 ripe tomatoes, peeled and seeded
150g (5¼ oz) courgettes, trimmed
chicken stock*

*500 ml (18 fl oz) milk
bay leaf
thyme
3 tablespoons vinaigrette
1 shallot, peeled and chopped very finely
4 attractive lettuce or curly endive leaves
120g (4½ oz) piquant mayonnaise
100g (3½ oz) tapenade
2 tablespoons basil purée
4 tiny bouquets of fresh green herbs
salt
freshly ground pepper*

Heat the oil in a heavy pan and add the chopped onion, with the thyme and sugar. Season with salt and pepper and cook gently until the onion is translucent Cut the tomatoes in thin slices. Score the courgettes with a channelling knife and slice as thinly as possible. Put 2 tablespoons onion into four ramekins. Arrange the tomato and courgette slices in overlapping layers on top, season and add chicken stock to cover. Seal the top of each dish with foil and cook for 5 hours in a 110°C/225°F/Gas ¼ oven. Remove, cool and chill in refrigerator.

Shell the cooked lobsters. Poach the cod in the milk with a bay leaf and thyme for about 3 minutes, according to thickness. Unmould the courgette *tians* on to the centre of four serving plates. Cut the lobster tails into 12 handsome medallions, and slice the cod into 12 thin leaves. Place three lobster medallions on one side of each *tian* and three leaves of cod on the other. Add the shelled claws, sprinkled with vinaigrette and chopped shallot, and lying on a salad leaf. Put a little piquant mayonnaise on each lobster medallion, and a teaspoon of tapenade on each leaf of cod. Brush the *tians* with basil purée and plant a tiny bouquet of herbs in the centre.

FOR FOUR PEOPLE

Banana trees flourish in the warm valley.

Lobster and Cod served with a Courgette 'Confit'

Saumon Grillé à la Peau au Beurre de Verveine et Pointes d'Asperges Vertes

Salmon cooked on an open grill with Lemon Verbena Butter and Green Asparagus Tips

*4 pieces of salmon fillet, weighing about 150 g
(5¼ oz) each, scaled, but with the skin on
8 shelled langoustines or Dublin Bay
prawn tails
3 tablespoons olive oil
24 green asparagus tips, cooked in salted water
4 langoustine shells, to decorate
4 sprigs of lemon verbena*

*Lemon verbena butter
3½ tablespoons wine vinegar
2 generous tablespoons finely chopped shallot
250 g (8¾ oz) unsalted butter, chilled
and diced
1 teaspoon finely chopped lemon verbena
salt and freshly ground pepper*

Make the lemon verbena butter. Bring the vinegar and shallot to the boil with 3½ tablespoons of water over medium heat and reduce for about 6 minutes or until you have barely 2 tablespoons of shallot 'marmelade' left. Lower the heat and whisk in the butter gradually until the mixture becomes creamy. Whisk more vigorously and raise the heat slightly to compensate for the cooling effect of the butter. Season with salt and pepper and add the chopped lemon verbena. Leave to infuse in a bain-marie or double boiler.

Season the salmon pieces all over with salt and pepper and brush with olive oil. Heat the grill rack until it is exceedingly hot, grease it with oil and place the salmon pieces on it, skin side down, diagonally across the bars. After 3 minutes, turn the fish over with a spatula and cook on the other diagonal for a further 3 minutes. Remove and keep warm. Season the langoustine tails, brush them with oil and grill for 1 minute on each side. Warm the asparagus if necessary, and coat four serving plates with the verbena butter. Place a piece of salmon on each plate with 2 grilled langoustines and the asparagus tips arranged in a fan round the langoustine shell. Decorate with verbena.

FOR FOUR PEOPLE

François the Gardener's Duckling with a Parsleyed sauce

Le Caneton Rose du Jardinier François

François the Gardener's Duckling with a Parsleyed sauce

*1 medium size duck – Chalosse for
preference
30 g (1 oz) turned carrots
40 g (1½ oz) turned courgettes
40 g (1½ oz) turned young turnips
2 heads of chicory
40 g (1⅓ oz) unsalted butter
2 tablespoons sherry vinegar
7 tablespoons chicken stock
1 tablespoon Noilly Prat or other dry
vermouth
1 tablespoon dry white wine
200 ml (7 fl oz) whipping cream
1 level tablespoon of parsley purée
salt and pepper*

Cook the turned vegetables separately in boiling salted water until they are just crisp, and refresh under cold running water. Split the chicory in two vertically then slice thinly across. Plunge into boiling water for 1 minute, refresh and squeeze out any surplus moisture. Melt 10 g (⅓ oz) butter in a small pan and sweat the blanched chicory without allowing them to colour. Season with salt and pepper. Pour in the sherry vinegar, cover and cook gently for 6 minutes. Keep hot.

Preheat the oven to 230°C/450°F/Gas 8. Season the duck inside and out and roast, breast-side down, for 10–20 minutes. Leave the cooked duck to rest for 10 minutes in a warm place.

To make the sauce, bring the chicken stock, vermouth and wine to the boil and reduce for 2 minutes. Add the cream and reduce for 3 minutes, then whisk in the remaining butter, diced. Keep hot.

Have ready two hot serving plates. Lift off the two duck breasts and slice them finely. Arrange the cooked chicory in a half-moon round the front of each plate, with the duck slices behind them. Keep hot while you put the turned vegetables into the pan with the sauce to heat through before arranging them round the top of the plates. Mix the parsley purée into the remaining sauce, stir briskly and spoon the sauce round the duck breasts.

FOR TWO PEOPLE

Feuillantine d'Ailes de Cailles 'Truffées' de Cèpes

Quail Wings in Puff Pastry, 'Truffled' with Ceps

*2 quails, marinated for 12 hours in the
following: 7 tablespoons red wine, 200 ml
(7 fl oz) cognac, 1 tablespoon olive oil, 1 carrot
and 1 shallot (both chopped), 1 crushed garlic
clove, 1 juniper berry and a bunch of
fresh herbs
120 g (4½ oz) chicken livers
40 g (1½ oz) lard
80 g (2¾ oz) shallots, peeled and
finely sliced
120 g (4½ oz) ceps, very
finely chopped
160 g (5½ oz) button mushrooms, very
finely chopped
½ teaspoon lemon juice
150 ml (¼ pint) cognac
200 ml (7 fl oz) whipping cream
350 g (12⅓ oz) puff pastry dough
80 g (2¾ oz) foie gras
500 g (1 lb) evenly sized potatoes, cooked in
their skins
100 g (3½ oz) butter
salt and pepper*

Sauce
*75 g (2⅔ oz) each carrot and onion, coarsely
chopped
150 g (5⅓ oz) unsalted butter
10 g (⅓ oz) black peppercorns
1 bouquet garni
7 tablespoons red wine vinegar
50 ml (2 fl oz) cognac
7 tablespoons red wine (preferably Tursan
from the Landes)*

Remove the wings and legs from the marinated quails (use the breasts for another purpose – in a warm salad, for example – and the carcases for making stock). Bone the wings. Do not bone the legs.

Prepare the stuffing. Chop the chicken livers and cook them in a frying pan over a low heat with the lard and chopped shallots. When the shallots are softened, add the chopped ceps and mushrooms and moisten with a little lemon juice. When everything is nicely browned, deglaze the pan with the cognac, season with salt and pepper and add the cream. Heat through and then set aside to allow to cool.

Preheat the oven to 190–200°C/375–400°F/Gas 5–6. Roll out the puff pastry dough paper-thin and cut out four rounds 12 cm (4¾ inch) in diameter. Put a spoonful of the cooled (but not chilled) stuffing in the centre of each, then a boned quail wing and a leg, of which the bone will protrude from the pastry. Divide the foie gras between the rounds, and top with a little more stuffing. Fold the pastry over to form a semicircle and pinch the edges tightly together. Transfer to a baking sheet and cook in the preheated oven for 8–10 minutes according to the size of the quail.

Meanwhile prepare the sauce. Brown the coarsely chopped carrot and onion in 50 g (1⅔ oz) butter with the peppercorns and the bouquet garni. After 5 minutes, add the vinegar and cognac and reduce until the mixture is almost dry. Add the red wine and reduce by a third. Strain the sauce into a clean pan and whisk in the remaining butter, diced. Taste for salt and pepper, and if necessary sharpen with a few drops more wine vinegar.

Cut the cooked, unpeeled potatoes into 2 cm (¾ inch) thick discs. Heat 100 g (3½ oz) butter in a sauté pan, and fry the slices for about 2 minutes on each side.

To serve, pour the wine sauce on to two heated plates, place the quail feuillantines in the centre and place a pile of fried potatoes on one side of each plate.

FOR FOUR PEOPLE

Last minute preparation

Millefeuille à la Crème Legère

Millefeuille with a Light Cream

360 g (12²⁄₃ oz) puff pastry dough
250 g (9 oz) crème pâtissière, made with the following:
250 ml (8 fl oz) full-cream milk
a piece of vanilla pod, split lengthwise
75 g (2²⁄₃ oz) sugar
3 egg yolks
10 g (¹⁄₃ oz) plain flour
10 g (¹⁄₃ oz) cornflour
40 g (1¹⁄₃ oz) icing sugar
80 g (3 oz) chilled whipping cream

Preheat the oven to 220°C/425°F/Gas 7. Roll out the puff pastry dough until you have an oblong sheet 20 × 45 cm (8 × 18 inches), and paper thin. Cut the dough into three equal strips and place on a very lightly greased baking sheet. Prick all over with a fork to prevent the pastry rising too much. Bake for about 20 minutes, then place on a rack and allow to cool completely. The crust should be a nice light brown colour.

To prepare the *crème pâtissière*, boil the milk with the vanilla and a third of the sugar. Beat the remaining sugar in a bowl with the egg yolks until they are pale. Whip in the flour and cornflour gradually.

Remove the vanilla pod and pour half the boiling milk on to the egg mixture, whipping constantly. Pour this mixture back into the remaining milk in the pan. Raise the heat and stir for a minute without boiling, making sure the mixture does not 'catch' on the bottom of the pan. Pour into a cold bowl and whip until cool, incorporating as much air as possible as you do so.

Add 10 g (¹⁄₃ oz) icing sugar to the well chilled whipping cream. Whip gently for 1 minute to incorporate air and then briskly for 5 minutes, or until the cream forms stiff peaks. Fold the whipped cream into the *crème pâtissière* with a wooden spatula. Using a metal spatula, spread half the cream on to one of the strips of cooked pastry. Cover with a second strip and the rest of the cream, and top with the last strip of pastry, smooth golden side up. Dredge with a thick, even layer of icing sugar. Serve the millefeuille on a rectangular plate and slice it at the table, perhaps with a few fresh berries in a fruit purée or poached pear slices in a light caramel sauce.

FOR FOUR PEOPLE

La Corne d'Abondance aux Fruits Glacés

A Cornucopia with Iced Fruits

350 g (12¹⁄₂ oz) puff pastry dough
flour for the pastry board
60 g (2 oz) icing sugar
4 tablespoons crème Chantilly (sweetened whipped cream)
300 g (10¹⁄₂ oz) raspberry purée
1 kiwi, peeled, cut in four, then into fan shapes
4 slices of mango, cut in fan shapes
1 pear, cored and cut in four, then into fan shapes
250 g (8³⁄₄ oz) fresh raspberries
1 small bunch of grapes, divided into four equal portions and peeled
fresh mint leaves
fresh lemon verbena leaves
250 ml (8 fl oz) pistachio ice-cream

Preheat the oven to 220°C/425°F/Gas 7, and have ready 4 metal cornet moulds 5 cm (2 inches) in diameter, lightly buttered on the outside. Flour the working surface, and roll out the dough to a rectangle 12 × 40 cm (4³⁄₄ × 15³⁄₄ inches) and 2 mm (¹⁄₈ inch) thick. Using a sharp knife, cut out four strips 3 × 40 cm (1¹⁄₄ × 15³⁄₄ inches). Starting at the tip, wrap each strip in a spiral round a buttered mould. Turn the edges of the pastry over the lip of the moulds. Sprinkle the pastry lavishly with icing sugar, place on an oiled baking sheet and bake in the preheated oven for about 20 minutes. The cornets should be puffed up and an attractive golden colour. Place them on a rack to cool completely.

To serve, cut through the pastry just below the outer rim of the moulds and slip the cornets off. Fill each cornet with a tablespoon of crème Chantilly and place it facing inwards from the top of the serving plate. Make a pool of raspberry purée over the rest of the plate, and arrange the fans of kiwi, mango and pear, the whole raspberries and the grapes on top of the purée. Spike with mint and lemon verbena. Place a scoop of ice-cream in the opening of each cornet.

Note: the fruits and purée should be thoroughly chilled before serving.

FOR FOUR PEOPLE

A Cornucopia with Iced Fruits

Marc Meneau

L'Espérance

Vézelay

Marc Meneau was born in 1944, less than a hundred yards from his now celebrated restaurant in Saint-Père-sous-Vézelay, in the house (now a newsagent) where his parents had a small bar-restaurant. His father died when he was a small child, but his mother still helps in the restaurant, where she makes chocolates and a variety of other items. He is unique among all the chefs featured in this book in that, apart from a period spent studying hotel management in Strasbourg, and the time taken to complete his military service (a compulsory absence), he has never moved from his home region or, indeed, home village. He married Françoise, the daughter of local restaurant owners, in 1966 and they took over the family bistro for three years before opening L'Espérance.

He has never been tempted, despite his success and international reputation, to accept lucrative offers to lend his name to restaurants overseas or to accept contracts from manufacturers in return for sponsoring their goods. 'I have no wish to run around the world. It's not my philosophy.' True, he has a shop selling Meneau wines and china in L'Espérance itself, and has published a book, *La Cuisine en Fêtes*, and true, he has helped devise menus for French astronauts, but that is the extent of his public exposure outside L'Espérance itself. He is, as he says with evident pride, rooted in the area surrounding the 'holy hill'

of Vézelay, crowned with perhaps the most beautiful church in France. He and his wife and their adopted son Pierre now live in Vézelay itself, in a comfortable prosperous burgher's house immediately north of the basilica, with spectacular views across Burgundy and Morvan. To the south of the hill he has, in co-operation with others, reclaimed a whole stretch of derelict vineyard and replanted it, mainly with Chardonnay grapes, and it seems likely that these will provide some notable wines in the future.

Saint-Père-sous-Vézelay crouches at the foot of the holy hill, and is a basically agricultural village full of the sounds of chickens and other livestock, with a rather battered Gothic church, a *charcuterie* through the kitchen window of which can be seen strings of *saucissons* hanging from the ceiling, and the various craft and other enterprises which inevitably spring up round a tourist attraction such as L'Espérance. For indeed, this has become an essential stop for the serious gastronomic traveller, especially now that the Meneaus have added additional rooms in a charming converted mill in the village. Visitors come with high expectations – who wouldn't, to a restaurant called 'The Good Hope' and lauded in every guide book as one of the best in

The conservatory-dining room

Marc Meneau in the garden at L'Espérance

France? – and they are not disappointed. The food is of such Burgundian richness that several days of strict fasting both before and after would probably be appropriate for most people without iron digestions.

The best known speciality of the house is the *cromesquis de foie gras*. These are cubes of chilled *foie gras* breaded and deep fried. They are presented in a napkin, with a stern injunction from the waiter that they must be eaten in one bite, as the hot *foie gras* is liquid. They explode in the mouth like magic and are the nearest thing to culinary perfection that can be imagined – and tricky to make, according to the young American girl trainee chef one of whose jobs it is to prepare them. And these *cromesquis* are merely an *amuse-gueule*, an appetizer. After them will follow, on a typical menu, oysters in a sea-water jelly, a millefeuille of *foie gras*, Parma ham and truffle, a chicken roasted on the spit and then fried in boiling oil, or any number of other rich dishes, followed by a variety of puddings, many of them chocolate-based, and a tray of petits fours.

Not everything is rich. The Assiette de Modestie (Lambs' Brains with Sweetcorn Pancakes, Beef marrow and Onion Purée, see page 31) was deliberately – almost mischievously – introduced as a contrast, and has successfully shown that simple ingredients, simply cooked, can make an interesting and unusual addition to a menu. There is also a delicious vegetable consommé made of tiny cubed vegetables, slow-cooked in a glass preserving jar at the back of the stove and strained into a soup bowl with a few of the same vegetables, freshly steamed.

Marc Meneau is a very private man, whose spare time is spent in his remarkable library of antiquarian books, but his public persona is ebullient and irrepressible. In the sparkling modern kitchen, which he redesigned in 1986 as a model of practicality and efficient use of space, he commands his staff through a loudspeaker, reading out the orders as they come through from his wife or his maître d'hôtel, checking each plate and dish as it leaves the kitchen, and making a constant stream of jokes. This does not conceal (or adversely affect) the extraordinary precision with which everything works, but the pleasure which his unusual approach gives is obvious. His staff, male and female, do not wear the traditional tall toques, but the flatter baker's boy white caps. This is a deliberate policy on Meneau's part: he explains that the cooks can express their moods and personalities by changing the angle of their caps and, indeed, it is obvious who is feeling good and who depressed or defiant.

Marc Meneau himself is almost entirely self-taught, and never served a formal chef's apprenticeship. As a young man, however, he spent much time reading culinary literature and long hours talking to Alex Humbert, the celebrated retired chef of the almost legendary Maxim's, who passed on to him the knowledge acquired through a lifetime's cooking. He was also strongly inspired by the three great books by Eduard Mignon, published at the beginning of the twentieth century. 'People don't get pleasure simply from the palate, they get it from their memories.' For this reason, although modern transport makes it relatively simple to obtain out-of-season or exotic produce, he prefers to use local seasonal fruit and vegetables which, in his hands, are far from dull or mundane. 'If it is cabbage-time, I use plenty of cabbages. The art lies in showing people that

The kitchen staff at L'Espérance do not wear the traditional chef's toque, but flatter, baker's-boy caps. Marc Meneau believes that the cooks can express their personalities – and their moods - by the way they wear their hats and the angles at which they tilt them. This typifies the warm relationshp that exists between him and his staff. A similar rapport exists between Françoise Meneau and the waiting staff.

L'Espérance is the most elegant house in Vézelay, built of honey-coloured stone and with shuttered windows. It is seen here in night-time floodlighting from the 'English' garden.

an apple, properly treated, is superior to a kiwi. I know and care little about the new technology, except for one *sous-vide* machine which I keep for the experiments on food for astronauts.' In his kitchen, in spite of its modernity, mixers and blenders are used very sparingly because he feels they tend to make all sauces look and taste the same.

His staff all clearly hold him in the highest esteem, not only for his skills but also because he notices their moods – hence the caps – and listens carefully to what they have to say. In particular, the waiters are encouraged to report the customers' comments (favourable and unfavourable), to explain why someone has not finished his helping or – when someone has been especially critical or, more usually, appreciative – to relay their comments in detail to the kitchen. This process of two-way communication results in a constantly creative atmosphere; new dishes are experimented with almost daily and the constantly changing menu represents not just the season's produce, but Marc Meneau's own current preoccupations and the ideas his

cooks are encouraged to develop. This makes the waiters' task extra difficult because they have to learn to to present and explain a new dish to the customers every day.

Produce in so rich an area as Burgundy (though Vézelay itself lies in the Morvan, which has a reputation for infertility) is hardly a problem. In addition the great wholesale markets of Rungis and Lyons and the poultry breeding centres of the Bresse are only a few autoroute hours away to the south. The Loire produces salmon and, to the west, exceedingly efficient Breton distributors supply oysters and a range of other seafood. Vegetables are locally grown, wherever possible, and the Meneaus are creating a *jardin potager* which will eventually be a cornucopia of salad plants and herbs.

L'Espérance itself is the grandest house in the village, a honey-coloured stone building with shuttered windows, set back behind a courtyard shaded with trees, and floodlit at night. At the back, overlooking a garden full of fruit trees, with an alley of pollarded limes, a conservatory has been constructed to hold the main dining room and bar. It is full of elegance and light, with charming touches like the ornamental cabbages used for table decorations. This is Françoise Meneau's empire and it is run with almost telepathic communication between herself and Patrice Martin, the young head waiter, whose sympathy with his métier matches that of the chef. Of the sixty places – all booked weeks ahead in season – roughly half are occupied by foreign tourists, but businessmen and weekenders from Dijon, Lyon and Paris also visit regularly.

Of course, L'Espérance gains from its position under the holy hill and close to the main routes south to the Midi and Italy, but the quality of the food and the sheer exuberance of the place completely justify its Michelin three stars – meaning that it is *'vaut le voyage'*.

Oysters in Sea-Water Jelly with Watercress

Huîtres en Gelée

Oysters in Sea-Water Jelly with Watercress

30 absolutely fresh oysters,
No 3 'specials' for preference
½ leaf of gelatine, or powdered gelatine
(see method)
30–40 g (1–1½ oz) shallots,
peeled and chopped
50 g (1¾ oz) butter
150 ml (¼ pint) single cream
juice of ¼ lemon
a bunch of watercress, about 280 g (10 oz),
washed and stalked
salt and freshly ground pepper

Check that you have enough ice, cubed or ready cracked, to serve the oysters on. Open the oysters over a bowl so that you lose none of their juices. Remove the oysters from their shells and lay them on a clean cloth.

Heat the oyster juices to 40°C/104°F (just over blood heat), while you soak the leaf gelatine in cold water. When it is soft, squeeze out excess moisture and stir very gently into the warmed juices until it dissolves. (If you are using powdered gelatine, measure the volume of oyster juices, then follow the instructions on the packet for setting to a light jelly.) Cool in the refrigerator.

Take six of the oysters and chop them finely. Sweat the chopped shallots in the butter and then cool. Mix the chopped oysters, cooled shallots, single cream and lemon juice in a bowl and season with pepper. Set aside to chill in the refrigerator.

Wash 24 of the concave shells and scrub them with a stiff brush. Wipe dry and put a teaspoon of the oyster cream in each shell. Put a whole oyster on top, give it a brisk grinding of pepper, and cover with watercress leaves. The jelly should by now be just set to a wobbly consistency (certainly not hard or chewy): if it is too liquid put it in a bowl of cracked ice. Spoon the jelly over the top of the watercress leaves, and if you are not serving the oysters for half an hour or so, return to the refrigerator.

Present on a dish or individual plates on a bed of cracked ice.

FOR FOUR PEOPLE

Saumon de la Loire Braisé au Champagne

Loire Salmon with a Champagne Butter Sauce

800 g (1¾ lb) fillet of salmon, in one piece
10 g (⅓ oz) unsalted butter
7 tablespoons concentrated fish stock
7 tablespoons champagne
200 g (7 oz) small leeks, washed and trimmed
salt and pepper

Sauce
3½ tablespoons juice from a roast of meat
7 tablespoons whipping cream
7 tablespoons single cream
2 tablespoons champagne
juice of ¼ lemon
fine salt and freshly milled pepper

Preheat the oven to 160°C/325°F/Gas 3. Butter a roasting pan lightly and place the seasoned piece of fish on it. Sprinkle with the fish stock and champagne and bring to a simmer over a low flame. Transfer to the oven and cook for 10–12 minutes, turning it once. Remove and drain the salmon, keeping all the juices separately in a bowl. Place the salmon on a dish to rest in a warm place, covered with a sheet of foil to keep warm.

Cook the leeks in a pan of boiling salted water for about 8–10 minutes. When you can push in the point of a knife easily, they are cooked. Remove, drain and keep hot.

Meanwhile, make the sauce. Reduce the meat juice and salmon cooking juices together in a pan, until you have one third of the original quantity. Add the whipping cream and reduce until the sauce will coat the back of a spoon. Immediately add the single cream and champagne and bring to the boil, whisking all the time. Remove from the heat and season with lemon juice, salt and pepper. Keep warm.

To serve, remove the skin from the salmon and place it on a heated dish with the little leeks round it. Pour a little of the sauce over the fish and serve the rest in a sauceboat.

Note: Marc Meneau often uses the defatted juices which have run out of a roast of beef or veal or a roast chicken to enrich his sauces, rather than the traditional meat glazes, which he feels can make everything taste the same, with a palate-jading result.

FOR FOUR PEOPLE

Loire Salmon with a Champagne Butter Sauce

Omelette Soufflé au Jus de Viande

Soufflé Omelette with Savoury Meat Sauce

10 eggs
7 tablespoons cream
7 tablespoons cold water
50 g (1¾ oz) unsalted butter, softened
150 ml (¼ pint) juice from a roast of veal or chicken
3½ tablespoons arachide oil
salt and pepper

Preheat the oven to 150°C/300°F/Gas 2. Break 5 eggs into a bowl and add the yolks of the rest. Whisk in the cream, water, butter, and seasoning. Whip the egg whites and fold into the mixture.

Put the meat juices to heat in a small pan; taste for seasoning. Heat the oil in a large sauté pan with an ovenproof handle. Pour in the omelette mixture and place in the oven for 3–4 minutes until the top and bottom of the omelette are browned. Do not turn the omelette. When the omelette feels cooked (press it with the tip of a finger), turn out on to a heated serving plate and pour round the hot meat juice.

FOR FOUR PEOPLE

Vol-au-Vent à l'Ancienne

Sweetbreads and Foie Gras in a Pastry Case

100 g (3½ oz) chicken breast meat
135 ml (4¼ fl oz) double cream
250 g (9 oz) puff pastry dough
1 egg yolk, beaten
200 g (7 oz) sweetbreads,
blanched and trimmed
unsalted butter for frying
200 g (7 oz) raw fresh duck foie gras
salt and pepper

Sauce
6–7 tablespoons port
1 shallot, peeled and chopped
300 ml (½ pint) single cream
juice of ½ a lemon
40 g (1½ oz) sliced truffles

Several hours in advance, prepare the quenelles. Process the chicken breast meat and add a quarter of the cream. Push the mixture through a very fine tamis or sieve and refrigerate for 20 minutes. Add the next quarter of cream, mix again and refrigerate for 20 minutes. Repeat two more times. Season with salt and pepper as needed. When the mixture is finally ready, use two wet teaspoons to mould it in little quenelles. Arrange them on a lightly oiled baking sheet.

Preheat the oven to 200°C/400°F/Gas 6. Roll out the puff pastry dough to 3 mm (⅛ inch) thick, and cut out two circles 20 cm (8 inches) in diameter. Scrunch up a sheet of aluminium foil until you have a reasonably firm ball the size of a tennis ball. Place it in the centre of one of the pastry circles. Brush the edge of the circle with beaten egg yolk and cover with the second round of pastry. Press the edges of the two circles together, and brush the whole vol-au-vent with beaten egg yolk. Bake in the preheated oven for 20 minutes. When it is cooked, remove to a rack and cut round with a sharp knife to separate the lid from the base. Discard the aluminium foil, and any pastry which has not completely cooked in the interior.

Heat the port in a small pan and sweat the chopped shallot until the liquid has all but evaporated. Add the single cream and reduce by a third. Season with salt and pepper and finish with lemon juice. Strain into a warmed sauceboat, stir in half the

truffle slices to infuse in the sauce, set aside and keep hot.

Cook the little chicken quenelles for 5–6 minutes in the hot oven, and brown the sweetbreads in a little butter until they are crusty outside and melting inside – about 12 minutes. Cut the foie gras in 1.5 cm (½ inch) slices and fry for 2–3 minutes. Drain the sweetbreads and foie gras on kitchen paper and pat dry.

Arrange the sweetbreads, foie gras, chicken quenelles and remaining truffle slices in the vol-au-vent case. Replace the pastry lid and serve hot, with the sauce in a sauceboat.

FOR FOUR PEOPLE

Brochette de Polenta au Foie Gras

Fois Gras with Skewered Polenta

250 g (8¾ oz) fresh foie gras
7 tablespoons de-fatted juice from a roast
3½ tablespoons truffle juice (from the tin)
10 g (⅓ oz) unsalted butter
fine salt and freshly ground pepper

Polenta (12 hours in advance)
250 ml (8 fl oz) full-cream milk
65 g (2⅓ oz) fine corn meal
20 g (⅔ oz) grated parmesan
20 g (⅔ oz) black truffle,
very finely chopped
1 egg yolk

Make the polenta at least 12 hours in advance. Heat the milk in a heavy pan. As

Sweetbreads and Foie Gras in a Pastry Case

soon as it boils, trickle the corn meal through your fingers into the pan in a steady stream, stirring all the time. Lower the heat and continue to stir for 10 minutes. Remove from the heat and add the grated parmesan and truffle and then the egg yolk, stirring vigorously all the time. Taste for seasoning, and pour out to a depth of 2 cm (¾ inch) on a lightly buttered tray. Cool in the refrigerator.

Cut the foie gras in 2 cm (¾ inch) square cubes, and season with salt and pepper. Cut the polenta in cubes of the same size. Impale them alternately on four skewers.

Heat the meat juice over a medium flame and reduce by half. Add the truffle juice and the butter, allow to boil for a second and, off the heat, taste for seasoning. Keep warm.

Brown the brochettes for 2 minutes on each side, using a non-stick frying pan over a medium heat. Put one on each hot plate with a thin trickle of sauce on either side. Serve very hot.

FOR FOUR PEOPLE

Assiette de Modestie

Assiette de Modestie

Lambs' Brains with Sweetcorn Pancakes, Beef Marrow and Onion Purée

2 sets of lambs' brains, pre-soaked in cold water and trimmed
400 g (14 oz) beef marrow, pre-soaked in cold water for 24 hours
8 small heads of celery
50 g (1¾ oz) unsalted butter
400 ml (¾ pint) strong chicken stock
a little flour
unsalted butter for frying
coarse salt and freshly ground pepper

Sweetcorn pancakes
170 g (6 oz) sweetcorn kernels, cooked or tinned
60 g (2 oz) plain flour, sifted
1 egg and 1 egg yolk
250 ml (8 fl oz) single cream
2 tablespoons milk
a pinch of nutmeg
salt and freshly ground pepper

Onion purée
500 g (1 lb 2 oz) new season's (white) onions, peeled and coarsely chopped
200 g (7 oz) unsalted butter
6–7 tablespoons crème fraîche

Liquidize two-thirds of the sweetcorn kernels to a smooth purée. Beat the flour and eggs in a bowl and, still beating, add the cream and milk. There should be no lumps. Beat in the sweetcorn purée and then fold in the remaining kernels very gently with a wooden spatula. Season with nutmeg, salt and pepper. Keep this batter cold in an airtight container.

Twelve hours in advance, butter an ovenproof dish. Pack in the onions, dividing the butter between the layers. Place the dish in a roasting pan half-full of water and cook in the lowest possible oven for 12 hours. Remove from the oven and allow to cool. Liquidize the onions, and stir in the *crème fraîche*. Just before serving, push the purée through a fine sieve.

Poach the beef marrow for 15 minutes in barely simmering salted water.

Wash and trim the celery heads, reserving the outer stalks for stock. Season the hearts and soften with the butter in a small sauté pan on a low heat. Add enough stock to cover the celery and braise, covered, for 2 hours on a low heat.

Blanch the soaked and trimmed brains for four minutes in boiling salted water.

To assemble the *assiettes*, first make four sweetcorn pancakes 5 cm (2 inches) across and 1 cm (½ inch) thick, in the usual way, and keep warm. Cut the blanched brains in half lengthwise, flour lightly, and fry in butter. Warm through the onion purée and the beef marrow separately. Cut the celery hearts in half lengthwise and slice the beef marrow into 2.5 cm (1 inch) pieces. Make a pool of onion purée in the middle of four hot plates. Arrange the other ingredients round the edge of each plate as follows: four slices of marrow with grains of coarse salt on top of each, a piece of brain, two half celery hearts, a pancake, then two more half celery hearts and another piece of brain.

Note: this delicate and delicious dish can be prepared well in advance and assembled quickly at the last moment.

FOR FOUR PEOPLE

Poulet Goret Cuit à la Broche

Chicken Cooked like Suckling Pig

1 Bresse chicken weighing 2 kg (4 lb 6 oz)
150 g (5¼ oz) unsalted butter
a large thin sheet of pork back fat
10 g (⅓ oz) coarse salt
black pepper
4 litres (7 pints) arachide (or, better,
grapeseed) oil
a few sprigs of parsley

Rub the chicken all over with coarse salt and throw some into the cavity, with a few good grindings of pepper. Wrap the bird with the sheet of fat and secure with thread so that it does not fall off during cooking. Impale the bird lengthwise on the spit of a preheated rôtisserie, and roast for 35 minutes. Place a pan underneath the bird to catch the juices and use them to baste it frequently while it cooks. Meanwhile bring the oil to the boil in a heavy-bottomed saucepan.

Remove the chicken from the spit and keep the sheet of fat and the cooking juices carefully on one side. Using a wooden-handled metal fork with long tines, plunge the chicken into the boiling oil for 7–8 minutes. The skin of the chicken will brown and blister.

Carve the chicken on a board, dip the parsley sprigs briefly in the hot oil to crisp them, and cut up the pork bard into morsels. Arrange on a hot serving dish, and serve the cooking juices separately.

Note: as you can see from the photograph, this is a spectacular dish to prepare. It is also noisy, and the large quantity of very hot oil makes it potentially hazardous. Take great care that the oil does not catch fire from a neighbouring gas flame or spill on a hot plate. Also make sure that the oil is perfectly clear.

FOR FOUR PEOPLE

Impaling the chicken

Basting during roasting

Cooking in the oil is a hazardous business.

Gelée de Fruit Rouges

Red Fruit Jelly

1 kg (2¼ lb) red fruits
(strawberries or raspberries)
200 g (7 oz) caster sugar
4 leaves of gelatine
finely grated rind of 1 lime

Pick over and hull the fruit. Cut in quarters and sprinkle with the sugar, turning gently. Add 500 ml (18 fl oz) water and leave to macerate for 2 hours. Transfer the fruit to a muslin-lined colander and catch the juices in a bowl.

Soften the gelatine in a little water and squeeze dry, then add to the juices, (or if using powdered gelatine follow the instructions on the packet, having measured the juices). Stir until thoroughly dissolved and mix in the lime rind just as it begins to set. Divide between four chilled shallow dessert plates and put in the refrigerator. When the jelly has set, decorate with the fruit and serve.

FOR FOUR PEOPLE

A variation of Red Fruit Jelly

Glace Vanille Surprise et Gâteau Nivernais

Vanilla Surprise Ice-Cream with Redcurrant Spongecake

Vanilla Surprise Ice-Cream
750 ml (1¼ pints) full-cream milk
3 vanilla beans
12 egg yolks
150 g (5¼ oz) caster sugar

Soufflé mixture
2 eggs, separated
50 g (1¾ oz) caster sugar

Bring the milk and vanilla to the boil, stirring occasionally. Meanwhile whisk the egg yolks and sugar vigorously in a bowl. Remove the vanilla from the milk, then whisk into the egg yolks. Pour into a clean pan and cook very gently until the mixture has thickened. Test by dipping a spatula into the mixture and then running your finger across it. If the indentation in the cream remains, the mixture is ready to sieve and set aside to cool.

When the mixture is cool, make the ice-cream in a sorbetière or by whatever other method you normally use. It should be soft, not hard.

Spoon the ice-cream into a ring mould approximately 16 cm (6½ inches) in diameter and 4 cm (1½ inches) deep. Place in the freezer while you make the soufflé mixture.

Whisk the egg yolks with 50 g (1¾ oz) sugar in a metal or glass bowl over hot water. Work quickly, to achieve a frothy consistency without curdling the egg. Let it cool off the heat, continuing to whisk. Preheat the grill. Whisk the egg whites to a snow and add to the cooled yolks. Unmould the ice-cream on a baking sheet and entirely cover it with the soufflé mixture. Place under the grill until the meringue has turned golden brown, slide on to a dessert plate and serve immediately. Serve with a slice of Gâteau Nivernais, which you can make in advance.

Gâteau Nivernais
4 eggs, separated
70 g (2⅔ oz) caster sugar
35 g (1¼ oz) potato starch
35 g (1¼ oz) finely ground almonds
unsalted butter and flour for the mould
50 g (1¾ oz) redcurrant jelly

Preheat the oven to 150°C/300°F/Gas 2. Whisk the egg yolks with the sugar until they are pale; whisk the egg whites to a snow. Add the potato starch and the almonds to the yolks, and then fold in the egg whites. Spoon the mixture into a buttered and floured rectangular French cake mould, and bake for 25 minutes. Just before serving, make a vertical cut down the centre of the cake, taking care not to touch the bottom. Pipe the jelly into this 'letter-box'.

FOR FOUR PEOPLE

DOMINIQUE NAHMIAS

RESTAURANT D'OLYMPE

Paris

Dominique Nahmias may not have liked the recent reference to her by Patrick Lussac as 'un petit Bonaparte en jupons' even if he followed it up by describing her as the most inventive and important female cook in France. Nevertheless, it is true that she has achieved her present status through sheer determination, often in the face of opposition from the largely male world of French restaurateurs. Female apprentices are still rare but the young Dominique found it impossible to obtain a formal training, partly because she first studied law and would have been too late a starter. This fact makes her, like Raymond Blanc and Myrtle Allen, one of the breed of self-taught chefs who have proved that an adolescence spent slicing carrots for peanuts is not the only way to gastronomic stardom.

She comes from Corsican stock, hence the reference to Napoleon, and her family profession is the law – it was nearly hers, too. Her advocate father, however, was passionately interested in food and opened a restaurant near Toulon where she helped out during her teens. Her Italian mother and grandmother gave her a grounding in basic French bourgeois cooking, as well as teaching her to make pasta and polenta and to appreciate ceps and white truffles. This might not seem a basis for the hard life of the restaurant trade, yet, in 1972, when she was twenty, still a law student and already married to Albert Nahmias, she opened her first restaurant, which she describes as a cupboard, in Montparnasse. More fanciful admirers like to think that she christened it the Olympe because it served food fit for the gods of Mount Parnassus, but the truth is more mundane. There was already a Chez Dominique in the area and Olympe happens to be her other given name. Thus are legends born, and sometimes, as in this case, they become true. For the first Olympe, run then as now, jointly by Dominique and Albert, was a success from the start. To begin with, the menu was relatively unsophisticated, including many pasta dishes that she learned as a child, and the traditional dishes served in most small Parisian restaurants of the period. But this was also the time of the emergence of nouvelle cuisine and the young chef was quick to grasp the principles of lightness and originality which Paul Bocuse and the Troisgros brothers were preaching so successfully. The Olympe followed their trail, adding the extra dimension of an audacious use of exotic spices and unusual saucing – some influenced by Albert's memories of his North African childhood. He was building up his knowledge of wine and was already started on his indefatigable search for drinkable bottles from little-known sources which could be sold at modest prices alongside fine wines. Inevitably, prices rose, the student clientèle was left behind and fashionable Paris flocked to the Olympe.

Dominique and Albert Nahmias

The dining room at the Restaurant d'Olympe

Economy of space is everything in the Olympe kitchen.

When the Montparnasse premises had been outgrown, the couple bought the corner premises of a grocer and spice merchant off the Boulevard Pasteur in the 15th *arrondissement*, and set about, with a combination of skill and luck, in creating a stunningly attractive interior. The dominant colour is plum: gloss plum paint on the walls and iron stanchions supporting the matt plum ceiling. The chairs are mainly in plum velours and the table china is in plum and white. Curved brass rails continue the Thirties impression and the ceiling lights come from the liner *Normandie*. The greatest treasures, however, are the lacquer panels from the old Orient Express, and these, combined with panels of marble embossed with gold leaf, and other Thirties objets d'art, complete the decor. The atmosphere is intimate because the tables are well spaced, but the lighting level is high enough to ensure that those who have gone to be seen in the right company will indeed be seen by every other client. The restaurant is small, with 50 covers, and the layout is a miracle of compression. The space is roughly square, and of this two thirds contains the mixture of round and rectangular tables, and the remaining third, at a higher level, the bar. The L-shaped kitchen fits snugly and almost like a ship's galley round the inner corner of the room. A tiny servery at restaurant level has three hatches into the kitchen. Stairs lead down to washrooms, staff quarters, cold rooms and wine cellar, and a square of carpet just inside the main entrance conceals a hoist on which the daily deliveries from Rungis and specialist merchants descend to the stores below.

In the all stainless steel kitchen, economy of space is everything. As Albert Nahmias says, the larger the kitchen, the more potential for mess – there is no mess in this one. Dominique herself puts it somewhat differently: she claims ultra-efficiency is her only means of overcoming her natural laziness . . . Because everything is cooked to order and mainly briefly, there need be only two ovens – a baker's oven and a convection oven – a solid gas-fired hot plate and four gas rings. A grill and a gas blow lamp for caramelizing pastries complete the cooking arrangements; for chilling there are cold drawers and a freezer for ice-creams. During the service all unwanted equipment – the pasta machine used daily for making the noodles and pasta sheets for ravioli, stock pans, and so on – is stacked away on high shelves, to give the seven chefs maximum room.

The exterior is also painted in deep gloss plum, with a plum canvas awning discreetly lettered 'Restaurant d'Olympe' in gold and equally discreet gold lettering announcing the opening hours. The windows are shrouded in lace curtains, allowing the passer-by to see merely that something very special is going on inside, except for one which contains a single menu, spotlit, with prices high enough to deter any tourist who may have mistaken the Olympe for a neighbourhood bistro. For this is not a chic neighbourhood but a respectable *quartier* of doctors and residential blocks. The Olympe, like Michel Guérard's first restaurant, the Pot-au-Feu, in the dingy Asnières area north-west of the city all those years ago, proves the maxim that good chefs, like good mousetrap makers, will have the world beating a path to their door just as soon as the news gets round. And get round it did, as so often in Paris, where the new and unexpected is always the most chic.

The first Olympe reflected its creator's personality and her innovations like écrevisses simply grilled with curry and lobster ravioli are hers alone. They have become established attractions on the new menu, accompanied by other, spectacular new dishes. The menu is certainly expensive, though no more so than in other Parisian restaurants with a standard of cooking well below the Olympe's. Both ingredients and execution are superfine, and the most expensive item on the menu, the Lobster Ravioli, is a dish so marvellous that a high proportion of diners choose it every time. A card on every table reads 'N'oubliez pas ... Olympe' – quite unnecessarily, it might be thought by anyone who has tasted the ravioli, or the écrevisses, or the tripe in phyllo, or the duck with olives, or any one of a score of original and perfect dishes.

If Dominique Nahmias does not make any fuss about feminism ('aren't we all feminists?'), she runs her kitchen as absolute boss. Her sous-chef interprets her ideas with precision and skill during her infrequent absences: hers is one of those rare restaurants, perhaps because the specialities are so popular and so familiar a part of the kitchen routine, in which standards do not fall, however imperceptibly, during the absence of the chef. She is not, however, hidebound, and new dishes appear regularly, all aiming towards her ideal of a 'cuisine parfumée', combining flavours, textures and temperatures in a new and exciting way. When she began her career, French people travelled seldom, and there were fewer ethnic restaurants in Paris than there are today. Now, most customers are already familiar with oriental and Middle Eastern flavours, and she can use phyllo pastry and fresh coriander and rose water without fear of giving offence. She has also shed a little of her early dogmatism and will pay more attention to customers' different tastes, cooking her ducks and crustaceans well if asked to, though she herself and most of her customers share the modern preference for underdone meat and barely cooked fish. As she has never worked in any kitchen other than her own, it is a remarkable achievement to have acquired her skill almost from the air, and through a combination of application and intelligence.

The wine list is not cheap, with the most expensive bottle a 1977 Pétrus at 7,000 francs, but it is interesting in its range and variety. The wine is Albert Nahmias's special responsibility and while he recognizes the need for fine bottles at high prices, he also knows that they are not wanted by the successful young entrepreneurs who fill the Olympe every night. He and his sommelier therefore seek out unusual wines of good quality which are now making their way on to the wine list. He and Dominique have worked together from the beginning, sharing between them the joint responsibilities of the restaurants and of parenthood. Apart from handling the wine side, he also deals with the grinding chores of administration and finance.

A second and successful restaurant in Geneva proved too hard to monitor without constant travel and took Dominique away from her young daughter Sarah, for unacceptable lengths of time, so they took the realistic course of closing it down, and concentrating on a new venture nearer home. This is a new night-club restaurant Les Bains-Douches, with a kitchen staff trained by Dominique, and many dishes which have proved themselves on the Olympe menu. She has also published two books, *La Cuisine d'Olympe* and *Les Parfums d'Olympe* and takes part in a very successful, twice weekly radio programme in Paris. Away from the restaurant, she says that she just 'flops', spends precious time with Sarah, reads, goes to the cinema and shops in the local markets like any other Parisian woman.

One has the feeling that Dominique Nahmias, with her energy and elfin appearance, is capable of anything, and that she is on the verge of new and greater successes – ways of proving that a self-taught chef with a young child and the daily life of a 7th *arrondissement* household to run can also be a star. Her dynamism does not, however, derive from feminism. She believes firmly that women can achieve whatever they set out to do in a man's world without discarding or compromising their personalities as women, or adopting extreme attitudes. They just, she says, have to do everything that little bit better.

Dominique selecting cheeses in the local market

Lobster Ravioli

edges of the pasta with beaten egg yolk and place a second square of pasta on top. Press down hard with your fingers to make a tight seal, and finish the ravioli by trimming off the surplus pasta with a round biscuit cutter approximately 4 cm (1½ inches) in diameter.

The ravioli could now wait in a cool place for an hour or so, if necessary, but are better cooked as soon as possible. They should be poached for 2–3 minutes in simmering salted water, then removed with a slotted spoon, keeping the water to cook the claws later, and placed in a clean sauté pan with 200 ml (7 fl oz) cream.

Sweat the carrot and onion with the lobster shells, including the crushed head, in a little oil. Add the cayenne pepper, white wine and tomato purée, and 250 ml (8 fl oz) water. Bring to the boil and cook over a medium heat. Strain into a clean pan, stir in the remaining cream and the butter and reduce by half. Taste for seasoning. Remove from the heat and whisk in the reserved coral to bind the sauce without curdling. Keep hot in a bain marie, or over a pan of hot water.

Arrange the ravioli on a plate with the claw meat warmed through in the poaching liquid. Pour over the sauce and decorate with more chervil sprigs.

FOR FOUR PEOPLE

Raviolis de Homard

Lobster Ravioli

1 lobster weighing 400 g (14 oz)
2 tomatoes, peeled, seeded and diced
50 ml (2 fl oz) crème fraîche
a handful of fresh chervil, in sprigs
1 egg yolk, beaten
300 ml (½ pint) single cream
1 carrot, peeled and coarsely chopped
1 onion, peeled and chopped
4 tablespoons olive oil
½ teaspoon cayenne pepper
250 ml (8 fl oz) dry white wine
1 tablespoon tomato purée
25 g (1 oz) butter
salt and pepper

Pasta
4 egg yolks
2 whole eggs
a pinch of salt
300 g (10½ oz) flour

Make the pasta by mixing the egg yolks, eggs and salt into the flour. Knead, roll into a ball, wrap in clingfilm and rest in the refrigerator for 30 minutes. Then roll it out, by hand or with a machine, into very thin strips and cut them in 15 cm (6 inch) squares.

Kill the lobster by piercing the head with a skewer and remove the raw flesh from the tail and claws, retaining the shape of the claws as far as possible. Remove any coral from the head, sieve and set aside in a bowl. Slice the tail meat thinly. Keep the claw meat on one side.

Spread out half the pasta squares on a floured surface. In the centre of each put a few slices of lobster, three or four tomato dice and ¼ teaspoon of *crème fraîche*. Season with salt and pepper and add a teaspoon of chervil sprigs. Brush the

Écrevisses au Curry

Freshwater Crayfish with Curry

500 g (1 lb 2 oz) live freshwater crayfish
40 g (1½ oz) butter
2 shallots, peeled and sliced
2 tablespoons crème fraîche
1 teaspoon curry paste
1 tablespoon chopped fresh parsley
coarse salt and pepper

Do not shell or de-vein the live crayfish. Heat the butter in a sauté pan and throw in the crayfish and the shallot. Season with salt and pepper. When the crayfish are rosy-red, they are cooked and should be removed and set on one side. Discard the cooking butter.

Put the *crème fraîche* and the curry paste in the pan. Heat through over a good flame and return the crayfish to the pan. Allow to bubble a few times, giving the pan a good shake to coat the crayfish evenly with the sauce. Check the seasoning, sprinkle with parsley and serve on a very hot dish.

Note: this is one of Olympe's most famous and sought-after dishes, and depends for its success on having absolutely fresh, living, crayfish. In western Europe they are becoming scarcer, but Dominique Nahmias obtains good quality supplies from Poland, Turkey and Yugoslavia. They can be caught in small chalk or limestone streams in the British Isles, but patience and the knack are needed. You can substitute Dublin Bay prawns or langoustines; the result will be delicious ... but not quite the same as the Olympe's triumph.

FOR TWO PEOPLE

Daurade Crue en Filets

Raw Bream Fillets in an Olive Oil Sauce

1 bream, weighing
about 800 g (1 lb 12 oz)
3 tablespoons olive oil
3 tablespoons lemon juice
1 tablespoon light soy sauce
1 tablespoon mixed chopped fresh herbs
(coriander, mint and parsley)
salt and pepper

Obtain the freshest fish you can find and ask the fishmonger to skin and fillet it for you. Remove the fine bones with tweezers, then cut the fillets into the finest possible slices with an exceedingly sharp knife of the kind used for smoked salmon. Arrange the slices in a fan on three chilled plates and leave in the refrigerator for 15 minutes. Mix the other ingredients in a bowl with a wooden spoon, and brush the slices of fish generously with the sauce just before serving.

Note: raw salmon can be used with or instead of the bream for the dish. You can choose between the gilt-head bream, which has a golden ring between its eyes (the best) or other types. Bream are available all the year round, and their freshness can be judged by the firmness of the flesh and the brilliance of the scales and eyes.

FOR THREE PEOPLE

Freshwater Crayfish with Curry – one of Olympe's most famous dishes

Raw Bream Fillet in an Olive Oil Sauce

Croustillants de Lamelles de Tripes aux Piments

Millefeuilles of Tripe with Paprika

*1 kg (2¼ lb) mixed prepared
but uncooked tripe
1 carrot, 1 leek, 1 celery stalk, 1 onion, peeled
or trimmed and coarsely chopped
1 sprig thyme
2 pinches of cayenne pepper
1 teaspoon paprika
4 lemon slices, each cut in four
4 blanched cabbage leaves
8 sheets of pastilla
(North African puff pastry)
16 leaves fresh coriander
3 tablespoons arachide or sunflower oil
20 g (²⁄₃ oz) unsalted butter
salt and pepper*

Blanch the tripe in boiling water for 30 minutes. Drain and rinse in several changes of water. Transfer to a large pan and add the chopped vegetables and the thyme and water to cover. Simmer for 3–4 hours.

Remove the tripe and reserve the cooking broth. Cut the tripe in fine slices and put them in a large sauté pan. Strain the broth over the tripe, adding the cayenne, paprika and lemon slices. Salt if necessary. Simmer for 30 minutes. Remove the tripe to cool on a dish and reserve the broth, removing the lemon slices for use later.

Cut the cabbage leaves into eight squares. Spread out a sheet of *pastilla*, forming it into a rough square, taking care not to let it break, and place a cabbage square on top of it. Pile on an eighth of the tripe, one of the lemon pieces and a coriander leaf. Repeat the operation. Fold and seal lightly. Make three more millefeuilles in this way. Heat the oil in a big frying pan and brown the millefeuilles nicely over a medium heat. Reduce the liquid in which the tripe has cooked, swirling in the butter until you have a smooth thickish sauce. Taste for seasoning.

Have ready four heated plates and put one millefeuille on each, surrounded by the sauce and the remaining lemon and coriander leaves. Serve immediately.

FOR FOUR PEOPLE

Pigeonneaux au Miel

Pigeons in a Honey Sauce

*4 tender young pigeons
80 g (2¾ oz) runny honey
1 tablespoon wine vinegar
2 tablespoons dark soy sauce
1 teaspoon coriander seeds, crushed
1 teaspoon toasted sesame seeds, pounded
1 teaspoon arachide oil*

Noodles
*25 g (1 oz) thin Chinese noodles
½ teaspoon wine vinegar
½ teaspoon sesame oil
½ teaspoon light soy sauce
1 litre (1¾ pints) arachide oil for frying
120 g (4²⁄₃ oz) Chinese leaves, in strips
3 spinach leaves, torn
1 carrot, peeled and grated
salt and pepper*

Clean the pigeons. Season with salt and pepper, inside and out. Preheat the oven to its highest possible setting.

Mix the honey, vinegar, dark soy sauce, crushed coriander and sesame and a few grinds of pepper together in a bowl. Allow to stand for 20 minutes.

Lightly oil a roasting pan 20 × 30 cm (8 × 12 inches) and put in the pigeons. Roast for 10–12 minutes. Discard the fat from the bottom of the pan and pour over the honey mixture. Heat the roasting pan over a high flame until the honey has thickened and is turning brown. Reduce the heat to low, and baste the pigeons continually for 5 minutes, turning them occasionally. The honey should become slightly crusty and should stick to them.

Cook the noodles in plenty of boiling salted water until just tender. Drain and mix in a bowl with the vinegar, sesame oil and light soy sauce. Keep hot.

Heat the oil in a deep frying pan and plunge in the Chinese leaves, spinach and carrot for 30 seconds. Remove and drain on kitchen paper. Season with salt and mix gently with the cooked noodles.

Have ready a hot serving dish and heap the noodles in the middle, with the honeyed pigeons, cut in two, arranged round the outside. Brush them one last time with honey and serve immediately.

FOR FOUR PEOPLE

Millefeuilles of Tripe with Paprika

Canard aux Olives

Duck with Black Olives

2 ducklings
2 tablespoons arachide or sunflower oil
40 g (1½ oz) unsalted butter
500 ml (18 fl oz) light poultry stock
12 black olives, stoned
1 lemon preserved in lemon juice and
coarse salt
1 tablespoon chopped chives
salt and pepper

Cut each cleaned duckling into four pieces. Heat the oil and half the butter in a sauté pan and brown the pieces on both sides. Discard the cooking fat and add the stock. Season with salt and pepper. Add the olives and the lemon cut in eight slices. Cover and cook over a low heat for 15–20 minutes. Remove the lid and check the seasoning.

Remove the duck pieces to a hot dish and swirl the rest of the butter into the sauce, allowing it to reduce slightly. Add the chives, and pour over the duck. Serve immediately.

Small turnips cooked in water and butter go well with this dish.

FOR FOUR PEOPLE

Duck with Black Olives

Millefeuilles aux Fruits

Fresh Fruit Millefeuilles

250 g (8¾ oz) puff pastry dough
120 g (4⅔ oz) icing sugar
500 ml (18 fl oz) full cream milk
1 vanilla pod
160 g (5¼ oz) caster sugar
7 egg yolks
40 g (1⅓ oz) flour
500 ml (18 fl oz) crème fraîche
extra ½ teaspoon caster sugar
1 pineapple, or 500 g (1 lb 2 oz) wild
strawberries, raspberries or other suitable
soft fruit

Preheat the oven to 200°C/400°F/Gas 6. Roll out the puff pastry dough to 5 mm (¼ inch) thick on a baking tray and bake in the oven for 10 minutes so that the pastry can rise and 'puff'. Remove and turn the oven off, leaving the door open. Place a reversed baking sheet of the same size on top to press the pastry down, and dry in the turned-off oven for half an hour.

Cut the pastry into twelve rectangles, 10 × 5 cm (4 × 2 inches) and divide each rectangle in half lengthways to make a narrow strip. You will need three divided rectangles for each millefeuille – 24 in all. Dredge 40 g (1½ oz) of the icing sugar thickly over eight of the rectangles and put under a hot grill to caramelize the sugar. This is rather tricky: it has to be done very quickly, and must be watched all the time.

Make a *crème pâtissière*. Boil the milk with the vanilla pod and half the caster sugar. Mix the egg yolks, the remaining caster sugar and the flour in a bowl, then add it to the milk, having removed the vanilla pod. Whisk over a medium heat for 5 minutes. Allow to cool. Whisk the *crème fraîche* with the remaining icing sugar, and mix into the cooled *crème pâtissière*. Add the extra ½ teaspoon of caster sugar if necessary.

Spread the *crème pâtissère* and *crème fraîche* mixture on eight rectangles of pastry and top with the fruit. (If you are using pineapple, it should be very finely sliced.) Make another layer of pastry, cream and fruit and put on a caramelized pastry lid. Serve immediately.

FOR EIGHT PEOPLE

Citrus Cream with Pineapple

Crémet au Citrus et à l'Ananas

Citrus Cream with Pineapple

50 g (1¾ oz) sugar
3½ tablespoons water
juice of 4 good oranges
3 egg whites
50 g (1¾ oz) caster sugar
3 leaves gelatine
finely grated rind and juice of 3 lemons
500 ml (18 fl oz) whipping cream
250 g (8¾ oz) pineapple, finely sliced
a few mint leaves
orange slices

Make the sauce by reducing the sugar and water slightly over a medium heat for 5 minutes. Stir in the orange juice, strain into a bowl and allow to cool.

Whisk the egg whites with the caster sugar until they are firm. Soak the gelatine leaves in cold water. Bring the lemon juice to the boil with the rind, and add the drained and squeezed gelatine away from the heat. Stir well and allow to cool. If using powdered gelatine, follow the packet instructions.

Fold the cooled lemon juice mixture into the egg whites just as it is beginning to set, and then the cream whipped to a fine snow. On a baking sheet or flat board, set out eight 8 × 2 cm (3¼ × ¾ inch) biscuit cutters or circles of plastic or foil-covered card. Spoon a layer of citrus cream into each, cover with a layer of finely sliced pineapple and top with more cream, smoothing the surface with a spatula. Chill in the refrigerator for 3–4 hours.

To serve, place each cream in the middle of a dessert plate, using a broad spatula or fish slice. Slide off the mould and pour round the orange sauce. Decorate with mint leaves and orange slices.

FOR EIGHT PEOPLE

ROGER VERGÉ

LE MOULIN DE MOUGINS

Mougins

Roger Vergé, with his twinkling eyes and slightly piratical look, was always one of the most visible of the group of French chefs who changed the culinary world in the 1970s, and at nearly sixty he still epitomizes the image of 'chef as hero', both in his appearance and his personality. A man who has driven in the East African Safari Rally, who has orchestrated a flawless meal for six hundred motor-racing enthusiasts in the kitchenless Royal Albert Hall, whose business interests stretch from Japan to Florida and whose office sports a vast map of Air France routes, he exudes confidence and energy – 'I am much more of a businessman than I was ten years ago. But all this competition is fun, a challenge which I enjoy.' He is also keenly aware that his whole empire rests on one all-important image, that of his three-star restaurant the Moulin de Mougins, just inland from Cannes. He now does not travel at all during the summer season so that his high standards can be maintained and, if possible, improved – not always easy when 200–220 diners may be served in a single July evening, or during the Cannes Film Festival. At these times he does not work alongside his chefs; the kitchen routine is in the hands of his Chef de Cuisine, Serge Chollet, his trusted deputy for more than twenty years, but he checks all the dishes, discusses all the menus, and keeps watch on the freshness and quality which are the keynotes of his personal cuisine.

His two books, *Roger Vergé's Cuisine of the Sun* and *Entertaining in the French Style*, both convey a great deal of the man: the first shows his love of the flavours and people of Provence, and the second his gregariousness and style. All these qualities are apparent in the Moulin itself, a converted olive-press which crouches in a valley below the self-consciously picturesque hill-town of Mougins, a patch of coolness in the summer months when the heat shimmers over the white houses and the aromatic bushes of the surrounding countryside.

Roger Vergé and his second wife Denise opened the Moulin in 1969, and by 1974 the third star was theirs. Since then it has enjoyed enormous success, with an international clientèle. The staff is large: Serge Chollet has five senior chefs working under him, and M. Sylvain, the manager, five head waiters and two sommeliers. The total staff in kitchen and dining rooms combined can reach seventy-five at high season.

For such a large and minutely organized enterprise it is surprisingly intimate: the dark-beamed interior is divided into smaller spaces where diners can eat without feeling crowded, and the place is full of objects which recall Roger Vergé's early life as a chef and the passion for modern art and antiques which he shares with Denise. The decor is cosy rather than austere – flowered service plates and tapestried chairs somehow blend

Le Moulin de Mougins – the entrance

Roger Vergé with part of the original mill machinery

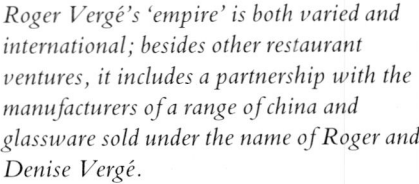

Roger Vergé's 'empire' is both varied and international; besides other restaurant ventures, it includes a partnership with the manufacturers of a range of china and glassware sold under the name of Roger and Denise Vergé.

At the passe, Chef de Cuisine and Roger Vergé's trusted deputy of more than twenty years, Serge Chollet (right with beard), spoons orange butter over seven scallop salads, before decorating them (see page 48).

happily with ultra-modern light fittings and sculpture. At the southern end of the room, sliding doors give on to a flowery patio and a tented area for summer dining – with the latest in electronic mosquito traps. In spring the hillsides are covered with anemones and meadow flowers under the mimosas, and in the autumn persimmons shine among the golden leaves.

By contrast, the kitchen is all stainless steel and white tiles, with every possible electric aid for the chefs, and an air of high seriousness. The young chefs who work here know that they are lucky to have been accepted, whether they are fully qualified, or *stagiaires* from the United States, England or Japan. Roger Vergé takes great pleasure in the fact that, whereas the majority of chefs used to be French (in the same way that the stereotype of the opera-singer was Italian), there are now talented aspirant chefs in every developed country. In England, for example, the cook used to be the person who simply delivered food to the table on time. Now it is a proper profession. He also says, with justified pride, that he and his colleagues made cooking a respectable and – for the really talented – a glamorous profession; and that even young chefs who will never get further than running their own modest restaurant or cooking at middle rank in a large kitchen, have a different attitude, look smarter and are, in short, proud of themselves. Like Michel Guérard, he worries about the pressures put on talented young chefs, both by financial temptations and by overemphasis in the media on innovation and eclecticism. In the United States in particular, though he loves the ferment of

culinary ideas, he finds that the mix has become too rich, disastrously so in all but the most skilled hands. He feels a very real responsibility, as a senior chef with power and resources, for guiding younger talent: time and time again in his conversation the words 'they need our help' crop up.

He acknowledges that among today's greatest cooks there are men and women who are largely or completely self-taught, but he fears for the future of some chefs who think they can emulate them without long years of experience. 'These cooks have accumulated little baggage in the way of experience and technique: there are things they can do well, but they lack the resources to cope with change or go beyond their original good ideas.' The inexperienced can also fall foul of the dangers which exist in every kitchen, for example the undercooked *foie gras* or fish which has all the journalists in raptures one day, and a dozen or more people seriously ill the next. Again: 'We must help them'. The proof of this concern is the dozens of young men and women who have passed through the kitchens of the Moulin since 1969 and gone on to run profitable and sometimes brilliant kitchens.

What they learn at the Moulin is consistency and organization, how to cope with a menu which changes every two weeks, and with providing for both the small intricate portions of a Menu Dégustation and the simpler demands of a customer who feels safe with something more straightforward. Standard Vergé dishes like the lobster cooked in a pepper sauce and the truffle ravioli, have become second nature. Absorbing the details and perfecting the techniques of a dish they have never heard of before is harder, but becomes a routine skill. Above all they learn to work as a team, in which as many as five chefs may contribute to a single plate. The *pâtissier* has made the puff pastry or *feuilletage*, a *chef garde-manger* has looked out and prepared the *foie gras* and truffles, the vegetable cook has turned and cooked the vegetable garnish, a meat chef has cooked the medallion or saddle for precisely the right time, the *saucier* has reduced the cooking juices with alcohol and perhaps cream or butter. Finally, the dish is decorated and checked by the chef at the *passe* – and the waiter presents the plate to the customer. At the bottom of the heap is the *plongeur* or washer-up, whose lot, as George Orwell pointed out fifty-five years ago in *Down and Out in Paris and London*, is often not a happy one.

Roger Vergé still takes great personal interest in the fish and vegetables which come to his kitchen. This partly stems from his having chosen to work in Provence, where the quality and variety of ingredients is second to none, and where courgette flowers picked in the morning can be ready for stuffing, with a farce of chicken and mushrooms surrounding a whole black truffle, by noon on the same day. The vegetables may now be raised by university-educated growers on the land once farmed by their peasant forebears, but the love and attention to the smallest detail is still there. In Roger Vergé's case, there is also the ever-present memory of his Aunt Célestine, described in his second book as a champion marketer, scourge of every stall-holder in his home town. Trotting round behind her, he learned to distinguish between good and stale, to recognize chickens whose gizzards had been gorged with grain to increase their weight, cheeses which had been stored at the wrong temperature and fish which had been splashed with water to give an illusion of freshness. This early training is one he has never forgotten. He says that if you haven't got a garden and poultry-yard of your own, the only way to learn is to study the art of shopping. Of course, like most senior chefs, he now no longer gets up at dawn to ransack the wholesale markets: a whole breed of professional middlemen has grown up in every area of produce, whether it be cheese, fish or vegetables and fruit, who have become experts in their field, and who know exactly what each restaurateur on their limited list of clients prefers and what his budget will stand. They can only survive through providing the right goods, and the chefs have come to trust them.

All this combines to make the Moulin what it is, and few guests go away disappointed. They can choose from the large à la carte menu, or can select either from the Menu du Jardin or the Menu Gourmand. Both are the same price, but the first is lighter – offering a scallop salad perhaps, with a steamed lobster surrounded by just-cooked vegetables and a herb sauce to follow, then a fruit sorbet, then mallard cooked with ginger and lemon and served with a spinach and pear tart. The second is more substantial: lobster salad and merlan de palangre with a salt cod sauce and tapenade, the same fruit sorbet and a saddle of hare with wild mushrooms. Both finish with a selection of cheeses from the Moulin's supplier, Maître Ceneri in Cannes, and one of the elaborate puddings for which the pâtisserie department is famous. All this will change the following week, and again in

another two weeks' time, perhaps to a menu which will include a fillet of roe deer with a raspberry sauce, an idea Roger Vergé picked up from a young woman contestant in a London competition. Monotony, the cook's enemy, is never a problem at the Moulin.

Meanwhile the empire rolls on. Some establishments, like the restaurants in Denmark and Luxembourg, are no longer under Vergé's control. Others are new joint ventures: in one he has formed a company with Paul Bocuse and Gaston Lenôtre to supply thousands of meals a day in the Disneyworld complex at Epcot, in Florida; in another he is in partnership with manufacturers to sell a wide range of glass and china under the name of Roger and Denise Vergé. Nearer home, he has a second restaurant, L'Amandier, up in Mougins village, which doubles as a cooking school, and a café in the Galerie du Sporting d'Hiver at Monte Carlo. These two enterprises, together with the Moulin, also serve as outlets for the Roger Vergé range of wines and oils, eaux de vie and attractively packaged Provençal specialities like herbs, vinegars and tapenades. A new cooking school has opened in Nice and one is planned for Monaco. This requires much administration, many meetings, wearisome travel. But Roger Vergé never forgets that the Moulin is the foundation on which everything rests, where his wife and family (two grown-up daughters by his first marriage, and nine-year-old Cordelia, a Peruvian child whom Denise and he adopted) live and where the painting of Tante Célestine's calm face greets the diners, reminding them that the art of cooking is based firmly in tradition.

Part of Roger Vergé's collection

The inner dining room with the conservatory and terrace beyond

La Salade de Noix de Saint-Jacques en Rosace et son Beurre d'Orange

Scallop Salad with Orange Butter

6 small purple artichokes
juice of ½ a lemon
200 g (7 oz) lamb's lettuce
12 large scallops
3 oranges
1 teaspoon caster sugar
1 tablespoon double cream
200 g (7 oz) cold unsalted butter
a few sprigs of chervil
salt and pepper

Remove the leaves from the artichokes and cook the central part for 15 minutes in boiling salted water with the lemon juice. Lift off the choke (bristles), trim the stalk end and cut the artichoke bottom into fine slices. Wash the lamb's lettuce, dry it carefully and select the finest leaves.

Cut each scallop into five horizontal slices (the corals are not used for this dish) and arrange each sliced scallop in an overlapping rosette on an individual sheet of baking paper. Season lightly with salt and pepper.

Peel one orange with a potato peeler and cut the rind into very fine matchsticks. Squeeze the other two oranges for juice. Cook the rind matchsticks in water with the sugar and 2 tablespoons of orange juice over a low heat until they are lightly caramelized. Remove the pith from the first orange and skin the segments. Reduce the remaining orange juice by half in a pan. Add the cream and bring to a rolling boil. Whisk in 150 g (5¼ oz) cold butter, little by little, over a minimum heat. Salt and pepper lightly and keep warm.

Put the remaining butter in a non-stick pan. Slide each sheet of paper with its rosette of scallop on to a plate and reverse over the pan so the scallops cook flesh side down until they have coloured lightly, for about 30 seconds. Remove with a fish slice and keep warm.

Arrange the lamb's lettuce leaves round 6 tepid plates, then the artichoke bottoms. Finally slide two scallops, cooked side up, off their paper on to the centre of each plate, retaining or re-forming each rosette. Pour over the orange butter and decorate with orange segments, sprigs of chervil and the caramelized orange rind.

FOR SIX PEOPLE

La Truffe Fraîche sous la Croûte de Sel et le Beurre de Champagne

Whole Truffles Cooked in a Salt Crust with a Champagne Sauce

6 fresh round black truffles of about 50 g
(1¾ oz) each, well brushed
6 thin sheets of fresh pork fat 10 × 10 cm
(4¼ × 4¼ inches)
150 g (5¼ oz) flour
90 g (3¼ oz) coarse salt
5–6 tablespoons good champagne
150 g (5¼ oz) good quality cold unsalted
butter, diced

Preheat the oven to 150°C/300°F/Gas 2. Season the truffles with freshly ground pepper. Do not salt. Wrap each securely in a sheet of pork fat. Make a dough of the flour, salt and 5–6 tablespoons of water and divide into six equal parts which should be rolled out on a floured board to a thickness of 5 mm (¼ inch). Enclose each truffle in a sheet of pastry, sealing it firmly by rolling between your hands. Bake in the preheated oven for 40 minutes in a small roasting pan.

Meanwhile, prepare the sauce. Bring the champagne to the boil in a small pan, and salt lightly. Keeping the liquid just below boiling point over a low flame, whisk in the cold diced butter, to make a smooth sauce. Pour into a heated sauceboat.

To serve, wrap the truffle, still in its crust, tightly in a linen napkin so that no whiff of the precious aroma is lost before this dish of kings is placed before the guest. Put the sauceboat on the table and accompany with hot toasted country bread.

FOR SIX PEOPLE

Scallop Salad with Orange Butter

Lobster Fricassée with Paprika

La Fricassée du Homard du Poivre Rose

Lobster Fricassée with Paprika

*6 small lobsters weighing 500 g (1 lb 2 oz)
each or 3 larger lobsters of 800 g–1 kg
(1¾–2¼ lb)
60 g (2 oz) unsalted butter
3 tablespoons chopped shallots
1 tablespoon sweet paprika
1 tablespoon tomato purée
4 tablespoons cognac
250 ml (8 fl oz) dry white wine
3 sprigs fresh tarragon
500 ml (18 fl oz) whipping cream
3 tablespoons chopped fresh chervil
salt and pepper*

Kill each lobster by inserting the point of a sharp knife into the head and then use the blade to cut in half lengthways. Remove the coral from the head and reserve. Remove the intestinal tract.

Melt the butter in a 25–35 cm (10–14 inch) sauté pan, and soften the chopped shallots. Add the paprika and mix well with a spatula. Stir in the tomato purée. Lay the half-lobsters flesh-side down in this hot sauce. Cook briefly over a medium heat to seal in the juices, then flame with the cognac. Pour in the white wine and add the tarragon. Turn the lobsters over so that the flesh side is uppermost. Cover the pan and cook on a gentle heat for 20 minutes if you are using small lobsters and 30 minutes if you are using larger ones. Check the liquid level from time to time.

Take out the lobsters and remove the meat from the tails and claws. Then remove the meat from the head. (The photograph shows a single lobster arranged with its shell and legs, but this method is easier for the home cook.) Divide the meat between six heated soup plates and keep warm.

Return the sauté pan to the heat and reduce the cooking liquid by half. Add the cream and boil gently for 5 minutes to let it thicken. Mix in the reserved coral off the heat. Season with salt and pepper. Strain through a fine sieve into a clean pan and heat through. Add the chopped chervil and pour over the lobster.

FOR SIX PEOPLE

Le Turbotin Rôti avec sa Fondue d'Oranges et de Citron à l'Huile d'Olive

Roast Baby Turbot with Citrus-flavoured Olive Oil

*2 baby turbots weighing 800 g–1 kg
(1¾–2¼ lb) each
unsalted butter
3 lemons
5 seedless oranges
150 ml (¼ pint) olive oil
salt and pepper*

Clean and scale the turbots, trimming off the fins with a pair of scissors, but leaving the heads and tails on. Preheat the oven to its hottest setting. Butter and season a roasting dish or dishes and strew the bottom with a little grated lemon and orange peel to flavour the fish while they cook. Put in the turbots, dark skin uppermost. Sprinkle with olive oil and spread it evenly with your fingers or a pastry brush so that every part of the skin is covered. Roast in the oven for 25–30 minutes. Sprinkle with more olive oil from time to time and, if you are using two pans on different levels, change them over after 15 minutes. (The cooking time will depend on the thickness of the fish and on the maximum heat of your oven, but a good test is to slip in the point of a knife under a fillet at the head end of the fish. If the flesh lifts easily, the fish is cooked.)

While the fish cooks, peel the citrus fruits with a very sharp knife until no trace of pith remains. Skin the segments over a bowl to catch the juices, transfer the fruit and its juices to a small pan and add 7 tablespoons olive oil. Heat through, but do not boil.

Serve the turbot on a heated dish and the citrus sauce in a sauceboat.

Note: this is a dish for summer, for a sunny day. The sharpness of the lemon is tamed by the sweetness of the orange and olive oil.

FOR SIX PEOPLE

Roast Baby Turbot with Citrus-flavoured Olive Oil

L'Aumonière de Volaille Farcie au Foie Gras et le Coulis de Truffes

Chicken Breasts stuffed with Foie Gras in a Truffle Sauce

6 chicken breasts, boned and skinned
1.5 litres (2½ pints) chicken stock
200 g (7 oz) pasta dough
100 g (3½ oz) chopped ceps or 50 g (1¾ oz)
dried ceps, soaked
10 g (⅓ oz) chopped truffles

Stuffing
200 g (7 oz) chicken breast meat
2 slices of white bread, without crusts, soaked
in milk
90 g (3¼ oz) cooked foie gras
400 ml (14 fl oz) whipping cream
salt and pepper

Sauce
3 tablespoons truffle juice (from the tin)
40–50 g (about 1⅔ oz) chopped truffles
a small glass of white port
2 tablespoons concentrated veal stock
300 g (10½ oz) cold unsalted butter, diced
salt and pepper

Begin by making the stuffing. Have all the ingredients and the processor bowl thoroughly chilled beforehand. Process the chicken meat with ½ teaspoon salt and a few turns of the peppermill. Add the squeezed bread and process again. Cut the cold foie gras in dice and process for a few seconds before starting to add the cream in a thin stream. When the mixture is smooth, remove to a bowl and keep cold.

Using a sharp knife, make each chicken breast into a pocket or pouch. Flatten gently with the side of a heavy knife. Place each on a square of clingfilm and season with salt and pepper. Fill with the stuffing, and form each breast into a round shape, wrapping the clingfilm tightly so that it keeps its shape. Secure with thread and poach these 'aumonières' (literally 'alms purses') for 25 minutes in the chicken stock.

Roll out the pasta dough to a thickness of 1 mm (paper thin). Using a fluted biscuit cutter, make 24 rounds of 7 cm (2¾ inches) in diameter. Place a teaspoon of chopped ceps and truffles in the centre of each, brush the edges with cold water and seal the raviolis carefully with your finger and thumb. Poach in chicken stock for about 5 minutes after the ravioli has come to the surface.

For the sauce, reduce the truffle juice with the chopped truffles in a small pan until you have barely a tablespoon. Add the white port and reduce by half. Add the veal stock, bring to the boil and pour the contents of the pan into the liquidizer. Drop in the cold butter bit by bit as you liquidize until you have a smooth emulsion. Season and warm through if necessary.

Carefully remove the clingfilm from the 'aumonières' and place one on each of six heated plates. Arrange the raviolis aound the 'aumonières'. Pour the sauce round and decorate with, perhaps, some diced raw tomato, a bay leaf, sprigs of chervil and, if you are feeling extravagant, strips of truffle arranged in a star shape over the 'aumonières'.

Note: only clingfilm whose manufacturer specifically states that it is suitable for cooking should be used for poaching food.

FOR SIX PEOPLE

Les Mignons d'Agneau à la Fleur de Thym

Medallions of Lamb with Thyme

a saddle of lamb weighing about 1.6 kg
(3½ lb)
4 tablespoons olive oil
50 g (1¾ oz) shallots, peeled and chopped
2 cloves of garlic, peeled and crushed
a bay leaf
1 tablespoon tomato purée
7 tablespoons wine vinegar
250 ml (8 fl oz) red wine
4 peppercorns
2 whole heads of garlic, separated into cloves
and peeled
3 tablespoons thick cream
50 g (1¾ oz) cold unsalted butter
4 good sprigs fresh thyme in flower
salt and pepper

Remove the fillets from the saddle. Slice them in medallions, trimmed of all membrane and fat, and keep cold in the refrigerator. Heat 3 tablespoons oil in a heavy pan while you crush the bones of the saddle, and then brown the bones and the lamb trimmings.

Chicken Breasts stuffed with Foie Gras in a Truffle Sauce

Medallions of Lamb with Thyme and an Aubergine Mould

Pour off nearly all the olive oil and add the chopped shallots, two garlic cloves, the bay leaf and the tomato purée. Let them sweat together for a minute or so, then pour in the vinegar and the wine. Add a few peppercorns, and reduce the liquid by three-quarters. Add sufficient water to cover and simmer gently for about 30 minutes or until the liquid has reduced to half.

While the stock is reducing, put the peeled cloves from the two heads of garlic in a pan of cold water and bring to the boil. Repeat this process four more times, then drain the garlic and purée finely.

Preheat the oven to 200°C/400°F/Gas 6. Strain the reduced lamb stock into a clean pan and add the cream. Cook for a few minutes, then add the garlic purée, which will bind the sauce. Whisk in 40 g (1½ oz) of the cold butter, diced, pass through a fine sieve into a bowl and taste for seasoning. Add 2 sprigs of thyme, cover and leave to infuse for 10 minutes in a warm place.

Heat a roasting pan with the remaining oil and butter. Season the lamb med-allions, brown them on both sides over a medium flame and place the roasting pan in the oven to cook for 7–8 minutes.

Strain the sauce to remove the thyme sprigs. Pour the sauce on to a heated serving plate and arrange the medallions. Garnish with the remaining thyme sprigs and serve with an aubergine mould (see below).

FOR SIX PEOPLE

Gâteau d'Aubergines

Aubergine Mould

4 medium aubergines
olive oil
1 red pepper
2 eggs
2 tablespoons cream
2 tablespoons chopped fresh parsley
40 g (1½ oz) fresh white breadcrumbs
2 leaves fresh basil
2 cloves of garlic, peeled
salt and pepper

Preheat the oven to 200°C/400°F/Gas 6. Wash the aubergines and cut them in two lengthwise. Season with salt and pepper, sprinkle with a little olive oil and bake in the preheated oven for 30 minutes. Trans-fer the flesh of the aubergines to the food processor bowl, and set aside. Keep the skins to line the ramekins. Char and peel the pepper. Remove the seeds and dice it finely.

Reset the oven to 110°C/225°F/Gas ¼. Purée the aubergine flesh and then add the eggs and cream to the processor bowl. Blend well and add the diced pepper, chopped parsley, breadcrumbs, basil leaves, salt and pepper. Blend again. Line six oiled ramekins with the aubergine skins cut in ribbons, fill with the auber-gine mixture from the food processor, and cook in a roasting pan, with enough hot water to come half-way up the sides of the moulds, for 30–35 minutes in the oven. Turn out, and serve either with the lamb medallions and their sauce or on a separate plate (see opposite).

FOR SIX PEOPLE

Apple Tart with Vanilla Ice-Cream and Caramel Sauce

Le Croustillant aux Fraises des Bois et le Coulis de Fruits Rouges

Wild Strawberry Millefeuilles with a Red Fruit Sauce

500 g (1 lb 2 oz) puff pastry dough
75 g (2⅔ oz) icing sugar
250 ml (8 fl oz) whipping cream, chilled
75 g (2⅔ oz) caster sugar
250 g (8¾ oz) cultivated strawberries
250 g (8¾ oz) raspberries
500 g (1 lb 2 oz) wild strawberries
6 leaves fresh mint

Roll out the pastry as thinly as you can. Cut 24 rounds 10 cm (4 inches) in diameter. Prick each with a fork and allow to rest for 20–30 minutes in the refrigerator. Preheat the oven to 230°C/450°F/Gas 8. Coat six of the rounds thinly with icing sugar. Place all the rounds on a lightly greased baking sheet or sheets and cook in the preheated oven for 10 minutes. Remove the rounds from the baking sheets to cool on racks.

Make a Chantilly cream by whipping the cream in a bowl, adding the caster sugar gradually as you do so until you have a thick cream which clings to the whisk. Set aside in the refrigerator.

Wash and hull the cultivated strawberries and the raspberries and then liquidize them, adding a little sugar if they seem too sour. Pick over and hull the wild strawberries.

To assemble the millefeuilles have ready 6 dessert plates. On each, place a round of puff pastry, spoon or pipe over a little crème Chantilly and dot with wild strawberries. Cover with another round of pastry and repeat until you have three 'storeys'. Finish with one of the caramelized rounds and decorate with mint leaves, a small piping of cream and a wild strawberry. Pour round the fruit sauce (you can make an attractive pattern round the edge with a little cream if you have time) and serve.

FOR SIX PEOPLE

La Petite Tarte 'Tatin', la Glace à la Vanille et la Sauce au Caramel

Apple Tart with Vanilla Ice-Cream and Caramel Sauce

250 g (8¾ oz) puff or shortcrust pastry
200 g (7 oz) sugar
7 tablespoons water
7 tablespoons whipping cream, whipped
100 g (3½ oz) cold unsalted butter, diced
1.6 kg (3½ lb) eating apples
12 scoops of freshly made vanilla ice-cream

Roll out the pastry to a thickness of 3 mm (⅛ inch) and cut out six 9 cm (3½ inch) rounds with a plain cutter. Prick with a fork and keep cold until needed.

To make the caramel sauce, put the sugar in a heavy small pan with the water. Bring to the boil and cook until you have a golden brown caramel. Fold in the cream, remove from heat and, stirring continuously, mix in the diced butter.

Butter six moulds 9 cm (3½ inches) wide and 4 cm (1½ inches) deep. Pour a little caramel into the bottom of each. Keep the remaining sauce hot.

Preheat the oven to 200°C/400°F/Gas 6. Peel and core the apples and cut each into 6 vertical slices. Arrange them in the moulds, rounded sides up. Cook in the oven for 20 minutes. Place a pastry round on top of each mould and return to the oven for 10–15 minutes, or until the pastry is golden. Remove the moulds from the oven, and place a reversed serving plate over each. Leave for 1–2 minutes, then turn over to unmould the tarts. Pour the remaining sauce round and add 2 scoops of ice-cream.

FOR SIX PEOPLE

Wild Strawberry Millefeuille with a Red Fruit Sauce

GERMANY

DIETER MÜLLER
ECKART WITZIGMANN

Dieter Müller

Schweizer Stuben

Wertheim

There are few restaurants in the world where an elderly gentleman and his wife, having progressed decorously through the most expensive set menu, accompanied by some truly noble wines, could greet a bill large enough to feed a family for a month with blissfully closed eyes and the muttered word 'Wunderbar!' But it did happen in the Schweizer Stuben, and was no less than a proper tribute to the meal they had just eaten. Perfectly orchestrated, it had consisted of a single salmon ravioli served in a hinged egg-shaped container with a grape sauce; fillets of sole in parsleyed breadcrumbs with a medallion of lobster, curry sauce and wild rice; lobster served on fresh samphire, followed by the most delicate of tomato consommés (this to refresh the palate; sorbets are thought to spoil the taste of the wine). The main course was briefly roasted saddle of roe deer with shallots and mushrooms, with a venison reduction and chanterelles, garnished with a few cranberries, mange-tout peas and a potato dumpling glazed with butter and sugar and filled with rosehip syrup (perhaps the only false note). A selection of cheeses, arranged fan-wise round the plate in order of strength of flavour, followed, then a hot plum tart with a plum brandy cream sauce and white chocolate ice-cream. It would have been memorable on any occasion, and meals of equal sophistication and the same faultless execution from a constantly changing menu are now drawing customers from all over the world.

At first glance, the site of the Schweizer Stuben does not seem promising. A tennis club complex in a small, modern suburb of a sleepy town on the river Main in the north of the German province of Baden-Württemberg, it has charm and tranquillity, but could easily be missed as travellers press on west towards Frankfurt and the Rhine, or south-east towards Bavaria and the Alps. Yet in 1988 this restaurant was recognized as one of the two greatest in West Germany – the other being the Aubergine in Munich. It is the creation of the Schmitt family. Adalbert Schmitt, whose family owns the large plastics factory a few kilometres away, where the meeting of the Main and Tauber rivers is guarded by the red-roofed old town of Wertheim, is a passionate wine lover and gastronome. He founded the Schweizer Stuben in 1971, and it is now under the direction of his son Andreas, whose speciality is the astonishing wine list.

The *maître chef de cuisines* is Dieter Müller, a young-looking thirty-nine year-old, who has cooked at the Schweizer Stuben for fifteen years. He first learned to cook in his parents' simple Black Forest restaurant and later trained at Mulheim and in the Schweizerhofen at Berne, where he first encountered French cooking. He counts among his mentors Escoffier, Paul Bocuse and Fredy Girardet, and regards his style as mainly French, with

The Schweizer Stuben

Dieter Müller

the principles of the nouvelle cuisine applied to German ingredients and tastes. To begin with, he worked at the Schweizer Stuben alongside his elder brother Jörg, but unlike other famous chef-brothers such as the Troisgros and the Haeberlins they decided to work separately, and Jörg now runs the almost equally celebrated resort restaurant Nosse on the North Sea island of Sylt.

Müller has always known that to attract customers to Wertheim he must provide only the best and the freshest. In this he is lucky, because the Franconian streams provide fresh saibling, waller, trout and zander and the forests venison, hare and rabbit, not to mention wild berries collected by local children and wild mushrooms such as chanterelles, ceps and morels, gathered by experienced collectors in season. The fertile Main valley is a good source of the freshest vegetables and fruit, and with the Schmitts' backing he is able to bring in refrigerated lobsters and seafish from the Atlantic coast, Aberdeen Angus beef from Scotland, cheeses and poultry from France, goose liver from Hungary and exotic fruit and scarce ingredients from wherever he can find a good supplier. He freezes only fruit purées and occasionally stocks, but because of the unpredictability of supply, and also because he feels it is a more satisfactory method of ageing than hanging, he matures his meat in vacuum packs, having trimmed it and divided it in four-person quantities. Goose liver is treated the same way.

Apart from stocks and certain desserts, and the bread which is made to his specification by the leading baker in Wertheim, everything is cooked to order. Specialist breads and pastries, pastas and ice-cream are made daily, and the morning and early evening routine of the kitchen is a steady process of preparation to ensure that everything is ready and to hand when the first orders come in. Fish is prepared and put away in refrigerated drawers, herbs and garnishes are picked over and prepared, and the *saucier* can be seen carefully labelling his pans with a felt-tip pen so that there can be no confusion, as the tempo increases, between a veal or a venison reduction. Müller, with his sous-chef Michel Baader and chef *pâtissier* Ingo Holland (who says he gets the same satisfaction out of an exquisitely presented plate as Luciano Pavarotti out of a perfectly executed aria) heads a *brigade* of eleven who work smoothly together in the ultra-modern stainless-steel kitchen, where even the samurai-style suit of butcher's chain mail is polished.

There is little waste, because the less prestigious parts of a deer, for example, or any excess stocks, can be absorbed in the cheerful adjoining restaurant the 'Schober', which uses the same kitchen and serves less elaborate meals at family prices. If the Schober is all red gingham and pine, the Schweizer Stuben is all traditional elegance. A modern interior is decorated with dark wood tables and upholstered chairs with individual table lamps and fine place settings. Flowers are everywhere, even on the elaborate silver serving trays carried by the dining-room staff of ten formally-suited waiters and waitresses in black dresses and white aprons.

When pressed, Dieter Müller will say that the secret of fine cooking is that it must be consistent in quality and must be done from the heart. His greatest pleasure comes from being told by a respected customer that a dish has been perfect, and as much a

pleasure to the eye as to the palate. Although he believes that everyone must start by learning the basic rules, and can in any case get nowhere without that certain indefinable talent which marks out the great cook, he also feels that a personal style is essential. His recipes are mainly his own creations, though some are worked up by his staff. He has no stake himself in the restaurant, although the style and reputation of the cooking are almost entirely due to his presence. He knows that without financial backing on a massive scale it is very difficult for a chef to start independently in Germany today, Eckart Witzigmann being one of the few to have succeeded. One day, when his two young sons are grown up, he might open a restaurant on the scale of his parents', but for the present he is happy to work with the finest resources in this beautiful valley, free from the pressure of running the finances and administration of a complex and capital-intensive business.

He radiates calm, even at the most hectic moments, and much prefers to work with a basic kitchen staff of Germans, because although the kind of multi-national *brigade* found in most kitchens gives a certain stimulus and exchange of experience, he also finds it makes for tension and difficulties – therefore the kind of mistakes which no major restaurant can afford. Even his *plongeurs* are local women and the nearest he has to a foreign cook

The dining room at Schweizer Stuben, with its contemporary glassware and silver ware, Tiffany-style lamps and upholstered chairs, is a model of traditional elegance combined with modern luxury and comfort.

Pedro Sandvoss, chief sommelier, inspects a bottle in Schweizer Stuben's legendary cellar. Many truly great burgundies and bordeaux have been laid down for drinking in a decade or two's time.

is a young man whose Neapolitan parents brought him to Germany as a child. True, he travels every year to give demonstrations and cook special menus but his favourite diversion is to give courses in Wertheim to 'hobby cooks', fourteen at a time, who pay to learn a complete menu, which they cook and eat, together with the appropriate wines.

A few hundred metres away, within the complex, Andreas Schmitt lives in a modern house over a cellar housing some two thousand bottles of red wine (the white wines have a separate cellar). The resources needed to have built up this amazing reserve of great wines, many of which have been laid down for drinking in fifteen or eighteen years time and do not yet appear on the wine list, must amount to millions of Deutschemarks, and the energy and application which has gone into its organization are truly impressive. German wines are of course represented, mainly by white wine, but the glory of the collection is in its red bordeauxs, taken from every major grower, and its burgundies. Ranged round the cellar in wooden bins, with more boxes bearing almost every name of distinction, they are rivalled only by a remarkable collection of Italian reds, especially from Gaja. These, unlike bottles collected for their rarity or age and

probably destined never to be drunk, are all wines bought with care for serious drinking. This philosophy runs over into Dieter Müller's kingdom, where 2,000 Deutschemarks' worth of wines and liqueurs are issued every month for sauces and puddings. Either Andreas Schmitt or his chief sommelier Pedro Sandvoss, or both, taste every dish in order to ensure that customers are given the right recommendations, and in return, Dieter Müller and his colleagues taste the wines to make sure that no dish will interfere with their quality. A new vinaigrette, for example, will be carefully tested for acidity.

Increasingly, country restaurants, especially those which now draw a considerable proportion of their clientèle from among foreign and domestic travellers-for-pleasure ('tourists' does not seem quite the right word for the people who seek out this place), must also offer accommodation. Recently, therefore, a luxurious building offering eight suites for restaurant customers only was opened and more were completed in 1988. This, with the calm of the wooded Main valley with its puttering barges and allotments and the sound of running water heard from the geranium-hung balconies and Japanese-style garden, make the Schweizer Stuben even more attractive.

One of the famous goose liver recipes

Langostinos in der Safrancruste

Langoustines in a Saffron Crust

8 langoustines, or Dublin Bay prawns,
peeled, heads and shells reserved
vegetables for stock (see below)
juice of ½ a lemon
salt and freshly ground pepper
oil for deep frying

Saffron crust
125 ml (4 fl oz) dry white wine
a pinch of saffron
a pinch of salt
a pinch of sugar
100 g (3½ oz) flour

Sauce
7 tablespoons thick home-made mayonnaise
1 tablespoon stock made with
the langoustine heads and shells
a pinch of saffron
a pinch of curry powder
2 teaspoons cognac
1 drop Tabasco
juice of ¼ lemon
1 tablespoon crème fraîche
salt

Make a stock with the langoustine shells and heads, and aromatic vegetables (carrot, celery, onion, a quarter clove garlic, tomatoes, thyme and peppercorns). Strain and reduce to a tablespoon. Cool.

Make the crust by mixing the wine, saffron, salt and sugar together and then beating in the flour.

Beat the mayonnaise with all the other sauce ingredients except the *crème fraîche* until it is stiff. Place in a bowl and pipe the *crème fraîche* in a decorative spiral on top.

Remove the black vein from the langoustine tails and season them with salt, pepper and lemon. Flour them lightly. Roll out the saffron crust, divide into eight and use to wrap the langoustine tails. Have ready a pan of arachide or sunflower oil at 175°C/350°F and fry each for 2 minutes until golden brown. Serve with the sauce and a fresh seasonal salad.

FOR FOUR PEOPLE

Soufflé von fränkischen Bachsaibling mit Rote-bete-sauce

Char with Beetroot Sauce

2 char, 400 g (14 oz) each
1 egg, separated
250 ml (8 fl oz) single cream
butter for the moulds
salt
lemon juice

Sauce
1 raw beetroot weighing about 50 g (1¾ oz)
80 g (3 oz) butter, softened
500 ml (18 fl oz) fish stock
7 tablespoons dry white wine
7 tablespoons double cream
4 teaspoons champagne
salt
lemon juice
1 tablespoon whipped cream

Fillet the fish and select the best fillets. The selected fillets should be poached for 2 minutes in stock just before serving.

Make the soufflés. Preheat the oven to 200C°/400°F/Gas 6. Cut the remaining pieces of fish into small pieces, season with salt and lemon juice and mix with the egg yolk. Put the fish and the single cream in the freezer to chill, then process them finely in a liquidizer or food processor. Push through a very fine sieve to eliminate any bones and season with salt and lemon juice. Beat the egg white until stiff, and fold it into the fish cream. Butter four ramekins and three-quarters fill them with the soufflé mixture. Stand them in a roasting pan with enough hot water to come half-way up the sides and cook in the preheated oven for 12–15 minutes, until puffed and golden.

Peel and dice the beetroot and liquidize with the butter; chill. Reduce the fish stock and the white wine to 150 ml (¼ pint) in a small pan. Add the double cream and cook through. Before serving, whisk the beetroot butter into the reduction, then the champagne with more salt and lemon juice to taste. Finally, fold in the whipped cream.

Arrange the sauce, fillet and soufflé on the plate, with fresh vegetables.

FOR FOUR PEOPLE

Char (omble chevalier) *with Beetroot Sauce*

Sweetbreads with Asparagus (only green asparagus is used here)

Piccata von Kalbsbries auf Weissen und Grünen Spargeln

Sweetbreads with White and Green Asparagus

400 g (14 oz) veal sweetbreads, well soaked
1 small onion, peeled and spiked with a small bay leaf and 2 cloves
1 sprig thyme
a splash of vinegar
8 white asparagus spears
8 green asparagus spears
200 ml (7 fl oz) crème fraîche
50 g (1¾ oz) cold diced butter
juice of ½ a lemon
200 ml (7 fl oz) red wine sauce
scant 3 tablespoons truffle juice
scant 3 tablespoons port
a pinch of cornflour
2 tablespoons flour
50 g (1¾ oz) clarified butter
1 large fresh egg
20 g (⅔ oz) finely chopped black truffles
salt and pepper

Bring the spiked onion, thyme and vinegar to the boil with water and cook the sweetbreads in this for 12 minutes. Drain the sweetbreads cool, skin and cut into four equal pieces.

Peel and trim the asparagus, and cook in a little boiling salted water. Rinse in iced water and trim the tips to 4 cm (1½ inches) long. Cut the remainder of the stalks into 1 cm (½ inch) pieces. Make the sauce for the asparagus by reducing the *crème fraîche* with the diced butter, whisking all the time, and season with salt and lemon. Keep both asparagus and sauce warm.

Make the sauce for the sweetbreads by reducing the red wine sauce, truffle juice and port to about 6 tablespoons, then whisking in the cornflour until the sauce is very smooth and shiny. Season with salt and pepper to taste.

Just before serving, coat the cooled sweetbreads in 1 tablespoon of seasoned flour and cook quickly in clarified butter. Drain on kitchen paper while you mix the large egg with the second tablespoon of flour and add the chopped truffles and salt. Place the sweetbreads in a pan with the egg and truffle mixture and cook gently over a medium heat until the egg is set.

Place the asparagus tips round the edges of four warm plates, arrange the short pieces of asparagus and their sauce in the middle and top with the sweetbreads and a spoonful of red sauce. Arrange slices of egg and truffle mixture around the sweetbreads. Serve immediately.

FOR FOUR PEOPLE

Salatvariationen mit Rehleber und Pfifferlingen

Venison Liver Salad with Chanterelles

1 roe deer liver of approximately 400 g (14 oz)
80 g (2¾ oz) butter
200 g (7 oz) small chanterelles
seasonal salad leaves
7 tablespoons reduced venison stock
salt and pepper

Vinaigrette
50 g (1¾ oz) shallots, peeled and chopped
200 ml (7 fl oz) strong veal stock
2 tablespoons sherry vinegar
7½ tablespoons walnut oil
4 tablespoons grapeseed oil
4 tablespoons arachide or sunflower oil
freshly chopped herbs (e.g. parsley, chives, chervil)
salt and pepper

Make the vinaigrette by cooking the shallots in the stock. Cool and mix well with the other ingredients. Season, and add the chopped herbs at the last moment.

Remove the skin and veins from the liver and trim carefully. Pan-fry in 60 g (2 oz) of the butter and then cook in a medium oven (180°C/350°F/Gas 4) until it is cooked but still rosy inside. Let it rest in a warm place while you sauté the cleaned chanterelles in the remaining butter for approximately 1 minute.

Have ready the salad leaves on four plates, and season with the vinaigrette. Slice the liver quickly and lay the pieces in a fan shape adjacent to the salad. Top with the chanterelles and a tablespoon or so of reduced venison stock. Serve immediately.

Note: venison liver has always been a favourite dish in Central Europe and is gradually gaining acceptance elsewhere, although it is likely to be difficult to obtain except, in season, from a local marksman. Farther south, in Bavaria, an air-cured ham made from roe deer calves' flesh is a special delicacy.

FOR FOUR PEOPLE

Venison Liver Salad with Chanterelles

Rehrücken mit Lebkuchensauce, glacierter Birne und Spätzle

Saddle of Roe Deer with Gingerbread Sauce, Glazed Pears and Spätzle

600 g (1 lb 5 oz) saddle of roe deer, boned and trimmed
40 g (1½ oz) clarified butter
20 g (⅔ oz) butter
salt and freshly ground pepper

Gingerbread sauce
60 g (2 oz) pain d'épice
400 ml (14 fl oz) strong venison stock
2 teaspoons armagnac
4 teaspoons port
2 juniper berries
½ teaspoon crushed white peppercorns
4 allspice berries
10 g (⅓ oz) chilled butter, diced
salt and freshly ground pepper

Poached pears
4 ripe Williams pears
3 tablespoons pear eau-de-vie
3 tablespoons dry white wine
3 tablespoons caster sugar
40 g (1½ oz) unsalted butter
40 g (1½ oz) sugar

Spätzle (small dumplings)
250 g (8¾ oz) sifted plain flour
4 egg yolks
salt
nutmeg
warm water
butter

Cranberry sauce
200 g (7 oz) cranberries, washed and picked over
6–7 tablespoons red wine
300 g (10½ oz) sugar
¼ cinnamon stick
arrowroot

Preheat the oven to 190°C/375°F/Gas 5. Divide the boned saddle into four equal slices, and season well with salt and pepper. Put the meat in a roasting pan with the clarified butter and roast for 5 minutes. Add the fresh butter and roast for 3–5 minutes more. Remove from the oven and allow to rest in a warm place.

Cut the *pain d'épice* in cubes and put in a small heavy pan with the stock, armag-nac, port and spices. Reduce by half over a low heat. Liquidize the sauce and pass through a conical sieve into a clean pan. Season with salt and pepper and keep hot. Just before serving, whisk in the butter.

Peel and quarter the pears, then core and trim them. Macerate in the pear spirit, white wine and caster sugar for 15 minutes. Melt the butter in a hot pan, and sprinkle in the sugar. Stir well with a wooden spoon and dip the macerated pear quarters carefully into the hot syrup. Turn in the syrup, then remove and keep warm.

Make a loose dough with the flour, egg yolks, salt, nutmeg and a little warm water. Have ready a pan of boiling salted water and very carefully flip in little oval pieces of the dough from the work surface with a knife. When the spätzle rise to the surface, lift them out of the pan with a slotted spoon and refresh under cold water to stop the cooking process. Toss in butter and keep warm. (Unless you are very skilled this step may have to be done in two or more batches.)

Boil the red wine with the sugar and add the prepared cranberries. They should cook until they are soft but not mushy. Take off the heat, add the cinnamon and leave to cool. Mix the arrowroot with a little of the wine and return to the pan. Remove the cinnamon before serving.

Cut the pieces of venison into slices and arrange in a fan shape on four heated plates. Pour the gingerbread sauce over the meat and arrange the pear quarters, spätzle and cranberries around them.

FOR FOUR PEOPLE

Saddle of Roe Deer with Gingerbread Sauce

Hot Plum Tart with Plum Cream and White Chocolate Ice-Cream

Zwetschgentorte mit Pflümlicreme und Weissen Schokoladeneis

Hot Plum Tart with Plum Cream and White Chocolate Ice-Cream

Pastry
150 g (5¼ oz) butter
75 g (2¼ oz) caster sugar
1 egg yolk
a small piece of vanilla pod
a small pinch of salt
50 g (1¾ oz) biscuit crumbs
100 g (3½ oz) flour
75 g (2¼ oz) toasted, finely chopped almonds

Ice-cream
250 ml (8 fl oz) cream
250 ml (8 fl oz) milk
60 g (2 oz) caster sugar
6 egg yolks
125 g (4½ oz) white chocolate

Vanilla cream
8½ tablespoons milk
8½ tablespoons cream
50 g (1¾ oz) caster sugar
a small piece of vanilla pod
2 egg yolks
20 g (⅔ oz) wheat starch, moistened in milk

Plum sauce
150 g (5¼ oz) crème fraîche
40 g (1¼ oz) caster sugar
2¾ tablespoons plum brandy
50 g (1¾ oz) whipped cream
18 ripe small purple plums (zwetschgen), stoned and sliced into eight
caster sugar
ground cinnamon

First, make the pastry. Mix the butter, sugar, egg yolk and flavourings together. Work the mixture briefly in a food processor with the biscuit crumbs, flour and almonds. Chill for at least an hour. Preheat the oven to 220°C/425°F/Gas 7. Roll out the dough to about 3 cm (1¼ inches) thick and use to make six 10 cm (4 inch) diameter tartlets. Bake in the oven until they are golden brown, and then cool on a rack.

Meanwhile, make the ice-cream. Heat the cream, milk and sugar and stir in the egg yolks. Let the mixture thicken a little, then

add the white chocolate in pieces, stirring until it has dissolved. Strain and allow to cool before freezing.

Make the vanilla cream by bringing the milk, cream, sugar and vanilla to the boil. Blend in the egg yolks and the wheat starch moistened with a little milk. Cook over a gentle heat for 2–3 minutes, cool and strain.

Mix the *crème fraîche*, sugar and plum brandy together and fold in the whipped cream to make a sauce.

Place the six tartlets on a baking sheet. Spoon in a layer of vanilla cream and arrange an overlapping layer of plum slices on top. Dust with fine sugar and a very little cinnamon and bake for 10 minutes in the 220°C/425°F/Gas 7 oven.

Transfer to plates, pour the plum sauce round and at the last moment add a scoop of white chocolate ice-cream. A raspberry sauce could also be served, and toasted flaked almonds and mint leaves used to decorate the dish.

FOR SIX PEOPLE

ECKART WITZIGMANN

RESTAURANT AUBERGINE

Eckart Witzigmann has a good claim to the title of Germany's senior chef – until 1988 his Aubergine restaurant in the smart Munich Maximiliansplatz was the only one to gain the top score of 19.50 points in the Gault Millau guide. He is certainly one of the most serious chefs, and it is significant that he was chosen to work alongside one of Germany's top medical nutritionists to devise the menus for the West German Olympic team at the Seoul Olympics. Born in 1941 in Badgastein, Austria, he was intended to succeed his father in the family tailoring business; he says now that because his two children, both almost grown-up, have no wish to follow him in the cooking profession, he understands his parents' bitter disappointment when he abandoned tailoring. Briefly, he considered taking up skiing professionally, the goldsmiths' or the opticians' trades, then finally and irrevocably decided to become a cook. It is significant that his three rejected professions, as well as his chosen métier, all require a high degree of technical skill, confidence and precision.

He trained in a Badgastein hotel, and then, apprenticeship completed, he embarked on a series of 'Wanderjahre', working in kitchens all over Germany and the Alps. It was in a ski-lift queue during his day off from a resort hotel that he made what was to be the most important contact of his life. He stood next to the Haeberlin brothers from L'Auberge de l'Ill at Illhaeusern, then,

as now, one of the finest restaurants in France. They talked, and young Eckart said that his greatest ambition was to work in France. At first, nothing happened, but they kept in touch, meeting again in Davos a few seasons later. Again silence, and then, just as the young chef was about to leave for a job in Johannesburg, the summons to Illhaeusern came. Since that day, the Haeberlins have been his greatest supporters and patrons. 'For me, personally, the Haeberlins were the springboard to success. I had already worked in the best hotels in Switzerland and Germany, but they gave me two years – in 1964 and 1967 – at Illhaeusern, and arranged for me to spend time with Paul Bocuse, Roger Vergé and other friends of theirs among the great French chefs.' He also worked in Stockholm and at the Café Royal in London. It was while he was at the Jockey Club in Washington, D.C. that the Haeberlins heard that the Tantris in Munich needed a new chef. Witzigmann was at first reluctant; he enjoyed America, the job was congenial, he had never thought seriously about working in Germany rather than in France. But the pull of Europe proved too much and he accepted the post. He still occasionally has doubts about leaving America, but says, 'I cannot complain. I can only thank God for everything I've achieved – I've had a career others can only dream of. Tantris turned out to be the place where I had the opportunity to use all

'God probably created me to be a cook.'

Restrained elegance is the trademark of the Aubergine decor.

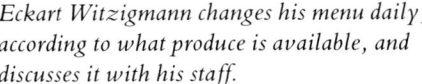

The Aubergine's cellar, which is small by comparison with, for example, the Schweizer Stuben's, is nevertheless expertly and imaginatively stocked. Eckart Witzigmann is particularly proud to offer a selection of his native Austrian wines as well as the finest German and French vintages.

Munich's produce market is one of the finest in Europe. Eckart Witzigmann inspects every ingredient used in the kitchen.

Eckart Witzigmann changes his menu daily, according to what produce is available, and discusses it with his staff.

the knowledge and cooking experience which I had acquired, and to make my own distinctive style. It is important to break away from your mentors at the right moment, whoever they are – the Haeberlins, Bocuse, Vergé – and think for yourself. Tantris was my chance.'

Eckart Witzigmann was the first chef to introduce the principles of the nouvelle cuisine to Germany, but he is now sceptical about much that has been written about the movement, and the ways in which it has been exploited. 'It is a very simple way of cooking, the logical process of combining good fresh ingredients which harmonize, whose colours combine well. The early mistakes came about because it is a cuisine without a foundation, no question about it. In my opinion, the basic prerequisite for making good nouvelle cuisine is the classic cuisine. The young people now don't know how to make a proper stew or ragoût.' In fact, he is one of those great chefs who have never made the mistake of disregarding the traditional and regional. In 1973, when the nouvelle cuisine vogue was at its height, he was cooking with Savoy cabbage and lentils, and using traditional Bavarian and Austrian recipes as well as dishes inspired by Bocuse and Vergé. For him, the client's pleasure is everything and his or her preferences come first. If oxtail soup, a simple grilled meat and salad or a full-blown meal is asked for, then it is provided. 'I want the customer to be satisfied: then I'm satisfied.'

The daily menu changes according to availability of ingredients, and offers full meals at various prices. For example, in June, a cheaper menu might offer a choice of two starters: pan-fried goose liver with a salad of lightly cooked green beans, or red barbel fillets with artichoke salad, both with the lightest of vinaigrettes: two soups: a rich fish soup with a creamy saffron base and an asparagus cream soup; then a fish course of cod served with courgettes and paprika in a balsamic vinegar sauce. A strawberry and rhubarb sorbet provides a respite before a choice between a sauté of Bavarian pigeon breasts with steamed pea shoots, or veal sweetbreads and kidneys with a selection of tiny vegetables. A varied cheeseboard precedes dessert, which could be either a confection of mangoes and wild strawberries or cherries and melon with a pistachio ice-cream. In August, a typical menu at the top of the price range starts with a salad of Breton lobster with artichokes, a warm salad of grilled quail breasts and green beans, a monkfish and fennel soup or a tomato paprika soup. This is followed by wild salmon with sorrel sauce, ragoût of wild mushroom with pasta, or saddle of venison cooked in caul fat. Cheese and a redcurrant sorbet follow, with a final choice between a compôte of fresh seasonal berries with almond ice-cream and a chocolate terrine with nougat sauce. Dishes on other days might be based on perch from the Chiemsee, omble chevalier, carp or other local fish or on more modest ingredients like rabbit or skate, all with a sauce and garnish contrived exactly to complement their special qualities.

The flower arrangements are spectacular and original

And on special occasions Maître Witzigmann will cook special dishes for groups of favoured customers – for instance a goose for the annual autumn goose festival.

The separate, short, and unutterably tempting dessert menu gives the Aubergine's North German pâtissier full scope for his artistic talents. As the photograph shows, he can arrange a variety of fruit ices and purées, scatter crushed pistachios and icing sugar and feather patterns into multicoloured sauces with virtuoso precision. The result may not always be to everyone's visual taste, but the impact on the palate is unforgettable.

The limitations of space in a city like Munich make a cellar on the scale of the Schweizer Stuben's impracticable, but the wine list is wide-ranging and well chosen.

For the future, Eckart Witzigmann sees his cooking developing in two streams, to meet people's needs at various times and for various purposes. On the one side, there is the healthier style, with plenty of wholefoods and lighter menus; on the other, the meal as an experience. 'The guests come into the restaurant – perhaps they are celebrating something, an anniversary, a new love – and they want a cordial reception, the chicken carved at the table, a flambé dessert. The future lies in making action around the guest, a little show, not a circus, perfectly executed.'

Certainly nothing could be more conducive to a celebration than the Aubergine, which Witzigmann launched in October

1978. Its ambience is one of calm perfection. The restaurant's name is echoed in the purple carpet which stretches from door to kerb, and repeated in the key pattern carpets and interior decor. Austere white paper collages hang on the walls. The tables are widely spaced and accommodate forty diners. Each is covered with a snowy cloth and is simply set with single lilies in plain vases. Upstairs, in the bar which overlooks the restaurant through three convex *oeil-de-boeuf* windows, the decoration is more ornate, and the flower arrangements are enormous and spectacularly original. The guests are greeted charmingly by Frau Witzigmann and the ten waiters move with well-oiled precision, explaining dishes to new clients, serving the habitués unobtrusively.

The kitchen staff numbers fourteen, all of whom are expected to stay at least eighteen months. Each is allotted a specialist 'station' after a trial period in each of the various kitchen areas to allow their particular talents and preferences to show themselves. The '*chef-tournant*', as he wryly remarks, is Eckart Witzigmann. His eye, as his staff will tell you, is on everything. He inspects every ingredient (bought always from the best available source, be it Brittany or the huge wholesale produce market in Munich) and every dish himself, and is virtually never absent on the foreign consultancy trips and television appearances which take so many famous chefs away from their stoves – often with disastrous results. His only outside activity is his writing and his leisure time is more limited than most people could endure. He himself regrets this, regrets not having had more time with his children when they were young. He says he may rethink his career, may decide to do something else. 'I enjoy cooking enormously, but sometimes I feel I never want to cook again. After a couple of days, though, I want to get back to the kitchen. God probably created me to be a cook.'

Kalbszungensalat mit Bries

Calf's Tongue Salad with Sweetbreads

1 calf's tongue of about 450g (1 lb)
1 veal sweetbread of about 300g (11½ oz)
a selection of seasonal vegetables
drawn from: beetroot, carrot, celery, parsley
root, potato, white radish
a selection of salad leaves, including lettuce,
lollo rosso lettuce, iceberg lettuce, lamb's
lettuce, curly endive, and a few radishes

Vinaigrette
7 tablespoons corn or sunflower oil
3 tablespoons fruit vinegar
a pinch of sugar
chopped chives
grated horseradish
salt and freshly ground pepper

Cook the tongue in salted water for approximately 2½ hours, until the tip is easily pierced with a knife. Cool under cold running water and peel off the skin. Slice the tongue thinly. Soak the trimmed sweetbread (overnight if possible) and simmer them for about 20 minutes on a low heat, so that they remain slightly pink inside. Allow to cool, remove from the pan, drain well, and slice thinly.

Cook the vegetables and slice thinly or chop them finely. Wash and pick over the salad leaves and toss them with the vinaigrette. Arrange the tongue and sweetbread on four individual plates or a large serving dish in a fan pattern and decorate with the salad leaves and the cooked vegetables.

FOR FOUR PEOPLE

Salat von Jacobsmuscheln mit Krevetten und Grünem Spargel

Scallop Salad with Prawns and Asparagus

28 scallops, sliced horizontally
28 uncooked prawns, shelled
4 tablespoons oil
1 tablespoon butter
a selection of salad leaves including radicchio,
lambs' lettuce, lollo rosso lettuce, ordinary
lettuce
28 green asparagus spears, cooked and
trimmed
vinaigrette (see previous recipe)
salt and pepper
a small bunch of chervil
a few small tomatoes, peeled, seeded and diced

Scallop Salad with Prawns and Asparagus

Cook the sliced scallops and prawns very briefly in a mixture of hot oil and butter. Wash the salad leaves and arrange on four plates, together with the asparagus spears. Sprinkle with vinaigrette and place the warm shellfish around the salad and asparagus. Season, decorate with the chervil and tomatoes and serve warm.

FOR FOUR PEOPLE

Taubensalat mit Taubenleber und Pfifferlingen

Salad of Pigeon with Chanterelles

4 pigeons of about 250g (8–9 oz) each
the pigeons' livers
a selection of salad leaves made up from
radicchio, iceberg lettuce, lamb's lettuce, lollo
rosso lettuce, rocket and curly endive, plus
other salad vegetables as available
4 tablespoons of diced savoury jelly
a few fine chanterelles

Vinaigrette
(you will need only a little; keep the rest for
other salads)
4 tablespoons apple or other fruit vinegar
2 tablespoons balsamic vinegar
6 tablespoons olive oil
6 tablespoons corn or sunflower oil
¼ teaspoon made mustard
salt, freshly ground pepper and sugar to taste

Roast the pigeons whole (about 20 minutes at 230°C / 450°F / Gas 8 will produce cooked but rosy breast meat. If you are using your oven at a lower temperature for another dish increase the cooking time). Allow the birds to rest for 10 minutes in a warm place, then slice the breasts thinly. Keep the carcases for stock.

Wash and pick over the salad leaves and vegetables. Divide them equally between four plates and sprinkle with some of the vinaigrette. Arrange the pigeon slices in an attractive pattern on the salad and garnish with the diced savoury jelly. Cook the chanterelles very briefly in hot oil, fry the pigeon livers briefly, and garnish the salad with them. It should be served warm.

FOR FOUR PEOPLE

Salad of Pigeon with Chanterelles

Monkfish with Beetroot Sauce

Seezunge auf Kresseschaum

Sole with Watercress Sauce

2 small soles of about 400 g (14 oz) each
4 medium potatoes, halved
24 mussels, in their shells
1 shallot, peeled and chopped
1 clove of garlic, peeled
a small sprig of thyme
2 parsley stalks
oil for frying
4 tablespoons dry white wine
salt, freshly ground pepper and lemon juice
watercress leaves
3 tomatoes, peeled, seeded and diced

Watercress sauce
1 small shallot, peeled and chopped
a nut of butter
a dash of Noilly Prat or other vermouth
8 tablespoons dry white wine
250 ml (8 fl oz) fish stock
150 ml (¼ pint) double cream
a handful of watercress, washed and picked over
about 225 g (8 oz) butter, chilled and cut into 30 cubes
1 tablespoon whipped cream
salt, cayenne pepper and lemon juice

Remove the fillets from the soles and skin them. Wrap each round a raw potato half and secure with a toothpick. Season with salt, pepper and lemon juice and poach very gently.

Scrub and debeard the mussels, throwing away any which are open. Sauté the shallot, garlic, thyme and parsley stalks in a little oil in a pan large enough to contain the mussels, then add the white wine and steam the mussels, covered, over the simmering liquid until they open. (If any fail to open, throw them away.) Remove them from their shells.

To make the watercress sauce, soften the chopped shallot in the butter in a sauté pan, add the vermouth and white wine and reduce. Add the fish stock and reduce again. Add the cream and bring to the boil again. Remove from the heat, season with salt, cayenne pepper and lemon juice to taste, and strain. Cook the watercress in boiling water, refresh under cold running water, squeeze dry and chop finely. Add to the hot sauce and liquidize or rub through a fine sieve. Gradually whisk in the cubes of cold butter, a few at a time, over a very low heat and finally add the whipped cream.

Pour a layer of watercress sauce on to four heated plates. Carefully remove the sole fillets from the potatoes, and place two fillets on each plate. (Discard the potatoes.) Decorate with the mussels, watercress leaves and a little diced raw tomato.

FOR FOUR PEOPLE

Seeteufel auf Roter Betesauce

Monkfish with Beetroot Sauce

1 large monkfish tail of about 1 kg (2¼ lb)
1 shallot, peeled and chopped
1 tablespoon butter
1 medium beetroot
250 ml (8 fl oz) fish stock
150 ml (¼ pint) double cream
a dash vinegar
20 g (⅔ oz) cold cubed butter
1 tablespoon whipped cream
1 small potato, peeled and cubed
1 tablespoon oil
salt, pepper and lemon juice
chives, grated horseradish and perhaps a few mussels for decoration

Bone the monkfish tail and cut it into eight equal-sized medallions. Soften the shallot in butter.

Dice the beetroot and bring to the boil in the fish stock, then let it reduce slowly. Add the cream, and bring to the boil again. Season with salt, pepper and lemon juice to taste. Add a dash of vinegar and liquidize or sieve the sauce. Return to the pan and gradually whisk in the cold butter, a few cubes at a time, over a very low heat, finally adding the whipped cream.

Fry the potato dice in hot oil until they are golden. Pan-fry the monkfish medallions very briefly.

Pour a layer of foamy beetroot sauce on to each of four heated plates, arrange the monkfish and potato dice attractively and decorate with chives and a little grated horseradish.

FOR FOUR PEOPLE

Crepinetten vom Lammsattel

Saddle of Lamb cooked in Caul Fat

a saddle of lamb weighing about 900 g (2 lb)
usual vegetables and seasonings for making stock
50 g (1¾ oz) pork caul fat
15 g (½ oz) bread dice
50 g (1¾ oz) butter
25 g (1 oz) cooked ham, sliced finely into strips
20 g (⅔ oz) blanched and drained spinach, coarsely chopped
1 tiny piece of garlic, finely chopped
pinch of nutmeg
pinch of thyme
1 teaspoon chopped chervil
1 tablespoon olive oil
sprig of thyme or rosemary
crushed clove of garlic
salt and freshly ground pepper

Bone the saddle of lamb and trim the fillets, which should be cut into 4 medallions weighing approximately 80 g (2¾ oz) each. Lightly flatten them with the side of a cleaver. Use the bones and trimmings with a selection of vegetables and seasonings to make a strong stock.

Meanwhile, fry the diced bread in 30 g (1 oz) of butter until golden brown; keep warm on a plate, reserving the butter. Sweat the ham, spinach and garlic in the butter. Add salt, pepper, nutmeg, thyme and chervil and mix well.

Spread out the sheet of caul fat on a work surface or board, having washed and drained it carefully. Divide it roughly into four equal pieces. Divide slightly more than half the drained spinach mixture between each piece of caul fat. Place a lamb medallion on each mound of spinach and season it with salt and pepper. Cover with the remaining spinach mixture and wrap up the caul fat parcels as securely as possible, using toothpicks or small skewers if necessary.

Melt the remaining butter with the olive oil in a heavy pan until it foams and then fry the little parcels for 5 minutes on each side. Remove and keep warm while you flavour the hot cooking juices with a sprig of thyme or rosemary and a crushed clove of garlic. Use this, together with any juices which have run out of the lamb parcels and the vegetable cooking juices, to make a strongly flavoured reduced sauce and strain over the lamb parcels on individual heated plates or into a sauce boat.

These *crepinetten* can be served with green beans, cabbage, artichokes, carrots and perhaps also with noodles, or, as in the photograph, with mange-tout peas and a green pea purée

Note: caul fat can be obtained from your butcher, but should normally be ordered in advance.

FOR FOUR PEOPLE

Saddle of Lamb cooked in Caul Fat

Duck with Savoy Cabbage

Ente mit Wirsing

Duck with Savoy Cabbage

1 duck
4–5 tablespoons olive oil
12 round potatoes
1 Savoy cabbage
170 g (6 oz) scraped carrots
170 g (6 oz) peeled onions
170 g (6 oz) washed parsley roots
60 g (2 oz) salted butter
250 ml (8 fl oz) clarified stock or water
30 g (1 oz) parsley, chopped
20 g (²/₃ oz) butter
salt and freshly ground pepper

Season the duck inside and out and truss it. Preheat the oven to 170°C/325°F/Gas 3. Sear the duck, breast-side down, in 2 tablespoons of hot oil, then roast for 1½ hours in the oven, basting frequently. Peel and turn the potatoes and blanch them for 3-4 minutes in boiling salted water. Cool.

Remove any tough outer leaves from the cabbage. Cut the heart in quarters. Cook the quarters in boiling salted water for 4 minutes, then refresh in cold water. Trim and turn the cleaned carrots, onions and parsley roots, then brown them very lightly in 40 g (1½ oz) foaming salted butter in a flameproof casserole. Moisten with the stock or water. Drain the blanched cabbage quarters and re-form as a heart, squeezing gently to eliminate any excess water. Place the cabbage among the other vegetables in the casserole. Season with salt and pepper, then put into a preheated 200°C/400°F/Gas 6 oven to braise. (If you do not have two ovens, this operation can be carried out either in a Dutch oven or in covered casserole on the top of the stove.) Take care that the liquid does not evaporate completely and moisten with stock or water from time to time if it seems necessary.

Meanwhile heat the cooled potatoes in the remaining olive oil and the remaining salted butter. When the potatoes are sizzling in the fat, place the pan in the oven with the vegetables (or continue to cook on top of the stove) until the potatoes can be easily pierced with a skewer.

When the duck is cooked, and about 15 minutes before serving, place the vegetables and potatoes round the bird in a clean ovenproof serving dish, and return to the 170°C/325°F/Gas 3 oven, continuing to moisten the vegetables as necessary. Remove the fat from the pan in which the duck has cooked and deglaze the pan with a little water and the juices from the vegetables. Add the chopped parsley, check the seasoning and pour over the vegetables. At the same time, make *beurre noisette* – butter heated until it is nut-brown – and pour it carefully over the bird.

Note: at the Aubergine, the cabbage is placed in the cavity of the duck as the dish is finished; and for the photograph, Chef Witzigmann has decorated the bird with whole parsley.

FOR FOUR PEOPLE

Passionsfruchtcreme mit Joghurtmus

Passion Fruit Cream with a Yogurt Mousse

Passion fruit cream
150 g (5¼ oz) strained passion fruit pulp
60 g (2 oz) caster sugar
4 g (2 leaves) of gelatine, softened in warm water
125 ml (4½ fl oz) double cream
2 egg whites
20 g (⅔ oz) caster sugar
a few drops of fruit vinegar

Yogurt mousse
170 g (6 oz) plain yogurt
90 g (3½ oz) caster sugar
juice of two lemons
4 g (2 leaves) of gelatine, softened in warm water
125 ml (4½ fl oz) double cream
2 egg whites
20 g (⅔ oz) caster sugar

peeled segments of pink grapefruit
very thin strips of mango

Add the 60 g (2 oz) sugar to the passion fruit pulp and heat gently with the softened gelatine, whisking until the gelatine has dissolved. Add the cream and stir thoroughly. Keep warm while you beat the egg whites and 20 g (⅔ oz) sugar to a snow, and then fold into the passion fruit mixture with the fruit vinegar.

Make the yogurt mousse in the same way, dissolving the gelatine in the lemon juice and adding the yogurt with the cream.

Arrange peeled grapefruit segments equally between four plates and arrange scoops of the yogurt mousse and passion fruit cream on top of them. Decorate with mint leaves and very thin strips of mango.

Note: Eckart Witzigmann's pâtissier is a culinary surrealist whose boss rightly gives him complete freedom in producing his amazing puddings. All chefs are football fans – most of the restaurants in this book have their own teams which regularly play against neighbouring restaurants – so the Bayern Munich red colours are frequently used.

FOR FOUR PEOPLE

Karamelisierte Birne mit Sauerrahmcreme auf Himbeercoulis

Caramelized Pear with a Sour Cream Mousse with Raspberry Purée

4 ripe pears (preferably Williams), with stalks
500 ml (18 fl oz) Muscat de Lunel
200 ml (7 fl oz) pear eau-de-vie
1 stick cinnamon
1 vanilla pod
80 g (2¾ oz) sugar
zest and juice of 1 lemon
icing sugar
mint leaves

Sour cream mousse
300 g (12½ oz) sour cream
4 leaves of gelatine
juice of 3 oranges
120 g (4 oz) caster sugar
250 ml (9 fl oz) double cream, whipped
4 egg whites
30 g (1 oz) caster sugar

Raspberry purée
300 g (12½ oz) raspberries
200 ml (7 fl oz) raspberry eau-de-vie
juice of 1 lemon
80 g (2¾ oz) caster sugar

Peel and core the pears from the bottom, leaving the stalks intact. Meanwhile heat the wine, pear eau-de-vie, cinnamon, vanilla, sugar, lemon zest and juice in a pan. Poach the pears in this liquid for 10 minutes, and leave them to cool in the liquid. When cool, remove them and pat dry, then slice them thinly, retaining the original shape of the pear (see photograph). Sprinkle with icing sugar and caramelize under a hot grill.

Soften the gelatine in the orange juice, add the 120 g (4 oz) sugar and warm through until the gelatine has completely dissolved. Beat the sour cream lightly with a fork and add gradually to the gelatine mixture, beating all the time. Heat again but do not boil.

Whip the egg whites with the 30 g (1 oz) sugar till stiff, add the whipped cream and fold into the sour cream mixture. Refrigerate till set.

Mix the ingredients for the raspberry purée together and liquidize and sieve.

To serve, make a pool of raspberry purée on each plate, then arrange the sliced but whole pear with two scoops of sour cream mousse on it. Decorate.

FOR FOUR PEOPLE

Caramelized Pear with a Sour Cream Mousse with Raspberry Purée

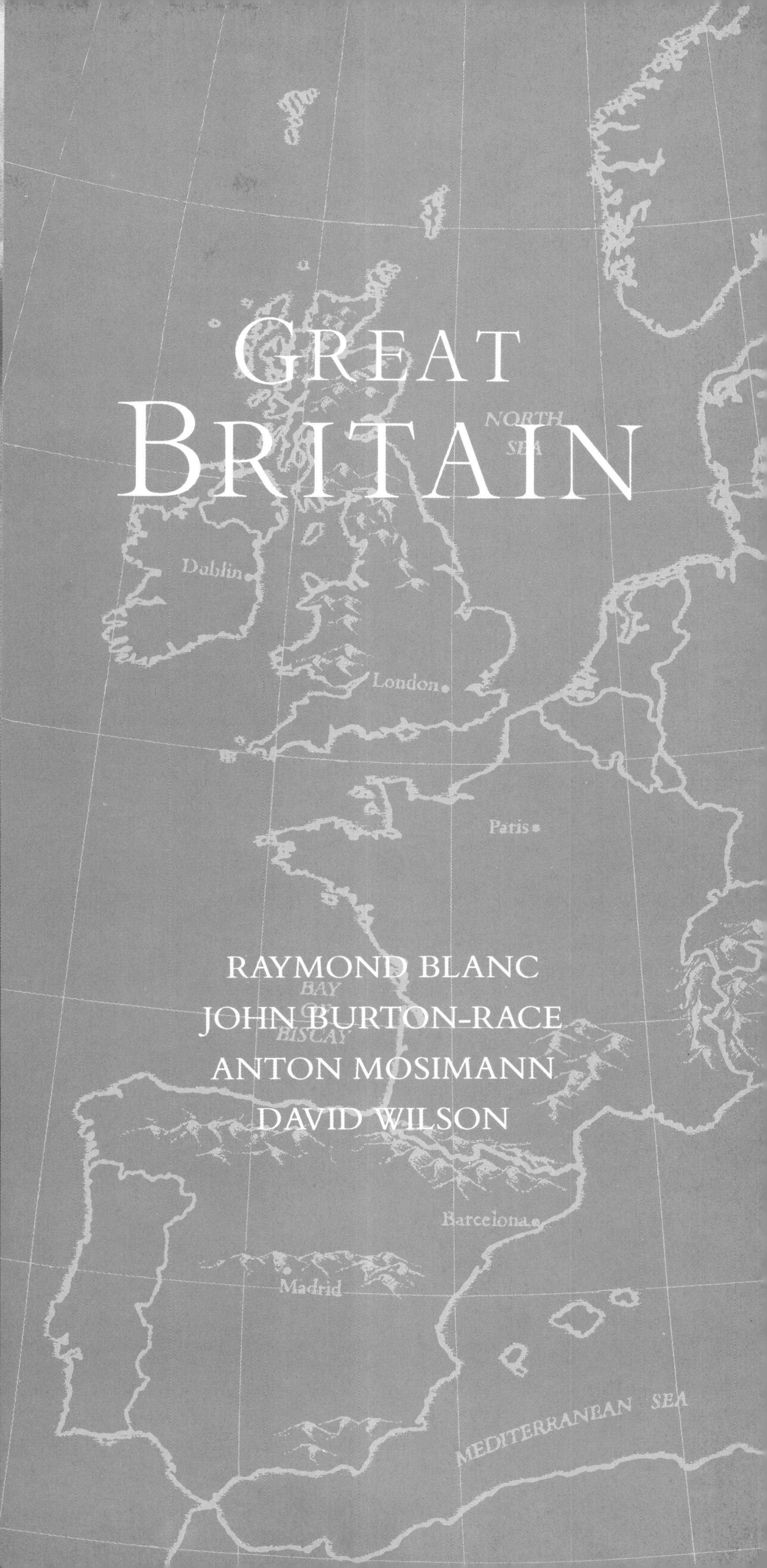

GREAT BRITAIN

RAYMOND BLANC

JOHN BURTON-RACE

ANTON MOSIMANN

DAVID WILSON

RAYMOND BLANC

LE MANOIR AUX QUAT' SAISONS

Great Milton

Raymond Blanc was born in a country village near Besançon in the Franche-Comté in 1949. He looks like a man still in his twenties, slim and like one of Stendhal's heroes with his dramatic good looks and flashing soulful eyes. Today, he is widely thought to be the most talented chef working in Britain, and when his Manoir aux Quat' Saisons outside Oxford achieves its third Michelin star, as it surely must very soon, he will be the youngest to reach that level. The journey from French country boy, son of a skilled watchmaker in Besançon, to his present position has been one of the more remarkable success stories of recent years, not least because he is one of the few major chefs who are 'autodidacte' or completely self-taught. He came late to the culinary world, having tried various jobs before applying to the Palais de la Bière in Besançon. He wanted a kitchen post but was told that, at nineteen, he was too old: apprentices must start at fifteen. So he became a waiter and soon picked up the rudiments of restaurant life and an understanding of that curious and unpredictable animal, the customer.

In 1972 he came to England to learn the language, picking a small riverside hotel restaurant on the Thames out of the Jobs Vacant column. The Rose Revived at Newbridge was the beginning of his adventure. He fell in love with and married the owner's daughter, Jenny, and eventually found himself filling in when the chef left suddenly. He had read *Larousse Gastronomique* and also Escoffier, whom he admired as a codifier of culinary knowledge and leader of cooks. His first reaction to the great man's recipe for quenelles de brochet – that the quantities of flour and cream must be a printer's error – is already legendary. Apart from that, he had to learn everything, by watching others, by experimentation and by constant trial and error. By 1975 he had moved to the head waiter's job at the fashionable Sorbonne restaurant in Oxford, and in 1977 he and Jenny, now with a son, Olivier, felt able to start up on their own.

The Blancs looked at Cambridge, but in the end settled on the only Oxford premises they could afford. As he says, a scruffy space between a corset shop and Oxfam was not exactly the most auspicious place for a new restaurant, but it was the best they could do. They cleaned it up themselves, decorated in a homely bistro style, and opened for business. At first, the menu was cautious, possibly because of the influence of the two English girl cooks he had employed at The Rose Revived, or the reassuring and succinct style of *The Cordon Bleu Cookery Book* by Constance Spry, that was much leaned on in the early stages. The moment at which Raymond Blanc felt he was breaking free was when he

Le Manoir aux Quat' Saisons

Raymond Blanc

introduced avocado with crab and ginger in place of the conventional vinaigrette or shrimps in flavoured mayonnaise. This now seems like an elementary step, but then it was a departure into realms unknown for a middle-range restaurant in an English provincial city. Oxford was, perhaps, the ideal place, not because it is full of rich people – most undergraduates and dons are not rich – but because it is one of those places which, sooner or later, everyone passes through, and if a remarkable and much talked about restaurant suddenly appears, they come sooner rather than later.

It was never easy: the premises were cramped and inconvenient, the work grindingly, sometimes almost defeatingly, hard, and the young chef had always to contend with his own lack of basic knowledge and experience. Many would have failed; even his confidence sometimes faltered, but his innate talent and enthusiasm, and his demonic energy, backed up by Jenny Blanc's flair for organization, saw them through. 'That little place had something electric. It had to have.' In its way, the success of Les Quat' Saisons was as startling as that of Michel Guérard's Pot-au-Feu at Asnières – certainly the rewards came as soon and as abundantly. By 1979 Michelin had awarded a first rosette; the second came in 1982. Expansion was the natural way forward and, no larger premises being at that time available in the city, they decided to set up a country house hotel-restaurant. Again, the position helped: Oxford and the Cotswolds are on every moneyed tourist's route, and the English Tourist Board and admiring customers became shareholders in the company to help find the million pounds needed to buy and equip the fifteenth-century manor house at Great Milton as Le Manoir aux Quat' Saisons. Almost unprecedentedly, Michelin and other guides assumed its excellence in advance and in March 1984 it opened with two rosettes.

'Never accept second-hand information.'
Following his own advice, Raymond Blanc reassures himself that each dish achieves his standards of excellence by touching and tasting everything. He is everywhere in the kitchen at Le Manoir, his enthusiasm and dynamism apparent to all.

Self taught and constantly questioning accepted wisdom, Raymond Blanc, like all converts, is passionately keen that others should share his enthusiasm.

Great Milton was an inspired choice, both geographically, being just off the main motorway from London, and for the house itself, an attractive low-built stone mansion set in acres of established gardens. The house was tactfully gutted and turned into a series of ten suites offering every luxury. The flower garden was replanted and a vast kitchen garden planned. The finest equipment and tableware were bought for the kitchen and dining rooms. Blanc's fame ensured that he was able to attract the most talented and ambitious young chefs. At first he tried a fifty-fifty mix of French and English, but finding that the kitchen became a renactment of the Hundred Years War, reduced the numbers of his countrymen to a level at which they could be assimilated into a smoothly working team.

From the beginning, the aim was for excellence and innovation. Blanc was now completely confident of his own skills, though his combination of curiosity and modesty means that he has never ceased to experiment, reject and correct. The network of suppliers built up for the Quat' Saisons was expanded to the point where he could be certain of the best and freshest fish, meat and cheese. A bakery in Oxford, now run separately, produced all manner of breads and pâtisserie for other restaurants as well as for Le Manoir. The vegetable garden was built up until, with five gardeners and six polytunnels, it now supplies between 60 and 80 per cent of the fresh produce and herbs – at a loss on paper which will shortly be redressed by sales of delicate

items like herbs and courgette flowers to other restaurateurs. Raymond Blanc, a passionate conservationist, despairs of the quality of seed and plants available commercially. 'You can buy striped tomatoes, spotted tomatoes, but no real tomatoes, only sterile hybrids with no taste or character.' So he tries to grow his vegetables and salads as organically as the customers' preference for leaves without holes and blemishes will allow.

In the kitchen, the emphasis is on total professionalism, timing and precision: 'even ten seconds too long on the *passe* can ruin a dish'. Blanc's philosophy has changed little since he recoiled from Escoffier's quenelles de brochet and every element of it is expressed with fiery certainty. Like all converts, he is passionately keen that others should share his views: unlike most converts, he is fortunate in finding that they are delighted to do so. Lightness is everything, and the guests 'should go out with their minds and bodies in total harmony, feeling good and ready to start again next day', not sated with the 'deceitful lightness' of sauces which in fact conceal quantities of butter and cream. He feels that before nouvelle cuisine cooking had become stultified, the movement, poorly understood as it has been in many quarters, with the old excesses merely being replaced by new ones ('turbot with raspberries and all that nonsense'), has restored French cooking to its former pre-eminence and liberated a whole generation of chefs. Those men and women, encouraged

and backed by increasingly knowledgeable food journalists and much travelled customers, have lifted the profession of cook from a lowly one to among the most prestigious and are, in turn, training younger chefs who, Raymond Blanc prophesies, will change the face of cooking for the better. 'In France it took us 20 centuries to get cooking declared an art. In England it will take years longer. I can understand the reasons here. Food is dubious because it is associated with greed, hunger, excess of both kinds. Once people stuffed themselves until they nearly died. . . . Eating food is a moral issue, and until quite recently it was not thought polite in England to talk about the food at table.'

One cannot imagine Raymond Blanc ever ceasing to talk about food: as he says, he is intensely curious, and being self-taught has led him to explore in detail many things which conventional apprentices are expected to accept unquestioningly. Time and time again he says 'never accept second-hand information'. Always find out for yourself why, for instance, an egg – 'I could write a whole book on one egg' – behaves in the way it does, how its power to bind and lift can change so dramatically in a few days. 'If you can understand an ingredient or a process, you can control it, and control is everything.' All this might lead to a sterile, academic approach, but his enthusiasm and transparent pleasure in food will always prevent a Blanc restaurant or his menus becoming boring. This is what

has established and maintained his reputation and makes guests feel that, high as the prices are, a meal at Le Manoir aux Quat' Saisons is always an event.

Success has brought Raymond Blanc many rewards, and his book *Recipes from Le Manoir aux Quat' Saisons* is an enormous success and sold a record 50,000 copies in the first year in the UK. Unlike many chefs, he travels little, and has so far refused requests to endorse equipment and products. 'One bad product can ruin a chef.' In some ways a very private man, he plays tennis and rides for relaxation, listens to music and reads when he can. The long years of grindingly hard work in what must be the most demanding profession in the world left Raymond and Jenny Blanc precious little time for a family life. Perhaps inevitably, the strains this set up led to divorce, and Jenny Blanc now owns and runs the Oxford bakery business and plans new projects of her own. Their sons Olivier and Sebastian may be chefs one day, but for the time being Raymond is content to give them a good education. An apprenticeship in France might follow, but then it would be business school: 'chefs are controlled by money now, and too many are exploited, cheated'.

He is grateful to England for having given him the chance to cook, something which he feels – surely wrongly – would have gone on eluding him in France. 'I'm still very French at the core. If I play tennis with an Englishman I'm playing for France. I don't long for my country because by leaving it and living in England for 17 years I have come to understand it. You don't fall in love with England. I think it's a longer process.' When he arrived in 1972, intending only to learn the English which would help him advance as a waiter, he was full of Gallic prejudices about the climate, the food, the class-ridden structure of society. He still feels passionately about the social divides: 'in France we would have working-class people eating here'. He does not want to go back to France to live, at least not yet, although he loves holidays there. On visits to his home village he has been saddened by the changes he finds. When he was a boy, there were perhaps ten farmers, each with ten cows and a few hectares, and the mayor, the priest and the doctor ran the place. Now there is one gentleman farmer, the farming is mechanized, the people do not relate to each other any more. His mother learned to cook traditional and regional dishes from her mother and passed them on in turn to Raymond's sister. But his sister has a job and children, and no time to spend hours in the kitchen.

In all this, Raymond Blanc remains an entirely human figure, able to laugh at himself and at his past mistakes and failures, like the time when he decided to stock the lake at Le Manoir with écrevisses. The crayfish, imported from France, were ceremonially released – and vanished overnight. He even jokes about his appearance. 'I remember that Fernand Point, a huge towering man, would ask to see the chef if he went to a restaurant. If the chef was big he was OK, and he knew he would have a good' meal, but if the man was thin and unhappy, he would go away. If he was thin and happy, he would give him the benefit of the doubt – after all he might be a reformed fat man. A lot of *embonpoint* was a sign of success, of the ability to cook. In the nineteenth century I would have had no chance.'

Fricassée de Girolles et Trompettes de la Mort aux Racines de Persil

Fricassée of Wild Mushrooms and Parsley Roots

*400 g (14 oz) girolles (chanterelles), cleaned
and trimmed
200 g (7 oz) horn of plenty mushrooms
(trompettes de la mort), cleaned and trimmed
20 parsley roots
50 g (1¾ oz) butter
20 sprigs flat-leaved parsley
7 tablespoons water
2 shallots, peeled and chopped
juice of ¼ lemon
1 tablespoon finely chopped chervil
a tiny bunch of chives, finely chopped
30 g (1 oz) cold butter, diced
1 tomato, peeled, seeded and diced
salt and pepper*

*To serve
20 bread croûtons, 2.5 cm (1 inch square),
lightly rubbed with garlic and
fried in butter*

Place 10 g (⅓ oz) butter, a few parsley stalks, the water and a pinch of salt and pepper in a large saucepan. Bring to the boil and simmer the parsley roots for 7–10 minutes, according to size. Reduce until the parsley roots are glazed. Keep warm.

Blanch the parsley leaves from the sprigs in boiling salted water for 3 minutes. Drain and refresh.

Sweat the shallots in 20 g (⅔ oz) butter. Season the girolles with salt and pepper, add to the shallots and fry them briskly for 1 minute. Add a dash of lemon juice and cover, leaving the lid slightly ajar. Cook over a low heat for 3 minutes. Separately, cook the horns of plenty in the remaining butter in the same way. Keep aside in a warm place.

Pour the girolle cooking juices into another saucepan and add the chervil, blanched parsley leaves and chives, then whisk in the cold diced butter, until well blended. If necessary, thin with 1 tablespoon of water. Taste and correct the seasoning. Then add the diced tomato and keep warm.

On four large, warm plates, scatter the wild mushrooms and parsley roots and spoon over the sauce. Serve the croûtons separately.

Note: the photograph below shows this dish made with girolles (chanterelles) only. It is delicious without trompettes de la mort, but if you are lucky enough to obtain these rare mushrooms, their dark colour and velvety texture make a striking contrast with the chanterelles.

FOR FOUR PEOPLE

Fricassée of Wild Mushrooms and Parsley Roots

Nage de Poissons et Crustaces à la Coriandre

Fish and Shellfish Soup Scented with Coriander

80 g (3 oz) fillet of monkfish, cut in four
80 g (3 oz) fillet of turbot, cut in four
4 langoustine tails, shelled
80 g (3 oz) fillet of salmon, cut in four
4 large scallops, cut in half horizontally
400 ml (14 fl oz) nage (see below)
1 tablespoon cream
30 g (1 oz) cold butter, diced
8 leaves coriander, chopped
4 leaves basil, chopped
lemon juice
salt and pepper

Vegetable garnish
100 g (3½ oz) cucumber,
divided in 12 sticks and turned
100 g (3½ oz) carrots, peeled,
divided in 12 and turned
100 g (3½ oz) courgettes, divided
in 12 and turned
1 fennel bulb, cut in small triangles
1 tomato, peeled, seeded and
cut in small triangles

Fish and Shellfish Soup Scented with Coriander

Sprinkle salt over the cucumber and place in the freezer for at least 2 hours, then rinse under running water and reserve. Blanch the carrots for about 3 minutes, the courgettes and fennel for 1 minute. Place all the vegetables, including the tomato, together in 7 tablespoons of *nage*.

Place the remaining *nage* in a saucepan. Season the fish and, at just under simmering point, poach the monkfish for 3 minutes, the turbot and langoustine tails for 2 minutes and salmon and scallops for 1 minute. Put the fish aside and keep warm.

Strain the cooking juices into another saucepan, add the cream and whisk in the butter over a gentle heat. Taste, correct seasoning and 'lift' with a dash of lemon juice. Add the coriander and basil and infuse them in the *nage* for 1 minute.

Divide the fish and shellfish into 4 warm soupbowls. Adjust the seasoning. Strain the hot *nage* over them and scatter over the vegetable garnish.

FOR FOUR PEOPLE

Nage de Légumes, Herbes et Condiments

Clear-Scented Stock made from Vegetables, Herbs and Spices

½ onion, peeled and finely chopped
the white of 1 small leek, finely chopped
1 carrot, peeled and finely chopped
¼ celery stalk, finely chopped
trimmings of 1 fennel bulb, finely chopped,
or some fennel seeds
2 cloves of garlic, finely chopped
4 pink peppercorns
1 star anise
8 white peppercorns, crushed
thinly pared rind of 1 lemon
thinly pared rind of 1 orange
1 sprig thyme
a small bunch of tarragon, chopped
a small bunch of chervil, chopped
1 teaspoon chopped coriander leaves
or 5–8 coriander seeds, crushed
7 tablespoons dry white wine

Put all the vegetables, spices, citrus rind and thyme into a large saucepan and pour in 500 ml (18 fl oz) of cold water. Bring to the boil and skim, then simmer for about 10 minutes. Add the chopped tarragon, chervil and coriander, pour in the wine and simmer for a further 2 to 3 minutes. The gentle acidity of the wine will 'lift' the stock.

Take the pan off the heat and leave uncovered for 5 to 6 hours so that the flavours infuse. Using the back of a ladle, gently press the liquid and vegetables through a fine sieve into a suitable container. The stock will keep in a covered container for 2 to 3 days in a refrigerator or for several weeks in the freezer.

Note: this stock can be used as the basis for a sauce to accompany steamed fish; for four people, use 500 ml (18 fl oz) stock and reduce by half. Mix in 2 tablespoons cream, then whisk in 60 g (2 oz) cold diced butter. Season with salt, white pepper and lemon juice and add your own favourite herbs.

MAKES 400 ML (14 FL OZ)

Filets de Turbot et Tian de Coquilles Saint-Jacques aux Champignons Sauvages

Turbot with a Tian of Scallops with Wild mushrooms

4 small skinned fillets of turbot,
80 g (3 oz) each
1 shallot, peeled and chopped
1 teaspoon butter
2 button mushrooms, sliced
7 tablespoons dry white wine
4 tablespoons water
lemon juice
salt and pepper

Tian
150 g (5½ oz) scallops
1 egg yolk
130 ml (4½ fl oz) whipping cream, chilled
salt
cayenne pepper

Garnish for the tian
1 baby courgette, sliced into ribbons and
blanched for 1 minute
8 scallops, finely sliced horizontally
1 teaspoon melted butter
lemon juice
salt and pepper

To finish sauce
1 teaspoon cream
20 g (⅔ oz) butter
lemon juice
a tiny bundle of chives, finely chopped

Garnish
20 small firm girolles (chanterelles)
16 horn of plenty mushrooms (trompettes de
la mort) or other dark mushrooms, such as
Japanese shiitake
1 teaspoon butter
a dash of lemon juice
salt and pepper

First prepare the scallop tian. Purée the scallops in a food processor adding 2 pinches of salt, 1 pinch of cayenne and the egg yolk. Remove the mixture to a large bowl and refrigerate for 30 minutes. Slowly add the cold cream, beating it with a wooden spoon, getting as much air into it as possible to make the mousse as light as possible.

Take 4 round pastry cutters about 6 cm (2½ inches) diameter and 3 cm (1¼ inches) deep. Seal the bottoms with buttered clingfilm and line the moulds with courgette ribbons. Divide the mousse between the four rings (you will have surplus). Arrange the sliced scallops over the top of the mousse so that they overlap. Brush with melted butter and add a dash of lemon juice and pinch of salt to each. Refrigerate until needed.

Preheat the oven to 180°C/350°F/Gas 4. Place the tians in a small braising pan lined with greaseproof paper, with 1 cm (½ inch) water. Cover, leaving the lid slightly ajar, and cook in the preheated oven for 10 minutes. Remove from the oven and keep warm. Do not turn off the oven.

Season the turbot with salt and pepper. Sweat the shallot in 1 teaspoon butter, then add the sliced mushrooms and the white wine. Boil for 5 seconds to remove some of the acidity of the wine. Add the water and lay the turbot on top of the mushrooms. Cover and place in the oven to cook for 3 minutes. Remove from the oven and allow to rest for 5 minutes.

Strain the cooking juices from the turbot into a small saucepan. Keep the fish hot. To finish the sauce, whisk the cream and butter into the cooking juices. Taste, and add a pinch of salt and pepper, a dash of lemon juice and the chopped chives. Keep warm.

Season the wild mushrooms and briefly cook the two varieties separately in a tablespoon of very hot butter. Add a dash of lemon juice to the girolles.

Have ready four warm oval fish plates. Remove the tians on to a tray upside down. Remove the clingfilm, lift off the pastry cutters and, using a fish slice, place a tian on one side of each plate. Place a turbot fillet on the other side and sprinkle mushrooms around it. Spoon over the sauce and serve.

Note: the step-by-step photographs show this dish as served at Le Manoir. The turbot is criss-crossed with whole chives and lightly steamed leek ribbons have been added. A slice of black truffle adorns the scallop tian.

FOR FOUR PEOPLE

Making the scallop tian

1 Preparing the ingredients

Cooking the turbot

5 Cooking the turbot

Garnishing and serving

7 Removing the tian from the mould

2 Lining the mould with courgette ribbons

3 Filling the mould with scallop mousse

4 Arranging the sliced scallops on top

6 Testing the fish

8 Final adjustments

The final appearance on the plate

Blanc de Loup de Mer Poêlé au Jus de Poivrons Doux et Petits Légumes Farcis du Manoir

Sea Bass with a Sweet Pepper Sauce and Tiny Stuffed Vegetables

4 skinned fillets of sea bass, 150 g
(5½ oz) each
2 tablespoons olive oil
breadcrumbs made with 200 g (7 oz)
dried bread
50 g (1¾ oz) parsley, chopped
1 small clove of garlic, peeled and puréed
leaves of 3 sprigs thyme, finely chopped
2 tablespoons olive oil
a dash of Pernod
salt and pepper

Fish stock
350 g (12 oz) sea bass bones
½ onion, peeled and chopped
¼ fennel, chopped
1 tablespoon olive oil
15 g (½ oz) butter
7 tablespoons white wine
4 ripe tomatoes, finely chopped,
keeping juice and seeds
1 tablespoon purée of red pepper
300 ml (½ pint) water

Vegetables
4 courgettes and their flowers
diced tomato
basil
4 cherry tomatoes, skinned and seeded
100 g (3½ oz) parsley, blanched
4 teaspoons cream
2 tiny green peppers, blanched and cut in half
ratatouille
4 baby fennels, blanched for a few minutes
and refreshed

Saffron potatoes
4 potatoes, peeled and cut into barrel shapes
1 teaspoon butter
1 tablespoon olive oil
a few pistils of saffron
1 sprig thyme
50 ml (2 fl oz) water
salt and pepper

To finish the sauce
2 leaves basil
6 leaves coriander, finely chopped
1 tablespoon cream
220 g (⅔ oz) butter
lemon juice
salt and pepper

Make the fish stock. Sweat the onion and fennel in the olive oil and butter, add the sea bass bones and sweat for a further minute. Add the wine and boil for a few seconds and add the chopped tomatoes with juice and seeds, purée of pepper and water. Bring to the boil, skim and simmer for 20 minutes. Strain the stock through a fine sieve.

Meanwhile, prepare the vegetables. Blanch the courgettes for 2 minutes and the flowers for 30 seconds; drain. Fill the flowers with a mixture of diced tomatoes and basil. Fill the cherry tomatoes with a mixture of chopped, blanched parsley and 3 teaspoons of the cream. Fill the green peppers with the ratatouille. Cut the fennels in half, remove the centres and chop finely, then mix with the remaining cream and fill the fennel halves.

Put the courgette flowers, cherry tomatoes, green peppers and fennel halves on a lightly greased baking tray and set aside. For the saffron potatoes, cook the potatoes with the remaining ingredients until just tender. Set aside.

To finish the sauce, reduce the stock until you have 200 ml (7 fl oz), then add the basil and coriander and whisk in the cream and butter. Taste, adjust the seasoning and add a dash of lemon juice. Keep the sauce hot.

Sear the fillets of sea bass in hot olive oil without browning. Mix together the breadcrumbs, chopped parsley, puréed garlic, thyme leaves and Pernod and season to taste. Coat the fillets with the breadcrumb mixture and cook in an oven preheated to 180°C/350°F/Gas 4 for 5 minutes.

Briefly pan-fry the courgettes. Place the baking tray of other vegetables in the oven to cook for 5 minutes. Reheat the saffron potatoes.

Place the fillets on hot plates, arrange the vegetables around and pour the sauce on to the plates, but not on to the fish.

FOR FOUR PEOPLE

Sea Bass with Sweet Pepper Sauce and Tiny Stuffed Vegetables

Fillet of John Dory with Candied Aubergines

Filet de St Pierre Poêlé au Confit d'Aubergines, Jus de Volaille Parfumé au Romarin

Fillet of John Dory, Pan-fried, served with Candied Aubergines, its Juices Scented with Rosemary

*4 skinned fillets of John Dory
of 140 g (5 oz) each
2 tablespoons olive oil
lemon juice
salt and pepper*

Candied aubergines
*2 medium sized aubergines,
cut into 5 mm (¼ inch) slices
7 tablespoons olive oil
3 tablespoons white wine vinegar
2 teaspoons honey (acacia if possible)
4 tablespoons water
8 basil leaves, chopped
leaves from 2 sprigs thyme
salt and pepper*

Sauce
*200 ml (8 fl oz) jus brun de volaille
(brown chicken stock, see page 91)
1 sprig rosemary
1 sprig thyme
40 g (1½ oz) butter
juice of ¼ lemon
salt and pepper*

First, prepare the aubergines. Preheat the oven to 200°C/400°F/Gas 6. Season the aubergines with salt and pepper and colour them in a non-stick pan with the olive oil for about 1 minute on each side. Place the slices on a lightly greased baking tray and roast for 8 minutes.

Boil the vinegar and honey together for a few seconds, add the water and set aside. Remove the aubergines from the oven, drain on a piece of kitchen paper, place them on a large ovenproof tray, and pour the honey vinegar over them. Allow to cool, then sprinkle with basil leaves and thyme, cover with clingfilm, and refrigerate for a minimum of 24 hours.

To make the sauce, add the rosemary and thyme to the *jus brun de volaille*, bring to the boil and simmer for 2 minutes. In another pan, heat the butter until it becomes foamy and lightly browned (*beurre noisette*), then whisk into the chicken stock mixture. Taste, season with salt and pepper and enliven with lemon juice. Keep warm.

Preheat the oven to 180°C/350°F/Gas 4 and remove the aubergines from the refrigerator. Season and pan-fry the fish fillets in hot olive oil for 15 seconds on each side, then cook in the oven for another 3 minutes.

At the same time, place the marinated aubergines (on their tray) in the oven for 5 minutes, to reheat them.

Warm four plates. Arrange overlapping aubergine slices in the middle of each plate. Place the fish on the top, add a drop of lemon juice and pour the sauce around the fish.

FOR FOUR PEOPLE

Queue de Boeuf au Fumet d'Hermitage

Ballotine of Oxtail in a Red Wine Sauce

1 oxtail, boned with the tip of its tail cut off
1 pig's caul (the membrane, lining the
stomach)
4 tablespoons groundnut oil

Filling
80 g (3¼ oz) shallots, peeled
30 g (1 oz) butter
100 g (4 oz) button or wild mushrooms
5–8 young cabbage leaves (depending on size)
300 g (12 oz) lardons (strips of smoked bacon,
cut into small sticks and boiled for 1 minute,
then refreshed under cold water)

Sauce
Bones from the oxtail
1 tablespoon flour
1 carrot, peeled and diced
1 small onion, peeled and diced
100 ml (4 fl oz) red wine vinegar
500 ml (18 fl oz) red wine
200 ml (7 fl oz) jus brun de volaille (brown
chicken stock, see page 91), reduced to a
demi-glace
1 sprig thyme
¼ bay leaf
5 peppercorns, crushed
1 clove of garlic, crushed

Pan-fry the shallots in 20 g (¾ oz) of the butter, add a pinch of salt and pepper and cook, covered, for 10 minutes. Then remove the lid and cook to caramelize for a further 10 minutes. Allow to cool.

Pan-fry the mushrooms in the remaining butter for 2 minutes; put aside.

Blanch the cabbage leaves for 3 minutes in plenty of boiling, salted water. Refresh in cold water, pat dry and season with salt and pepper.

Unfold the pig's caul on the working table. Place the opened-up oxtail over it, season, then line with cabbage leaves. Arrange the filling (lardons, mushrooms, shallots) along a central line. Roll up together and secure with string.

The following two stages can be done either on top of the stove or in an oven preheated to 180°C/350°F/Gas 4.

In a roasting pan or frying pan, heat the oil and sear and brown the oxtail parcel all over for 20 minutes.

In a large cast-iron pan sear and brown the bones for 20 minutes, adding the flour

after 15 minutes. Add the diced vegetables and brown for a further 5 minutes. Add the vinegar and reduce until the vinegar is completely evaporated. Then add the red wine and reduce by one third.

Place the oxtail parcel on top of the bones, add the demi-glace and cover with water. Bring to the boil, skim, and add the thyme, bay leaf, peppercorns and garlic. Cover with the lid, leaving it slightly ajar, and braise in the oven for 2½ hours.

Remove the oxtail and keep warm. Strain the stock into a large saucepan and reduce until you obtain a light textured sauce. Taste and season, skimming off any fat.

Remove the string from the oxtail and any caul that is left and carve two large

slices per person. Arrange the slices in a large dish and pour over the sauce. The best garnish for this dish would be mostly root vegetables: parsnips, turnips, swedes, baby onions etc.

Note: this dish can be prepared 1–2 days in advance.

Ask your butcher to bone the oxtail for you and to remove excess fat. (He will have to slice lengthways through the oxtail, removing the bone without piercing the skin. This is difficult and I would recommend that you ask the butcher to do this for you.) Ask him for the bones too.

FOR FOUR PEOPLE

Ballotine of Oxtail in a Red Wine Sauce

Jus Brun de Volaille

Brown Chicken Stock

1½ kg (3¼ lb) chicken bones, finely chopped
4 tablespoons of cooking oil
2 onions, peeled and chopped
1 garlic clove, unpeeled
8 peppercorns, crushed
1 sprig thyme
1 bay leaf
1 litre (1¾ pints) water
1 teaspoon arrowroot

Preheat the oven to 220°C/425°F/Gas 7. In a large roasting pan, sear and colour the chopped chicken bones lightly in very hot oil. Place them in the oven and brown for 30 minutes.

Add the onions, garlic, peppercorns, thyme and bay leaf. Roast for a further 15 minutes until the bones and onions are of a good brown colour. Remove the roasting pan; tilt and spoon out excess fat. Add the water, scraping the bottom to dilute the caramelized juices. Bring it to the boil, then skim and simmer it for 30 minutes.

Strain through a conical sieve into a saucepan, leaving you with about 900 ml (1½ pints) of stock. Reduce down to 600 ml (1 pint) skimming from time to time, then bind the stock with the arrow-root diluted in a little cold water, boiling it for a further 5 minutes. Cool down and reserve in a container sealed with cling-film in your refrigerator or deep freezer.

Note: the colouring of the bones and onions is very important. If too light, the stock will be very pale and have little flavour. Also, on no account must the bones be burnt, or too brown, otherwise the stock will be bitter.

No salt should be added to the stock, since there is some sodium content in the meat and bones which will be released during the cooking.

As the stock has a very neutral, delicate taste, it will not interfere with the taste and the flavour of the cooked dish and can be used for all meat and fish dishes.

MAKES ABOUT 400 ML (14 FL OZ)

Good humour in the kitchen

Mousse de Citron Brûlée à la Giboulée de Cerises

Caramelized Lemon Mousse served with Cherries and its own Coulis

Mousse
200 ml (7 fl oz) milk
1 vanilla pod, finely chopped
finely grated zest of ½ a lemon
4 egg yolks
60 g (2 oz) caster sugar
juice of 2 lemons
3½ leaves of gelatine
200 ml (7 fl oz) whipping cream
3 egg whites
icing sugar for caramelizing the mousse

Coulis
1 kg (2¼ lb) cherries, stoned
100 g (3½ oz) sugar
7 tablespoons Sauternes
or other sweet dessert wine
2 tablespoons kirsch

Mix the milk, chopped vanilla pod and lemon zest in a heavy saucepan. Bring to the boil and infuse for a few minutes. Meanwhile, cream the yolks and 40 g (1⅓ oz) sugar, and add three-quarters of the lemon juice. Soften the gelatine leaves in cold water, then squeeze dry. Pour the milk over the egg and sugar mixture, then return to the pan and stir over a gentle heat until thickened. Add the softened gelatine and whisk until it has dissolved. Strain and cool. Whip the cream and set aside.

Whisk the egg whites until stiff, adding the remaining caster sugar and lemon juice. Mix with the lemon custard and fold in the whipped cream. Spread out the mousse on a 2.5 cm (1 inch) deep Swiss roll tin or in individual moulds and refrigerate for at least 2 hours.

Mix the cherries with the sugar and wine and cook for about 5 minutes. Remove about 40 cherries for the garnish. Purée the remainder with their liquid. Strain and reduce. Taste and add more sugar if necessary. Add the kirsch when cool.

Heat the grill or a salamander. Using 9 cm (3½ inch) pastry cutters, cut the mousse into rounds and slide on to a baking tray, with the pastry cutters still in position. Sprinkle the top of each mousse with icing sugar.

Caramelize the mousses under the grill or with the salamander. Alternatively, make a criss-cross pattern with a hot skewer. Place each mousse in the middle of a dessert plate and remove the pastry cutter. Pour the coulis and the reserved cherries around the mousse.

FOR EIGHT PEOPLE

JOHN BURTON-RACE

L'ORTOLAN

Shinfield

John Burton-Race has the reputation in some quarters for being an *enfant terrible* but this is largely exaggerated; he definitely does not, unlike some other chefs, behave on the mistaken assumption that customers enjoy being insulted and will come back for more, and that staff like being used as doormats. True, he says exactly what he thinks; true, some people find the going too hot in his kitchen; but the whole performance is designed to show the world that he can overcome the problems of his métier and cook creatively and well in a restaurant where he is completely in control. L'Ortolan at Shinfield is his present skirmishing ground, and to most outside observers it looks like the setting for a major victory. In the two and a half years since he took over the premises he has enhanced his reputation as a cook and built up an enviable number of regular customers.

Some of his defensiveness, even aggressiveness, stems from his youth – he was thirty-two in May 1989 – and background. His father was a chartered consultant civil engineer and his two sisters excelled at school. John, the elder son, resolutely refused to toe the line and threw up his public school A-level course. His father vetoed art school on the grounds that it was sissy, and agreed to catering only, John thinks, because his parents never

thought he would stick the grindingly hard apprenticeship. In fact, he is one of the ten out of eighteen chefs in this book who *really* started at the bottom, a teenage skivvy, doing all the messy boring chores. In between he took and passed the various professional diplomas – all useless to him now, he says, but nonetheless rungs on the ladder, and a contribution to his mastery of kitchen techniques. He worked under Carl Waddsack at Quaglino's and then at Chewton Glen, gaining experience in all the departments of the kitchen. He also met Marie Christine Bourdeau, who was on the management side there. Rashly as it seemed – they now believe it was the wisest thing they have done – they married. She is from near Tours, where she grew up in her parents' restaurant. At eighteen, after a course at the hotel school at Clermont-Ferrand, she came to England to improve her English and gain experience. They have no children yet, recognizing the difficulties which both children and parents face in this demanding trade if, as in their case, both husband and wife are essential to the success of the venture.

After Chewton Glen John moved to the Sorbonne in Oxford, favourite of a whole generation of dons and well-heeled undergraduates. In North Oxford Raymond Blanc was already making a big name for himself at the Quat' Saisons, and the two young chefs met and liked each other's work. Although Blanc

L'Ortolan

John and Christine Burton-Race

Meticulous attention to detail at the passe, *as each plate is inspected and given its final touches, is one of the hallmarks of L'Ortolan under the eye of John Burton-Race (right, without toque).*

A perfectionist with a distinctive style, John Burton-Race aims for lightness and delicacy, but scorns the fashion for absurdly small portions. He describes his cooking as 'straight down the middle', but this really does not do justice to his liking for strong flavours and the stylish and exciting way he experiments with new combinations.

couldn't offer John a job immediately, he found him a year's private post with a wealthy businessman, where there were the funds and the opportunities to experiment, and a more sophisticated audience than undergraduates to practise on. Then he moved to the Quat' Saisons, on the understanding that when Raymond and Jenny Blanc had set up the new luxury hotel-restaurant Le Manoir aux Quat' Saisons at Great Milton, he and Christine should run the old premises for them, as a cheaper, less grand restaurant. A year later, after what he feels was the most formative period of his career, working with Raymond Blanc in the old Quat' Saisons, he found himself in charge, for the first time in his life, of the kitchen of the re-named Le Petit Blanc. 'Off we went, and the first two years were for me a great success: we had a great deal of favourable publicity and awards from this and that magazine, then a Michelin star' – at that time a rarity in England. However the premises, a cramped shop in a modern shopping parade, had never been ideal and when his contract came up for renewal he opted for independence. With the help of the solicitor Sir David Napley, now chairman of the company which owns L'Ortolan, he found premises very quickly, and opened 7 October, 1986.

The Old Vicarage, Shinfield, a solid Georgian brick house in a few acres of land, just off the M4 motorway west of Reading, was previously run by Nico Ladenis who had decided that

country life was not for him and had returned to London to the highly successful Simply Nico. John Burton-Race approached Sir David Napley for advice, and as a result a new company, Burton-Race Restaurants plc, was formed under the Business Expansion Scheme, which has helped many British restaurateurs. The premises were bought as they stood, with capital put up by John and Christine themselves, by Sir David Napley and by some forty other investors. Christine's parents also supported the venture, and John's adoptive brother, James, joined him in the profession. (By now John's parents were positively proud of their mould-breaking son's success.) Nigel Marriage, who had trained at the Savoy and had met John at the old Quat' Saisons came as sous-chef, and a kitchen *brigade*, then as now, mainly British, was assembled. Meanwhile Christine recruited waiting staff, from the ranks of bright young French girls who, despite qualifications, were finding it hard to get work in good French restaurants.

L'Ortolan called on a chain of suppliers with whom John was already in contact to ensure top-quality produce, and built up its own contacts: for fish and shellfish in Scotland and Cornwall; with the Boucherie Lamartine in London for foie gras, wild mushrooms and truffles; with an ex-chef trade-only butcher; and with a first-rate vegetable supplier, Stephen Belcher in Reading, who understands exactly what kind of produce John needs. Everything (except at first the bread which was flown in, part-baked, from France) was made in the kitchens. Nothing except

Intense concentration in the kitchen

is put together from scratch, you might think "Is it worth it?". People come here on the odd quiet day and ask me why I have such a large team, but if you come on a Saturday when the place is full, I wish I had double the people because the work involved in preparing some of the dishes is enormous.' He regards himself as a working chef, not just as one who stands at the *passe* and tastes dishes cooked by other chefs, but he takes care to station himself where he can see everything, check as many dishes as possible, and act as troubleshooter – 'I am everyone's commis chef' – when something is going wrong. Nigel Marriage is his second pair of eyes, and with his French pastry-chef Dominique Cordier who has come to him via Tante Claire and his *chef-saucier* brother James is the core of his *brigade*. The commis-chefs and the occasional *stagiaire* from another restaurant, there to learn and help, also play a vital role. No one lasts long in the kitchen if they are not prepared to go all the way with John, to reach his own high standards and advance with him beyond them.

The recipes which follow are in their own way typical, though they happen to be from the winter menu, which features local game. The partridge recipe is one of John's favourites, combining five different flavours to make a single new one; all the recipes are original and stimulating without being outlandish. None depends on a luxury ingredient solely for luxury; foie gras there may be, but the menus are also rich in humbler ingredients like ox-tail, pigs' trotters and cabbage, raised to previously undreamt-of heights of deliciousness. The puddings, too, vary between complex and many-layered pastry confections and the simplest of perfect sorbets or soufflés.

batches of home-made puff pastry, ice-creams and sorbets, is frozen and there is no *sous-vide* (vacuum-packing) machine. There is a daily menu and a seasonally changed à la carte, with a special menu for Sundays.

John Burton-Race describes his cooking as 'straight down the middle' – meaning that his basic approach is between the modern classic cuisine of which he is an acknowledged master, and the eclectic exciting approach which is derived partly from his most important mentor, Raymond Blanc, and partly from his own determination to expand the frontiers of what he and his cooks can do. 'I am becoming, not a cheap imitation of Raymond Blanc, but someone with a style of my own, whether people like my food or hate it. I don't want to have a menu that never changes, it gets boring. If you are like me and you cook a dish twice, maybe fifty times, each time you try to perfect it. Then you get there, and it is time to move on, otherwise you start cooking like a robot.' He uses little flour and less cream and butter than many other chefs, but with the lightness he aims for he also likes strong pungent flavours and unusual, but carefully thought-out, combinations. He has nothing but scorn for the modish ideas dished up by some chefs ('fuss for fussiness' sake – rubbish') or for ludicrously small portions in wishy-washy sauces. His cooking is undoubtedly complicated and labour intensive. 'If you look at the basic structure of a dish, and how it

The interior, changed little since Nico Ladenis' day, is warm and welcoming, with an attractive plant-hung conservatory looking out on the mature quince and apple trees. The dominant colour is that of the apricot walls, hung with botanical and bird prints, and matched with the peach-coloured tablecloths. The waiting staff are still nearly all female, and in addition to waiting are responsible for arranging and checking the exceptional selection of cheeses and the flowers. The English sommelier, David Gaunt, looks after the well-chosen wine list, whose merit matches that of the kitchen. The success of the first year's trading encouraged the investors to plough back the profits into new furniture and service plates, extensive re-planting in the gardens and, most importantly, an enlargement and strengthening of the kitchen team. This has only enhanced the already high standards and added more complex dishes to the menu.

L'Ortolan is still comparatively new, but has been blessed by the talents of the Burton-Races and the support of their backers. Just off the major artery to the west, near several sizeable towns and within easy reach of London, it has a catchment area to match its quality and the prices which inevitably go with quality. The Burton-Races have no plans to add rooms – 'If we wanted a hotel we'd have one' – and it is this certainty, this determination to achieve perfection and then to go one better, which marks them out. As John says 'I want to be known for excitement, imagination – and progress.'

Delice aux deux Saumons, Crème de Ciboulette

Marinated and Smoked Salmon with a Chive Cream Sauce

Chive cream
60 g (2 oz) fresh chives, coarsely chopped
300 ml (½ pint) double cream, soured with a few drops lemon juice
1 teaspoon freshly grated horseradish
2 tablespoons live yogurt
half a Granny Smith or other tart eating apple, peeled and grated
half a yellow pepper and half a red pepper, diced finely, blanched for 30 seconds in boiling water and dried on kitchen paper
salt and pepper

Salmon moulds
4 large thin slices of smoked salmon
170–225 g (6–8 oz) lean fresh raw salmon, cut in 5 mm (¼ inch) dice
2 small shallots, peeled and finely chopped
2 teaspoons chopped fresh chives
1 teaspoon chopped fresh dill
half a small clove of garlic, peeled and finely chopped
juice of half a lemon
salt and pepper
1 tablespoon tarragon vinaigrette

Garnish
4 slices of lemon, channelled and halved
8 salmon caviar eggs
½ teaspoon caviar (optional)
1 tomato, peeled, seeded and finely diced, seasoned and sharpened with a few drops of lemon juice
4 raw quail eggs
a pinch of cayenne pepper
chervil sprigs

A day in advance, mix all the ingredients for the chive cream except the yellow and red peppers together in a bowl, cover and refrigerate for 24 hours, stirring the mixture occasionally.

Place the chive cream in a clean bowl, straining and setting aside 1½ tablespoons to finish the dish. Whip the rest until it forms soft peaks, then fold in the diced peppers. Season and keep cold.

Line four 5 cm (2 inch) ramekins with clingfilm and then with the smoked salmon, leaving enough overlap of salmon to fold back over the top.

To assemble the dish, arrange two half-slices of lemon on each of four cold plates and place 1 salmon caviar egg on each slice. Dip a dessertspoon in boiling water and make 2 small egg shapes of chive and pepper cream on each plate, and place a few black caviar eggs on each if used. Pile the tomato dice in four equal mounds and top with 2 sprigs of chervil.

Just before serving, put the raw diced salmon in a small bowl with the shallots, chives, dill, garlic, lemon juice and seasoning and stir gently with a wooden spoon. Pack into the lined ramekins and fold over the smoked salmon to cover the top. Turn out on to the centre of each prepared plate, peeling off the clingfilm, and brush with the tarragon vinaigrette to give a shine. Cut the tops off each raw quail egg and dust with a little cayenne pepper. Make a small indentation in the top of each salmon mould and place a quail egg in it. Place a tiny blob of the reserved chive cream next to two of the piles of diced tomato, and serve immediately with slices of warm brioche.

FOR FOUR PEOPLE

Marinated and Smoked Salmon with a Chive Cream Sauce

Pavé de Turbot Grillé au Jus de Veau

Grilled Turbot with a Veal Sauce, Potatoes and Truffles

4 slices of turbot – about 140 g (5 oz) each
without skin and bone
175 ml (6 fl oz) hazelnut oil
zests of 1 lemon and 1 lime cut in matchsticks
and blanched
1 small sprig fresh rosemary
2 cloves of garlic, peeled and sliced
115 g (4 oz) fresh foie gras, diced and tossed in
seasoned flour
a few lightly cooked spinach leaves
4 sprigs fresh dill

Stock
approximately 900 g (2 lb) veal bones cut in
small pieces
2 large onions
1 medium carrot, cubed
a quarter celery stalk
1 medium leek
1 sprig fresh thyme
half a fresh bay leaf
half a clove of garlic, peeled and crushed
12 black peppercorns, crushed
450 g (1 lb) button mushrooms, sliced
1 sprig fresh rosemary

Potato galettes
2 medium Maris Piper potatoes, peeled
a little clarified butter
salt and pepper

Sauce
300 ml (½ pint) veal stock (see above)
3 shallots, peeled and finely chopped
1 teaspoon chopped fresh chives
½ teaspoon chopped fresh tarragon,
blanched
½ teaspoon zest from the marinade
1 small sprig fresh rosemary
2 tomatoes, peeled, seeded and diced
1 teaspoon hazelnut oil
a few drops of lemon juice
1 teaspoon finely diced truffle
salt and pepper

Grilled Turbot with a Veal Sauce, Potatoes and Truffles

Twelve hours in advance, make a marinade with the hazelnut oil, citrus zest, rosemary and garlic in a bowl and put in the four pieces of turbot. Refrigerate. At the same time, put the veal bones in a large pan of cold water and bring to the boil. Drain and refresh under cold running water. Put all the other ingredients for the stock except the mushrooms and rosemary in a large pan with the bones and add cold water to cover. Bring to the boil, skim and simmer gently for 8 hours. Strain into a clean pan, add the rosemary and mushrooms, and reduce until the stock is amber in colour and very slightly syrupy. Strain and keep on one side.

Slice the peeled potatoes very thinly using a mandoline or food processor. Brush a small frying pan with clarified butter and arrange a single overlapping layer of potato slices on it. Season. Cook over a low heat until the edges begin to turn golden brown then turn over and cook the other side, adding a few drops of clarified butter to the pan as you do so. Repeat until you have four crisp galettes. Pat dry with kitchen paper, place on a rack and keep warm.

Heat the reduced stock in a pan and add the chopped shallots, chives, tarragon, citrus zest, rosemary and diced tomato. Lastly, whisk in the hazelnut oil. Season and sharpen with a little lemon juice. Just before serving, add the diced truffle.

Heat an iron griddle over a hot flame and place the marinated pavés of turbot on it upper side down. Cook for approximately 4 minutes, turning them over half way through. The fish should be only just cooked. Set aside to keep warm while you arrange the plates. Cook the diced foie gras in a very hot frying pan and keep warm.

Have ready four heated plates and put a galette in the middle of each, with a slice of turbot on top. Spoon round the veal 'jus' and its vegetables and herbs. Place a few spinach leaves at one side and decorate with a sprig of dill. Drop the diced foie gras into the sauce.

FOR FOUR PEOPLE

Choucroute de Perdreaux Rôti en son Jus

'Choucroute' of Partridge

4 young partridges
4 choucroute moulds (see separate recipe,
below)

Sauce
1 tablespoon clarified butter
half an onion, finely chopped
a quarter carrot, diced
1 small leek, trimmed and diced
a 4 cm (1½ inch) piece of celery stalk, diced
1 teaspoon butter
1 tablespoon white wine vinegar
115 g (4 oz) button mushrooms, sliced
1 sprig thyme
1 bay leaf
1 clove garlic, crushed
6–7 tablespoons madeira
550 ml (1 pint) good chicken stock
1 tablespoon meat glaze
30 g (1 oz) chilled unsalted butter, cubed
salt and pepper

Garnishes
7 large Comice pears
7.5 cm (3 inches) of black pudding, preferably
the French boudin noir
170 g (6 oz) assorted fresh wild mushrooms
(chanterelles, ceps, etc)
1 clove of garlic, peeled and chopped
2 shallots, finely chopped
1 teaspoon chopped chives
unsalted butter and clarified butter
flour to dust
sugar to taste
salt and freshly ground black pepper

Remove the legs, wings, wishbones and backbones from the cleaned partridges and chop these coarsely for the sauce, leaving the breasts attached to the ribs and breast bones. Seal the chopped bones in the clarified butter in a large, heavy sauté pan. Fry the diced vegetables in the teaspoon of butter in another pan, and add to the bones. Pour in the wine vinegar and reduce over a brisk heat till the liquid has almost all evaporated. Add the sliced mushrooms, thyme, bay leaf and garlic. Moisten with the madeira and reduce the liquid by half. Pour in the chicken stock and bring to the boil. Skim off any fat and impurities and simmer, uncovered, for 1 hour. Strain into a clean pan and reduce until the sauce is slightly syrupy. Add the

meat glaze and check the seasoning. Just before serving, whisk in the cold cubed butter.

Preheat the oven to 220°C/425°F/Gas 7. Season the partridge breasts with salt and pepper and gently rub them with a little butter. Heat a heavy frying pan and sear the breasts quickly. Transfer them to a roasting pan and cook for approximately 6 minutes in the preheated hot oven. Remove and allow the birds to relax for 10 minutes in a warm place before removing the breasts from the carcases. Set them aside in a warm place.

Prepare the garnishes as follows. Peel and core the pears and cut each into 12 segments. Sprinkle with a little sugar and freshly ground black pepper and caramelize in a heavy frying pan with a knob of butter. Keep warm. Slice the *boudin noir* into eight equal pieces and peel. Dust with a little flour and sauté for 30 seconds on each side in clarified butter. Keep warm. Sauté the wild mushrooms very quickly in a mixture of clarified and unsalted butter with garlic, shallots and chives.

To serve, turn out the choucroute moulds (see below) on to four heated plates and arrange the *boudin noir*, pear segments and wild mushrooms round the plate. Slice the warm partridge breasts and arrange between the garnishes. Strain the sauce round the meat and garnishes.

'Choucroute' of Partridge

Choucroute Moulds
2 large carrots, peeled
30 g (1 oz) melted unsalted butter whisked
with 150 ml (¼ pint) chicken stock and ¼
teaspoon blanched fresh tarragon to make
an emulsion
half a small Savoy cabbage
60 g (2 oz) unsalted butter
4 medium shallots, peeled and chopped
1 garlic clove, crushed
115 g (4 oz) rindless smoked streaky bacon,
cubed and blanched
120 ml (4 fl oz) dry white wine
300 ml (½ pint) chicken stock
salt and pepper

Slice the carrots lengthways on a mandoline to make long ribbons, and cook in the tarragon emulsion until tender. Remove with a slotted spoon and cool. Shred the cabbage and cook until *al dente* in boiling salted water. Refresh in iced water and drain. Melt the butter in a large sauté pan and cook the shallots and garlic until the shallots are translucent. Add the cubes of bacon, pour in the white wine and bring to the boil. Skim and reduce until the mixture is almost dry. Add the chicken stock and reduce until you have a sauce of a syrupy coating consistency. Add the drained cabbage and season with salt and pepper. Line four china or metal ramekins 7.5 cm (3 inches) across with the cooked carrot strips, laying them across the ramekins in a star shape and leaving sufficient length on each side to fold back across the top. Pack the choucroute mixture into the moulds, and turn back the ends of the carrot strips to the centre. Press down lightly to compact the choucroute. They are now ready to turn out and serve, but they can also be made in advance, covered with aluminium foil and heated through for 10 minutes in a medium oven.

FOR FOUR PEOPLE

Filet de Boeuf au Fumet de Sancerre Rouge et Saveurs des Sous-Bois

Pan-fried Beef Fillet with Wild Mushrooms and Beef Marrow

*4 medallions of beef fillet approximately
140 g (5 oz) each
15 g (½ oz) clarified butter
15 g (½ oz) unsalted butter
salt and pepper*

Sauce
*15 g (½ oz) unsalted butter
85 g (3 oz) shallots, peeled and sliced
450 g (1 lb) sliced button mushrooms
380 ml (13 fl oz) red Sancerre
a small piece of fresh bay leaf
1 sprig fresh thyme
2 cloves garlic, peeled and halved
a few fresh tarragon stalks
550 ml (1 pint) chicken stock
6–7 tablespoons meat glaze
30 g (1 oz) cold cubed unsalted butter
(optional)
a few drops of truffle juice
salt and pepper*

Garnish
*115 g (4 oz) beef marrow, in 1 cm (½ inch)
dice
340 g (12 oz) wild mushrooms (chanterelles
and oyster mushrooms, etc.)
1 clove garlic, peeled and crushed
1 tablespoon chopped fresh tarragon and chives
2 tomatoes, peeled, seeded and cut in lozenges
1 tablespoon basil-flavoured butter
sprigs of chervil*

To make the sauce, melt the butter in a large shallow sauté pan and sweat the shallots and mushrooms without letting them colour. Let the liquid evaporate almost completely. Add the red wine, bay leaf, thyme, garlic and tarragon stalks. Bring to the boil, skim and reduce until almost dry. Add the chicken stock and meat glaze and reduce by half. Strain through a fine sieve into a clean pan and keep on one side.

Season the beef medallions on both sides. Heat a small iron pan with the clarified butter, put in the medallions and add the unsalted butter. Fry for approximately 1 minute on each side. Leave to rest in a warm place while you finish the dish.

Heat a large frying pan over a fast flame, then toss in the diced beef marrow, mushrooms and garlic. Cook very quickly for 15–20 seconds, then add the herbs and season with salt and pepper. Meanwhile, reduce the sauce until it coats the back of a spoon, then whisk in the optional cold butter. Last of all, add the truffle juice but do not allow to boil, or the truffle flavour will vanish. Season.

Warm the tomato lozenges in a little basil butter. Have ready four heated plates.

Arrange the wild mushrooms and tomato lozenges on the four plates, and place a medallion in the middle of each. Strain the finished sauce over the meat and decorate with chervil sprigs.

FOR FOUR PEOPLE

Beef Fillet with Wild Mushrooms and a plate of seasonal vegetables

99

Suprême de Pigeonneau en Robe de Choux au Madère

Pigeon in a Cabbage Leaf with Madeira Sauce

*2 young pigeons (preferably Norfolk squabs),
with their hearts and livers
60 g (2 oz) fresh foie gras
4 shallots, peeled and coarsely sliced
2 cloves of garlic, peeled and halved
1 sprig thyme
a small piece of fresh bay leaf
1 tablespoon each of madeira, port and dry
white wine
120 ml (4 fl oz) chicken stock
300 ml (½ pint) double cream
4 Savoy cabbage leaves, 15 cm (6 inches)
across
1 tablespoon clarified butter
salt and freshly ground pepper*

*Sauce
carcases of the pigeons
1 tablespoon clarified butter
4 shallots, peeled and chopped
1 clove garlic, peeled and halved
1 sprig fresh thyme
a small piece of fresh bay leaf
2 tablespoons white wine vinegar
4 tablespoons dry aged madeira
400 ml (14 fl oz) clear chicken stock
115 g (4 oz) button mushrooms, sliced
1 tablespoon meat glaze
2 teaspoons very finely diced fresh truffle
30 g (1 oz) cold cubed butter
salt and pepper*

*Mushroom pastries
1 teaspoon clarified butter
170 g (6 oz) fresh mixed wild mushrooms
a quarter clove of garlic, chopped
1 teaspoon chopped chives
1 shallot, peeled and finely chopped
15 g (½ oz) unsalted butter
4 small cooked puff pastry cases*

Remove the breasts and legs from the pigeons, keeping the carcases for the sauce. Discard the breast skin, and set the breasts aside. Bone and skin the legs and place them with the hearts and livers in a non-metallic bowl. Add the foie gras, sliced shallots, garlic, thyme and bay leaf, then the madeira, port and dry white wine. Turn with a wooden spoon to mix the ingredients and marinate for 12 hours or overnight in the refrigerator.

Strain the marinade into a small pan and bring to the boil, skimming off all im-

purities. Reduce over a medium heat until syrupy, add the chicken stock, stir, strain and leave to cool. Remove and discard the shallots and herbs from the meat, which should be liquidized (including the hearts and livers) till very fine with two pinches of salt. Chill in the freezer for about 15 minutes and fold in the cream. Check the seasoning and pass through a fine sieve. Stir in the marinade and set aside in the refrigerator.

Blanch the cabbage leaves in boiling salted water until tender, refresh and dry on a cloth. If tough, the central rib should

be removed. Heat the clarified butter in a small frying pan and seal the seasoned pigeon breasts for 30 seconds on each side. Allow to cool.

Lay out the four dry cabbage leaves on a board and spoon a little pigeon mousse on to the upper half of each leaf. Place the pigeon breasts on top of the mousse, and cover with the remaining mousse, smoothing it with a palette knife. Fold the leaves over to form four neat parcels, press down the edges to seal and trim off any excess cabbage. Wrap each parcel securely in clingfilm and poach them in

Pigeon in a Cabbage Leaf with a 'saucepan' mushroom pastry

boiling water for about 10 minutes.

To make the sauce, seal the crushed pigeon carcases in hot clarified butter. Add the shallots, garlic, thyme and bay leaf and fry together for 2–3 minutes. Pour in the wine vinegar and reduce until it has evaporated, add the madeira and reduce by half. Pour in the chicken stock, bring to the boil and skim. Turn down the heat, add the sliced mushrooms and simmer for 1 hour. Strain the sauce into a clean pan and reboil. Skim and reduce by half. Stir in the meat glaze and keep warm. Just before serving, add the diced truffle, season and whisk in the cold cubed butter over a medium heat.

For the mushroom pastries, heat the clarified butter in a heavy frying pan and throw in all the other ingredients for the filling. Fry for 20 seconds. Season with salt and pepper, remove from the stove and spoon into the warm pastry cases.

To serve, remove the clingfilm from the cabbage parcels and cut each into five slices. Arrange in a semicircle on four heated plates. Place a mushroom pastry on each plate and spoon the hot sauce round the meat.

Note: John Burton-Race uses little sauce-pan-shaped vol-au-vent cases for his mushroom pastries, a small bar of cooked puff pastry making the handle.

FOR FOUR PEOPLE

Apricots in Puff Pastry with Rum Cream

Croustillant à l'Abricot

Apricots in Puff Pastry with Rum Cream

8 fresh apricots, peeled, halved and stoned
50 g (1¾ oz) sugar
50 g (1¾ oz) unsalted butter
3 tablespoons frangipane (made from 115 g
(4 oz) each of caster sugar, unsalted butter and
ground almonds, 2 eggs, 1 teaspoon flour and a
tiny amount of lemon zest mixed together)
1¼ tablespoons rum
1 tablespoon toasted blanched almonds, plus
1 teaspoon toasted flaked almonds
juice of 1 lemon
1 pre-cooked puff pastry case

Cook five of the apricots in the butter and sugar until they are caramelized and golden. Heat the frangipane in a pan and stir in the rum and toasted whole almonds. Put the pastry case in a 180°C/350°F/Gas 4 oven to warm through.

Put the remaining three halved apricots in a pan with the lemon juice, sugar to taste and 6–7 tablespoons water. Bring to the boil, simmer for 5 minutes, cool slightly and liquidize. Strain this sauce and keep warm.

Take the 'lid' off the pastry case and dredge it with a thick layer of icing sugar. Pass under a hot grill or salamander to glaze. Fill the heated pastry case with the rum frangipane and arrange the caramelized apricots on top. Sprinkle with the toasted flaked almonds and serve very hot with the apricot sauce poured round.

FOR FOUR PEOPLE

L'Ortolan's chocolate desserts

ANTON MOSIMANN

MOSIMANN'S

London

Since 1975, when he became first Executive Sous-Chef and, almost immediately, Maître Chef des Cuisines, of the Dorchester Hotel in Park Lane, Anton Mosimann has been one of the major figures of the British food world. On the catering side, he was the boss of one of the largest banqueting kitchens in London and on the gastronomic side, he proved himself an immensely skilled and innovative chef, author and communicator of proven success and the friend, counsellor and trainer of countless talented young cooks. Universally liked and admired, with every diploma, honour and rating achieved, it seemed to some that, at 41, he could go no higher. The logical step was to go it alone, as chef-patron instead of employee of a large organization, and there was much speculation as to where, when and how. The magnificent and elderly Dorchester kitchens, capable of serving up to 1,000 people in an evening, were reaching the end of their natural life and Mosimann himself was anxious for a smaller establishment where he could be more immediately involved with staff and customers. There would be no shortage of backers for a new luxury restaurant, whether in London or one of the prolific new breed of country restaurants with rooms. In the event, he took a bold and, to many people, unexpected step, and set up a private club, with membership limited to 2,000. The choice of premises was pure genius – a former Scottish Presbyterian church off Belgrave Square, complete with spire, gallery and impressive masonry façade.

The Belfry, as it was called before it became Mosimann's, was built in 1830, repaired and re-opened as The Belgrave Presbyterian Church in 1866 and reached its heyday in the late nineteenth century when it could seat 500 worshippers, with an additional afternoon service for the domestic servants of the neighbourhood. By 1923 the congregation had dwindled and the church was de-consecrated. It became a private house, and, in due course, a centre for spiritualism and the occult, venue of many high-society seances. At the end of World War II, the building changed again, becoming a club for ex-officers and, in 1954, under the control of Joseph Vecchi, a noted European restaurateur, it became a leading lunching and dining club for London society. Known as The Belfry, it continued under various managements until July 1988, when it was closed so that

the laborious and expensive process of converting it into Mosimann's could begin. Through all this, the building never lost its essentially ecclesiastical air, with its high raftered central hall, stained glass windows and octagonal gallery, and these, while extensively redecorated, have not been changed. Behind, or rather below, the scenes, all is relentlessly modern, glistening with the stainless steel and white tiling of one of the most sumptuous modern restaurant kitchens in Europe. Three new private rooms for functions, named respectively for Gucci, Wedgwood and Tiffany, have been created. The last, high up under the spire, has murals by Lincoln Seligman in the style of jeweller's drawings, representing some of Anton Mosimann's most famous dishes.

The gallery in the main hall has been transformed into a comfortable bar area, with views down into both West Halkin Street and the dining room below. The bar itself has no bottles in sight, but a mirror-backed display of sixty identical glass decanters with silver labels identifying the contents as a vast selection of spirits and liqueurs. The walls are hung with framed examples of the owner's remarkable collection of culinary ephemera, menus and bills of fare, prints and drawings. The organ recess on the inner wall has given way to a large glassed wine-cellar, panelled with the stencilled lids of boxes from the great vineyards of Bordeaux. Here members may browse and choose their wines from a list that is wide-ranging, both geographically and in terms of price.

Downstairs, the tables are discreetly spaced, with silver-grey linen and white porcelain; a maximum of 75 clients can be accommodated here and in a raised adjacent room. John Davy, an Englishman who was previously maître d'hôtel to Fredy Girardet at Crissier in Switzerland rules here with a staff of 20.

In the kitchen, Ralph Bürgin, a former colleague at the Dorchester, is Chef de Cuisine, with a kitchen staff of 15 and a formidable array of equipment. Most remarkable is the electric induction stove, a flat stainless steel central rectangular block divided into areas for cooking at different temperatures. Touch it, and it is merely warm. Place a metal pan on it, and cooking starts immediately. Economical to run, this Therma stove is the only one of its kind in Britain and was imported specially from Switzerland to Maître Mosimann's specifications. The pasta and puff-pastry machines, the ice-cream makers and the refrigerators

Anton Mosimann in his new kingdom

The main dining room

were equally carefully chosen from among the best equipment available. Everything in place, and the staff trained in every detail, Mosimann's opened with an oversubscribed membership list and deafening publicity in September, 1988.

Anton Mosimann, a dapper, quietly spoken, balding figure, is a man of terrier-like persistency and a perfectionism which has shown itself from his childhood. He was born in 1947 in the small town of Nidau near Biel in Central Switzerland, where his parents had a simple restaurant. At six years old he started to help with the washing up and portering, often returning from school to serve at lunch. (He was also a business prodigy, fattening rabbits for the local markets and organizing a gang of schoolfellows to salvage the filaments and fitments from discarded light bulbs for resale. That, however, was to finance a future car and, on his eighteenth birthday, he bought the Triumph Spitfire he had set his heart on.) It was then that he decided quite simply, that he would be a cook, come what may. 'I have never wanted to change my career. I have never looked back.' At fifteen, he left home to take up an apprenticeship at Twann, also near Biel, where he continued his academic schooling while attending a professional school one day a week. 'I had no private life in my teens, no life at all outside school, the college and the kitchen.' At Twann, he learned basic techniques; he also learned enough about how corners could be cut in the

kitchen to convince him that it should never happen. In 1964 he was the only chef of his section to pass the Swiss Chef's Diploma, and his cooking career was launched. Because Switzerland has many seasonal hotels which regularly exchange their *brigades* between summer and winter, his career history reads like a frantic scramble between Berne and Villars, Lucerne and St Moritz or Gstaad, but was, in fact, a steady progression round each section of traditionally run kitchens under a variety of chefs of varying temperaments. In the ski resort of Villars, for example, one of his first jobs was under a huge and irascible chef who on one occasion sent a risotto back seven times 'but flying, ZOOM, from the *passe*'. Perhaps this is why risotto with wild mushrooms is today one of Mosimann's most perfect dishes.

There were two overseas interludes, of which the first was in Montreal where he rose quickly through the *brigade* of the Queen Elizabeth Hotel. His efficiency and dedication took him to the post of Sous-Chef, and he learned both English and the routines of a vast kitchen (larger, even, than that of the Dorchester). Typically, however, he decided he had been promoted too quickly for his age and before he had perfected his mastery of technique, so he returned to the summer-winter slog of the Swiss resorts. The second was in 1970, when he travelled to Japan (meeting his future wife on the plane, though they were not to marry till some years later) to be Executive Chef at the Swiss Pavilion at Expo 70 in Osaka. Here he learned that presentation on the plate can be beautiful, something his French colleagues were beginning to practise under the influence of the nouvelle cuisine. He returned to the Swiss circuit, to increasingly senior posts, and meanwhile increased his collection of diplomas in every possible area of culinary art. He was never afraid to drop several ranks for a season to improve his techniques. For example, he went from summer Sous-Chef in Lucerne to winter Commis Pâtissier in St Moritz.

In 1975 he made a move which was to be decisive. He went to work with Adelrich Furrer, the most famous *traiteur* – producer of cold cooked foods and *charcuterie* – in Zurich. The two men, old and young, formed a friendship based on respect between fellow professionals, so deep that, on his death, Furrer insisted his unrivalled library of historic cookery books should be sold to Mosimann rather than to any of the many other eager bidders. It happened that, at that time, the Dorchester Hotel's head chef, Eugene Kaüfeler himself Swiss, was looking for a successor. He consulted Furrer, who suggested Anton Mosimann. The young chef, then 28 and recently married to his wife Kathrin, moved to London as sous-chef and was confirmed as Maître Chef des Cuisines in December 1975.

At that time the Dorchester kitchens were run on strictly traditional lines and promotion depended less on talent than on the retirement or departure of one of the older chefs. It was, therefore, a challenge (a word which typically appears very often in Mosimann's conversation about his career) but one to which he responded swiftly and efficiently, winning over the veterans and encouraging the more talented younger chefs. The kitchens were reorganized as far as possible and The Terrace Room restaurant built up to the point where it earned two Michelin rosettes in 1986. (Three stars are never given to employees of big hotels or private clubs so, unless the rules changes, Anton Mosimann will never join the elite group of three-star chefs, though he has long been regarded as their equal.) Even after he joined the Dorchester he continued the learning process, undertaking *stages* with Michel Guérard, Paul Bocuse, Roger Vergé and the Troisgros brothers, and taking yet another diploma, this time in advanced hotel management and restaurant business skills. He wrote four successful cookery books, of which perhaps *Cuisine Naturelle* (1985) was the most innovative, promoting a healthier, lighter diet in keeping with modern needs. He became a media personality, and the television documentary *Anton goes to Sheffield*, for which he cooked a budget meal in a Yorkshire bus-driver's kitchen, made him a national figure. He became British by adoption, and the first British chef to gain a genuinely international reputation. A workaholic, he is always in the news, winning this medal, judging this competition, teaching that course for young chefs, and all, remarkably, without arousing the jealousy or resentment of his fellows. A modest man, but absolutely certain of his own potential, he will admit, if pressed, that long ago in Canada the chef who promoted him had recognized his determination and potential, and that, deep-down, he himself knew it too. With his wife and two sons, whom he neither encourages nor discourages from following him into the profession, preferring that they finish their education before deciding, he lives a comfortable family life among his much enlarged culinary library, jogging several miles every morning.

This remarkable career is the springboard for his new venture at Mosimann's. The cooking will echo his own personal style rather than reflect the needs of a large hotel restaurant. His own special favourites – risotto, ravioli, lamb with rosemary, grilled home-made duck sausage with lentils and cabbage – and the lighter cuisine naturelle dishes, like a delicate chicken consommé with coriander and ginger, or the 'Orgy' of sorbets, will combine with new dishes perfected by Ralph Bürgin and his staff over numerous dummy runs. There will also be a 'Today's Market' menu offering two choices for each of three courses for a fixed price, and a six-course Menu Surprise including wines chosen by the *sommelier* at dinner. Finally, there is Anton Mosimann's most famous dish – Bread and Butter Pudding – which he, only half-jokingly, says will be compulsory.

There are, of course, great risks involved in establishing a club restaurant as opposed to one open to the general public, especially when the entrance and annual membership fees are very high, and prices, except for the fixed-price 'market' menus, match all but the most expensive public restaurants in London. The standards of food and service must be maintained at the highest level if members are not only to join but to use the club regularly, and the right mix of business and private members is needed to balance the lunch and the dinner services. Anton Mosimann has not previously run his own establishment without the back-up of a larger management structure; now, however high-powered his professional advisers, the responsibility for every last detail is his, and it is on his personality and leadership that the club will fail or succeed. So far, the auguries are good, and no chef-patron could have prepared himself more meticulously. 'I wake every morning and say "What can I do today which will be better than anything I have done before?" I have to have a new challenge all the time.'

John Davy and some of the staff

Marinated Salmon and Turbot

240 g (8½ oz) skinned and boned fillet of
salmon, preferably wild
200 g (7 oz) skinned and boned fillet of turbot
juice of 1 lime
1 teaspoon crushed white peppercorns
1 teaspoon crushed coriander seeds
50 ml (2 fl oz) olive oil
100 g (4 oz) tomatoes, peeled, seeded and diced
1 tablespoon finely chopped dill
salt

Remove any remaining fine bones from the fish with tweezers and slice into fine strips. Divide between four cold plates, which should have sufficient rim to pre-vent the marinade escaping. Sprinkle with the lime juice and season with the crushed peppercorns, coriander seeds and salt. Add the olive oil, diced tomatoes and dill.

Allow to stand for 3–4 minutes and serve with warm toasted French bread.

Note: if you wish to make the dish in advance, the fish can be sliced and ar-ranged on the plates with the pepper and coriander, and refrigerated for up to an hour under clingfilm. The lime juice, olive oil, tomato, dill and salt must not be added until just before serving.

FOR FOUR PEOPLE

Fisherman's Chowder

24 clams, scrubbed and cleaned
750 ml (1¼ pints) fish stock
25 g (1 oz) onion, peeled and diced
25 g (1 oz) leek, diced
25 g (1 oz) carrot, peeled and diced
50 g (1¾ oz) celeriac, peeled and diced
a clove of garlic, peeled and crushed
1½ tablespoons oil
a small bay leaf
25 g (1 oz) green pepper, seeded and sliced
100 g (3½ oz) potato, peeled and diced
2 tomatoes, peeled, seeded and diced
1 teaspoon chopped thyme
1 teaspoon chopped parsley
salt and freshly ground pepper

Place the clams in their shells in a large pan with the fish stock. Cover and simmer until the clams open, then remove them from the stock and leave to cool. Strain the stock through muslin or a fine sieve and reserve. Remove the clams from their shells and cut away the hard white tendons. Dice the flesh.

Sauté the onion, leek, carrot, celeriac and garlic in the butter without brown-ing. Add the bay leaf, green pepper, potato and reserved stock and simmer for about 7–8 minutes. Add the tomatoes and simmer for a further minute. Remove the bay leaf, then stir in the diced clams and chopped herbs. Season to taste with salt and pepper and either serve hot or refrig-erate before serving cold.

Note: clams can be replaced with scallops, monkfish or turbot.

FOR FOUR PEOPLE

Leek Terrine with Hazelnut Vinaigrette

1.2 kg (2 lb 10 oz) trimmed leeks, cut into
13 cm (5 inch) lengths
20 g (¾ oz) dried trompettes de la mort
wild mushrooms, soaked, blanched and drained
a bunch of chervil
vinaigrette made with hazelnut oil
salt and freshly ground pepper

Fisherman's Chowder

Slit the leeks lengthwise and wash them well. Tie into equal bundles and cook in boiling salted water until tender, but still *al dente* – about 3–4 minutes. Refresh in a large bowl of iced water, then drain well, squeezing out excess water.

Line a 9.5 × 15 × 7 cm (4 × 6 × 3 inch) terrine with foil, and pack the leeks in firmly. Season well with salt and pepper as you make alternating layers of green and white leeks and drained mushrooms, ending with a layer of leeks which should be above the level of the terrine. Place a piece of board or stiff card, cut to fit the inside of the terrine and covered with foil, over the top layer of leeks and invert the whole terrine on to a flat dish. Weight down the terrine with a kilogram (2¼ lb) weight and refrigerate for 6 hours or more. This will compress the leeks and extract any surplus water.

To serve, unmould the terrine on to a serving dish and remove the foil carefully. Decorate with chervil sprigs. Slice with a very sharp knife and serve with hazelnut vinaigrette.

Note: *trompettes de la mort* are best for this terrine because of their lovely black colour, but other dried fungi or fresh oyster mushrooms can be used.

FOR TEN PEOPLE

Chicken Hot-Pot Naturelle

1 chicken, about 2.2 kg (4¾ lb)
2 litres (3½ pints) white chicken stock
3 onions, peeled, each studded with 2 cloves
a bay leaf
2 cloves of garlic, peeled
a few white peppercorns
a bunch of mixed fresh herbs (for example,
thyme, rosemary, parsley stalks)
4 small carrots, peeled
4 pieces of celery, about 5 cm (2 inches) long
4 pieces of leek, about 5 cm (2 inches) long
4 small onions, skinned
1 small celeriac, peeled and cut into quarters
parsley sprigs
salt and freshly ground pepper

Leek Terrine with Hazelnut Vinaigrette

Bring a large saucepan of water to the boil. Add the chicken and bring back to the boil. Remove the chicken and allow to cool slightly. Meanwhile boil up the chicken stock with the onions, bay leaf, garlic, peppercorns and herbs and then simmer for 20 minutes. Add the chicken and poach for 20 minutes. Take out the chicken. Strain the stock, remove any fat with kitchen paper and return to the (washed) pan. Remove the skin from the chicken, and return the bird to the pan. Add the carrots, celery, leek, small onions and quartered celeriac and bring to the boil. Simmer for 10 minutes. Drain, reserving the stock, and keep the chicken and all the vegetables warm.

Reduce the chicken stock to half by boiling briskly and adjust the seasoning. Cut the chicken into eight pieces and arrange in four warmed soup plates with the vegetables. Pour over some reduced stock and decorate with parsley.

FOR FOUR PEOPLE

Palace Hotel Blanquette of Veal

Blanquette de Veau Palace

Palace Hotel Blanquette of Veal

900 g (2 lb) veal (boneless shoulder, breast or neck), cut into 40 g (1½ oz) cubes, trimmed of all fat
400 ml (14 fl oz) white veal stock
150 ml (¼ pint) dry white wine
a bouquet garni
25 g (1 oz) each of chopped onion, carrot and celery
25 g (1 oz) parsley
1 clove
½ bay leaf
40 ml (1½ fl oz) double cream, whisked with 1 egg yolk
25 g (1 oz) flour
1 tablespoon lemon juice
a pinch of grated nutmeg
25 g (1 oz) meat glaze
salt and freshly ground pepper

Blanch the veal quickly in boiling salted water, rinse under running water to remove any scum and return to a clean pan. Allow to cool and then add the cold veal stock to cover. Add the wine, bouquet garni, vegetables and seasonings and simmer, covered, for 1½ hours or until the meat is tender.

Transfer the meat to a warm dish and strain the cooking liquid through a cloth into a saucepan. Reduce the liquid to two-thirds of its volume, then lower the heat and stir in the cream/egg mixture. Blend the flour thoroughly with a few spoonfuls of the liquid and return to the pan. Stir constantly over a low heat until the sauce thickens.

Add the cooked veal, lemon juice and nutmeg, heat through, and taste for seasoning. Spoon the meat on to a large heated serving dish and pour a little heated meat glaze over the chunks. Surround with the sauce and serve with seasonal vegetables.

Note: this dish is named for the Palace Hotel, St Moritz, the long-established skiing resort in the Engadine – one of many where Anton Mosimann spent winter seasons as a young man.

In the photograph the chef has used sliced green beans, turned carrots and a cherry tomato.

FOR FOUR PEOPLE

Poached Fillet of Beef with Vegetables

Poached Fillet of Beef with Vegetables

four 150 g (5½ oz) slices of beef fillet, carefully trimmed
500 ml (18 fl oz) beef stock
100 g (3½ oz) each of white and red onions, peeled, quartered and broken up
150 g (5 oz) white part of leek, sliced diagonally
140 g (4¾ oz) Savoy cabbage leaves, roughly chopped
100 g (3½ oz) small Brussels sprouts, divided into individual leaves
1 tablespoon chopped mixed fresh parsley, chives and basil
salt and freshly ground pepper

Bring the beef stock to the boil in a small *sauteuse* (a round frying pan with slightly flared sides) just large enough to hold the fillets in a single layer, and allow to reduce a little. Blanch the vegetables briefly in boiling salted water, then drain. Add the beef fillets to the stock and simmer for 5–6 minutes. Remove and drain on a grid.

Put the blanched vegetables in the pan with the cooking liquid and bring to the boil. Add the meat and chopped herbs and season with salt and pepper. Remove the meat and vegetables and arrange the vegetables on a heated serving dish with the four fillets on top. Pour on a little stock and serve immediately. (This last phase has to be carried out very quickly if the meat is not to overcook.)

Note: to give this dish extra flavour, a whole peeled garlic clove may be poached with it and removed before serving. The vegetables may be varied according to the season – for instance carrots, celery, broccoli, mange-tout peas, broad beans or kohlrabi are all good.

FOR FOUR PEOPLE

Anton's Bread and Butter Pudding

250 ml (8 fl oz) full-cream milk
250 ml (8 fl oz) double cream
a small piece of vanilla pod
3 eggs
125 g (4½ oz) caster sugar
3 small white bread rolls, or slices of white
French bread
30 g (1¼ oz) butter
10 g (⅓ oz) sultanas, soaked in water
20 g (¾ oz) apricot jam, warmed
a little icing sugar
salt

Bring the milk and cream to the boil with a pinch of salt and the vanilla pod, while you mix the eggs and caster sugar together in a bowl. Add the simmering cream to the egg mixture, stirring thoroughly, and pass through a fine sieve. Cut the rolls into thin slices, keeping the crusts, and butter them. Drain the sultanas. Sprinkle a few sultanas over the bottom of a buttered ovenproof dish 10 cm (4 inches) deep with sloping sides and arrange the bread slices round the edges and bottom. Sprinkle with the remaining sultanas. Pour on the cream mixture and dot the top with the remaining butter.

Poach the pudding carefully for 45 minutes or more on top of the stove in a bain marie or roasting pan containing enough hot water to come three quarters of the way up the side of the pudding dish. Add more water if it seems to be evaporating. Alternatively, the pudding can be baked for 45 minutes in a 180°C/350°F/Gas 4 oven. When the pudding is done, spoon over the warmed apricot jam and dust with icing sugar.

Note: bread and butter pudding can be served with double cream or stewed fruit.

FOR FOUR PEOPLE

Fruit Terrine

6 leaves of gelatine, soaked in cold water and
squeezed dry or 3 teaspoons powdered gelatine
300 ml (½ pint) clear white grape juice
a bunch of fresh mint
100 g (3½ oz) mango flesh, sliced
150 g (5 oz) raspberries and strawberries,
picked over and sliced
200 g (7 oz) papaya flesh, sliced
100 g (3½ oz) bilberries or blueberries, sliced
100 g (3½ oz) black or white grapes,
halved and seeded
extra fresh fruit and mint sprigs to decorate

Raspberry sauce
300 g (12½ oz) raspberries,
puréed and strained
2 tablespoons icing sugar
juice of 1 small lemon

Put a 1.5 litre (2½ pint) china or glass terrine or dish in the freezer to chill. Dissolve the gelatine in a little warmed grape juice. Add the remaining grape juice and allow to cool until almost set.

Stand the chilled terrine in a larger bowl of ice and pour a layer of the nearly-set grape juice over the bottom. Allow to set and arrange a layer of mint leaves over the jelly. Turning the terrine, coat each side with jelly in turn, finishing with a layer of mint leaves.

Arrange the fruit in layers in the terrine, pouring a little grape jelly over each layer and allowing to set before continuing with the next, finishing with a layer of jelly. Chill for 3–4 hours until thoroughly set.

Meanwhile, make the raspberry sauce by mixing the puréed raspberries with the sugar and lemon juice. Chill.

To serve, run a knife dipped in hot water round the edges of the terrine, turn it out carefully on to a serving dish, and slice. Serve decorated with fresh fruit, raspberry sauce and mint sprigs.

FOR FIFTEEN PEOPLE

Fruit Terrine

Anton Mosimann's 'compulsory' Bread and Butter Pudding

DAVID WILSON

THE PEAT INN

Fife

A remote crossroads on a high, wind-whipped agricultural plateau in the Kingdom of Fife seems a strange place to find one of Britain's most individual restaurants, yet The Peat Inn, a few miles inland from St Andrews and an hour's drive from Edinburgh, with its Michelin star and host of other awards, is run by one of Britain's most individual chefs, and attracts visitors from all over the world.

David Wilson is a quiet man with a distinctive Scottish burr, and is one of the most unusual and talented self-taught chefs in a country which has a rich crop of them. Born in Glasgow in a family with absolutely no tradition of catering or cooking, he trained in marketing, marrying his wife Patricia – a textile designer – along the way. His first jobs were in business, and the Wilsons moved to London because he is a keen amateur jazz musician and it was easier to find bands to play with there. Their shared love of food and wine caused them to take the momentous and, with a new-born son, scary decision to change course entirely. David spent two years working in the restaurant trade to learn the rudiments, first with Somerset Moore, now at Flitwick Manor, in the kitchen and then as a waiter in the Strines Inn, a modest pub-restaurant in Derbyshire.

In 1972, with what David Wilson calls 'suicidal timing', (Patricia was eight months pregnant with their daughter) they bought the run-down inn at Peat Inn in Fife. Together they renovated it, building up the kitchen side, with David learning on the job and gaining new insights on working holidays in France, where he spent brief periods in the kitchens of Roger Vergé and the Troisgros brothers, and visited many more. The rooms where travellers had slept since the eighteenth century were abandoned immediately, but the public bar was kept on for the dwindling number of local small farmers and retired miners, until the restaurant had acquired sufficient reputation for the pub to be closed and for the kitchen to be extended as far as the limited area would permit and the dining room renovated to take 48 diners in luxury.

The Peat Inn itself will never be more than a charming, low-built whitewashed building, with low ceilings and dark beams, but Patricia Wilson's exuberant taste has created a most attractive interior. The furnishings are almost entirely from France, where the Wilsons spend most of their month-long holidays every year. Fabrics, tapestries and the comfortable sofas in the bar area with its enormous antique French fireplace and welcoming log fire, contrast with the almost prim black dresses of the waitresses. Recently, a modern extension to the rear, looking down on the peat moss Nature Reserve which gives the hamlet its name, has provided eight suites furnished to the highest standards of

The Peat Inn

David and Patricia Wilson

luxury. These are designed to attract foreign tourists and those people from Edinburgh who prefer, after sampling the fine wines for which The Peat Inn is world famous, to 'sleep where they dine', or those who spend a golfing holiday at nearby St Andrews and like to return refreshed to dine on the best of food and wine and sleep in great comfort.

The wine list is extraordinary, attested to by the dozens of citations – among them an Egon Ronay/Armagnac Cellar of the Year, and awards from German and French producers – framed on the walls. Very strong in German wines, the list is outstanding in Bordeaux and Burgundy vintages, many unusual and all underpriced by most standards. No wonder *Decanter* magazine dubbed it 'The Inn of Great Happiness'. Many customers leave the choice of wine up to the Wilsons and few are disappointed, because they have such an exact understanding of which wine best complements each dish. The choice never stands still: new producers are constantly sought and Australian and Californian wines have been added to the list.

This international flavour is in sharp contrast to the strictly local approach in the kitchen. David Wilson may have been influenced by the attitudes of such chefs as Guérard, Vergé and Marc Meneau, but he will never use an imported ingredient when something better and fresher is available locally. So far north (the Aurora Borealis can sometimes be seen from the Perthshire hills), tender vegetables cannot be obtained in winter, although the advent of polytunnels is changing that, especially for the fresh herbs which are bought in quantity from the local firm of Scotherbs. In season, however, there is no lack of tender baby vegetables of all kinds. Wild berries abound, and David has discovered two ardent local fungi experts who bring him morels, chanterelles, mousserons, ceps and other wild mushrooms – above all, the summer truffle, *Tuber aestivum* which, while less pronounced in its flavour than its European cousin, is a great delicacy. At first, these came from a Polish collector in Lothian; recently they have been found nearby by a friend who works as a National Trust gardener. *Crème fraîche* and *fromage frais* come from a Scottish dairy entrepreneur, and Scottish hard cheeses, including goat cheeses, are delivered regularly by an itinerant van. Soft cheeses are almost all French.

Fish comes from the nearby coast, although the choice is limited by the weather, as the local fishermen are mainly inshore and reluctant to risk their small boats in bad weather. Fish from Billingsgate Market in London or from Aberdeen is seldom used, because its freshness is unreliable; The Peat Inn therefore depends on its excellent contacts with fishmongers and fishermen in St Andrews and Pittenweem for monkfish (a special favourite), turbot and cod to obtain the best specimens, and David Wilson plans the menus round what is available. Excellent salmon and sea-trout are available both from netters and the fly-fishing rivers. Smoked fish is obviously a speciality, especially the Arbroath Smokie, a hot-smoked haddock with an intriguing flavour, which David gets from a specialist curer through his fish merchant in St Andrews. He uses them for a variety of first courses, and they are as inexpensive as they are delicious. Smoked salmon comes from the same source.

But, of course, the glory of The Peat Inn is its local game. Beef and lamb are offered, but they definitely take second place to

The dining room

venison, partridge, grouse and, above all, local wild pigeons. Few menus appear without a pigeon dish, cooked in any number of ingenious and delicious ways, all contrived to present the tender breasts cooked briefly to a rosy tenderness, with perhaps the legs slow-roasted to a succulent texture and the liver briefly sautéed for a garnish. The many carcases are turned into the stocks which are the basis of the finely flavoured reduced sauces. Venison is also important. Wilson and his staff are expert in cutting and roasting roe deer to perfection and The Peat Inn was one of the first British restaurants to serve venison liver, long a favourite in Central Europe, but at first sometimes a shock to British customers.

The puddings are simple but delicious, some of them, like the apple dish in this chapter, harking back to the tastes of childhood (as the Chinese novelist and philosopher Lin Yutang said 'What is patriotism but a love of the good food we ate in our childhood?'). Others, like the lacy biscuit cup filled with a praline ice-cream, would be equally at home in far more pretentious places. Local flavours are important here too. The home of a famous brand of porage oats is just down the road, so they are occasionally used as the basis of a pudding. Puff pastry is also frequently used.

So, the menu is truly one which the French would describe as based in the *terroir*, and is also one which depends on the availability of the best and freshest, and on a balanced meal, offering a proper combination of simplicity and richness of taste, of vegetable and starch ingredients, with right wines chosen to suit both the dishes and the customer's pocket. The kitchen is relatively modest, relying on propane gas from an outside tank for its burners and three ovens, and electricity for mixers, a pasta maker and an ice-cream maker. Bread is made daily, and ice-cream and stocks almost daily.

The staff of five is small, mainly local, and for most it is their first job. Some, including Angus Blackshaws, the sous-chef, have been with the Wilsons from the beginning. David's knowledge of technique and instinctive feeling for texture and flavour are so infectious that he is a teacher of talent. Although the restaurant rarely opens except under his supervision, he knows that all except the rawest recruit can understand and interpret his instructions and intentions. Everyone can do each kitchen task, and David himself is everywhere, helping to prepare ingredients or to assist with a particular dish when there is a sudden rush of orders. He also inspects each plate, arranging the final decorations of herbs or vegetables before it goes into the dining room. It is all a remarkable act of team work, without which a small restaurant with such extraordinarily high standards could not survive. All this serves to explain why in an isolated hamlet, which many would regard as being in the middle of nowhere, it has achieved its reputation. It is by no means the only restaurant in Scotland to have put the lie to Samuel Johnson's rude remarks about Scottish cooking, and the chefs are friends and allies to each other. David Wilson could move to larger premises, a more central location, at any time and would have no shortage of backers. But he and his family, whose privacy is protected by their holidays and the two days each week when the restaurant is closed, enjoy the clear wide skies of Fife and the life they live there, and though at the beginning they were often asked, and sometimes wondered, why they had taken such a risk, they rightly now have no cause for regret. The Peat Inn is firmly on the map.

David Wilson reckons to use over 1500 pigeons every year, and they are all locally shot young wood-pigeons. East Fife is an arable area, known for its baby peas and cereals, and the pigeon population is such a serious threat to farmers that they welcome the familiar figure of Iain Duncan, The Peat Inn's supplier, with his decoys and hide, his dog Jill and his gun. Mr Duncan also farms, but shooting has been his passion since he was a boy. He hopes to bag up to ten birds with each shot, shooting from his home-made hide set up on the edges of the woods where the birds congregate between their feeding forays. He always shoots alone, and remains in his hide for up to two hours, shooting at least sixty pigeons. What David Wilson is looking for is a plump young bird of 1–2 years old, healthy and undamaged. Iain Duncan plucks them himself, but does not gut them as David prefers to do it himself, partly as a double-check on the bird's health and also because the liver, which forms an important part of some dishes, stays fresher that way. Older birds go to commercial game dealers, the young ones all go to The Peat Inn, together with the roe deer which Mr Duncan culls for local farmers.

Iain Duncan and David Wilson (right) discuss a plump pigeon, watched by Jill.

'Feuilletée' of Potato and Smoked Salmon

140 g (4½ oz) smoked salmon, cut into 20 even pieces
140 g (4½ oz) peeled raw potato (ideally a large, regularly shaped potato), cut into 20 paper-thin slices of the same dimensions as the smoked salmon pieces
2 tablespoons double cream or crème fraîche
2 teaspoons finely chopped fresh dill, plus 4 sprigs
salt and freshly ground black pepper

Preheat the oven to 230°C/450°F/Gas 8. Parboil the potato slices in lightly salted boiling water very briefly. Drain and refresh under cold water. Have ready four buttered ovenproof ramekins. Pack in the potato and salmon slices, starting and finishing with potato. In a bowl, mix the cream with the chopped dill and black pepper and pour enough into each ramekin to cover the top layer.

Place the ramekins in a roasting pan with enough hot water to come half-way up their sides and bake for approximately 15 minutes, uncovered.

Turn out immediately on to four hot plates and decorate each with a sprig of dill. (In winter, green fennel tops would be an acceptable garnish.) Any remaining cream can be thinned with a little vegetable stock to make a sauce.

FOR FOUR PEOPLE

Escalope of Salmon in a Lemon Vinaigrette

Escalope of Salmon in a Lemon Vinaigrette

4 boned and filleted slices of salmon, each about 120 g (4 oz), skinned
2 lemons, with all peel, pith and membranes removed
6 tablespoons extra virgin olive oil
thin slices of a peeled cucumber
1 tomato, peeled, seeded and cut in triangles
pared peel of 1 lemon, cut in matchsticks and blanched
coarse sea salt

To make the sauce, purée the lemon flesh in a liquidizer, then add the olive oil gradually to form an emulsion. Strain through a fine sieve into a bowl.

Preheat the oven to 240°C/475°F/Gas 9. Sprinkle the salmon with sea salt, place on a baking tray and cook in the hot oven for about 5 minutes. (If you have to use a slightly lower oven temperature, the fish will have to cook for longer: the important point is that it should be slightly underdone.)

Warm the sauce over hot water or on the corner of the stove. Divide the sauce between four warm plates and arrange thin slices of cucumber in the centre of each. Place an escalope of salmon on top and decorate with tomato triangles. Strew the blanched lemon peel over the salmon and serve immediately.

FOR FOUR PEOPLE

Gratin of Arbroath Smokie with Smoked Salmon

1 pair of Arbroath Smokies (see note)
125 g (4½ oz) low-fat soft cheese
300 ml (½ pint) double cream
3 egg yolks
25–30 g (1 oz) smoked salmon
avocado and apple balls (if available)
freshly ground pepper

Heat the smokies gently in a cool oven or other warm place for 5–10 minutes (this makes it easier to remove the skin). Skin, split, and remove the spine and all other obvious bones. Process or liquidize the fish to a paste, add the cheese and cream

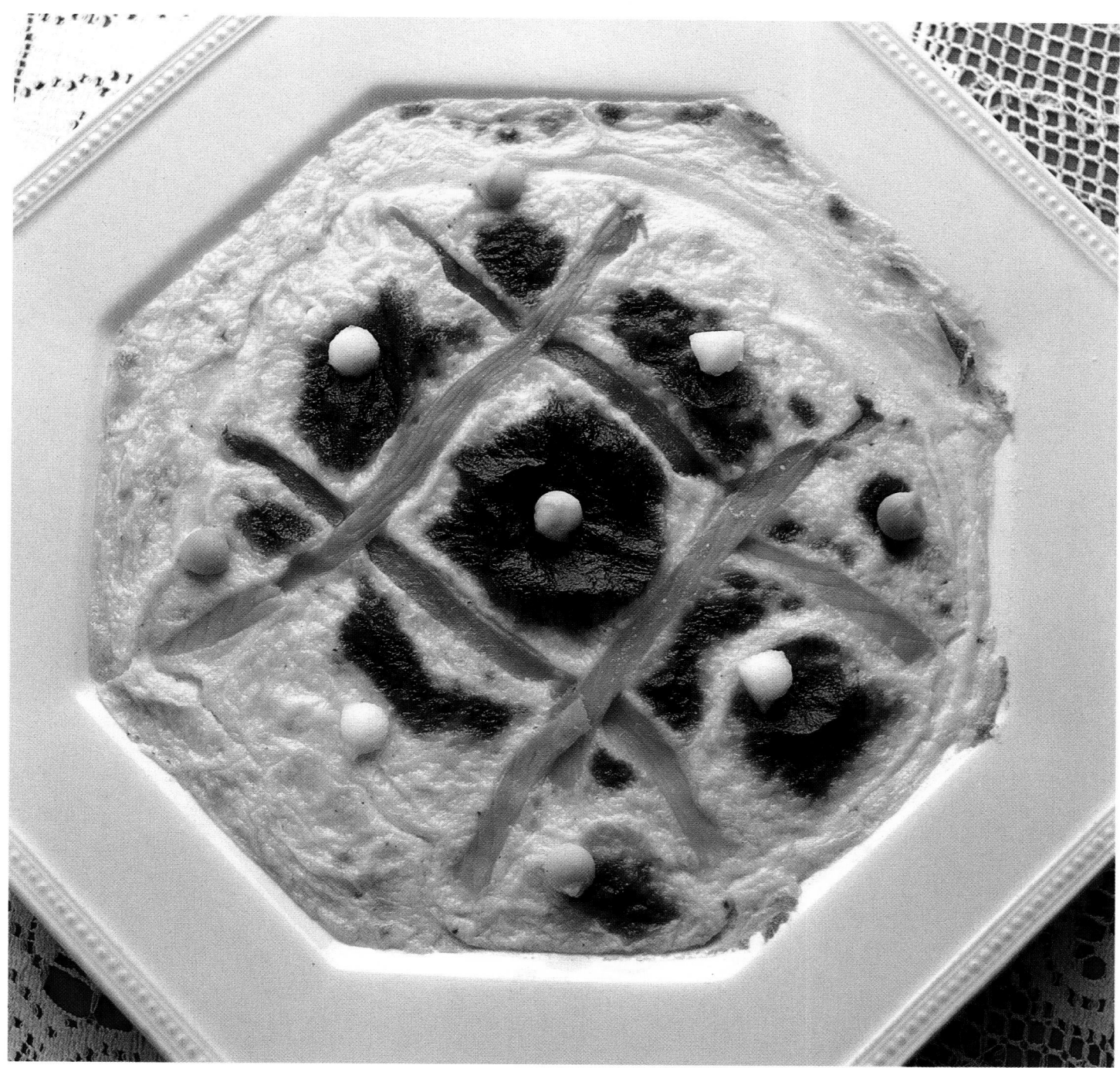

Gratin of Arbroath Smokie with Smoked Salmon

and process again. Pass, very carefully as the mixture is fairly thick, through a sieve to eliminate any remaining bones. Add the egg yolks and pepper and mix thoroughly. (This stage can be done up to a day in advance and the mixture refrigerated until needed.)

Preheat the grill to its hottest setting and spoon the mixture on to an ovenproof serving dish. Cut the sliced smoked salmon into thin strips and arrange in a lattice pattern over the top. Grill until the mixture sets, and is pleasantly browned. Place small balls of avocado and apple between the smoked salmon lattice.

Note: the Arbroath Smokie is one of the world's finest smoked fish, and anyone with a good supplier is fortunate indeed. David Wilson's recipe, especially with its decorative apple and avocado, is a triumph. It could be made as simply, and almost as deliciously, as a hot gratin without the smoked salmon or decoration. The most essential step is the sieving, as even the smallest fragment of bone ruins the dish. For convenience, this recipe is given for a single serving dish, but David Wilson prefers to prepare it on individual plates because it makes for better restaurant presentation.

FOR FOUR PEOPLE

Breasts of Pigeon on a Base of Pigeon Purée and Wild Mushrooms in a Juniper-Flavoured Sauce

4 young wood pigeons
60 g (2 oz) wild mushrooms, cleaned and picked over
1 egg
1 tablespoon double cream or crème fraîche
oil for frying
150 ml (¼ pint) red wine
1 tablespoon sherry vinegar
2 teaspoons redcurrant jelly
300 ml (½ pint) pigeon stock
4 juniper berries
60 g (2 oz) cold unsalted butter, diced
2 tablespoons each shredded red and white cabbage
salt and pepper

Begin by making the pigeon purée bases. Remove the meat from the pigeon legs and carcases, reserving the breasts, un-skinned. Liquidize or process the leg meat and wild mushrooms, add the egg and cream and process till smooth. Season with salt and pepper. Divide the mixture between 4 metal non-stick individual flan tins, approximately 8 cm (3½ inches) diameter and 2 cm (¾ inch) deep. The mixture should come up to only a quarter of the depth of the tins. Place the tins in a shallow roasting pan on the top of the stove, with enough hot water to come half-way up the sides of the flan tins.

Cook until the pigeon mixtures are set, which could take as little as 4 minutes. (This step can be carried out a few hours in advance and the pigeon bases reheated gently, if necessary.)

When you are ready to finish the dish, preheat the oven to 230°C/450°F/Gas 8. Sauté the pigeon breasts (skin on) for 1 minute on each side, then place, skin side up, in a shallow roasting pan with a little of the oil and cook for 5 minutes in the hot oven. Remove, drain and rest in a warm place while you make the sauce. Reduce the wine, vinegar and redcurrant jelly until it has almost evaporated, then add the stock and juniper berries. Stir well and reduce by approximately one-third. Whisk in the cold butter. Check seasoning and strain through a fine sieve or muslin. Keep warm.

Heat oil in a pan or wok for stir frying. Have ready four warm plates, and turn out a hot (or reheated) pigeon base on each. Surround with the hot sauce and keep warm. Quickly remove the skin from the pigeon breasts, cut each into 6–7 slices and arrange in a coronet around the bases. Finally, stir-fry the shredded mixed cabbages very briefly in the hot oil and place a crunchy spoonful in the centre of each base. Serve immediately.

FOR FOUR PEOPLE

Breasts of Pigeon in a Juniper-Flavoured Sauce

Julienne of Pigeon Breast with Brown Lentils

2 pigeon breasts, skin on
225 g (8 oz) brown lentils
½ small onion, studded with a clove
a bouquet garni
300 ml (½ pint) pigeon stock
30 g (1 oz) cold unsalted butter, diced
oil for sautéing
salt and pepper

Wash and pick over the lentils and soak in cold water for about 45 minutes. Discard the soaking water and cook in approximately 2.75 litres (5 pints) water with the onion and bouquet garni until tender. Drain, discarding the onion and bouquet

Julienne of Pigeon Breast with Brown Lentils

2 minutes. Remove the mushrooms and truffle with a slotted spoon and keep warm. Strain the stock and return to a simmer. Whisk in the remaining butter in small pieces, reducing the sauce to the point where it will coat the back of a spoon. Add the chervil and taste for seasoning.

Pour the sauce on to four warmed plates, and put a mound of mushrooms in the centre of each. Quickly remove the skin from the pigeon breasts, slice the meat into fine strips and arrange over the mushrooms. Serve immediately.

FOR FOUR PEOPLE

David Wilson's Vegetable Stock

David Wilson uses a great deal of vegetable stock, which is made up several times a week, as well as his game, fish and meat stocks. No fat is used, and the liquid is an equal mixture of dry white wine and water. The result is a marvellously aromatic liquid which enhances any sauce or soup.

garni. You will need 2 tablespoons of lentils for the sauce. Keep the rest warm.

Bring the pigeon stock and the 2 tablespoons of lentils to the boil, and then liquidize. Sieve, and return to the pan. Bring to the boil again and then, on a lower heat, whisk in the diced butter. If the sauce seems too thick, add a little more stock; if too thin, allow it to reduce over a very gentle heat. Taste for seasoning and keep hot.

Preheat the oven to 230°C/450°F/Gas 8. Heat a little oil in a sauté pan and sauté the pigeon breasts briefly to seal them. Place in a roasting pan and roast for 5 minutes. Leave to rest in a warm place for at least 10 minutes, then remove, skin and slice into fine matchsticks. Season with salt and pepper.

Have ready four heated plates and pour the sauce in an even layer on each. Place a mound of lentils on each plate and strew the strips of pigeon over the lentils.

FOR FOUR PEOPLE

Ragoût of Wood Pigeon, Wild Mushrooms and Truffle

*2 breasts from a plump young wood pigeon,
skin on
sunflower oil for frying
350 g (12 oz) assorted wild mushrooms,
cleaned and picked over
140 g (4½ oz) unsalted butter
150 ml (¼ pint) vegetable stock
4 thin slices of truffle
2 teaspoons freshly chopped chervil
salt and pepper*

Preheat the oven to 230°C/450°F/Gas 8. Sauté the pigeon breasts in oil for a minute on each side, then place skin-side up in a small roasting pan with a little of the oil. Roast for 5 minutes in the hot oven. Remove to a warm place to rest until needed.

Cut or slice the cleaned mushrooms into equal sized pieces, and cook in half the butter until the juices run out. Add the stock and truffle slices and simmer for

*1 white part of leek
1 carrot, peeled
half a fennel bulb
1 small onion, peeled
2 tomatoes, halved
6 cloves of garlic, peeled and crushed
1 sprig thyme
1 sprig tarragon
2 sprigs parsley
a bay leaf
a clove
1 teaspoon sea salt
1 teaspoon crushed black peppercorns
1 litre (1¾ pints) dry white table wine
1 litre (1¾ pints) cold water*

Roughly chop the leek, carrot, fennel and onion. Put in a stockpot with the tomatoes, garlic, seasonings, wine and water. Bring to the boil and simmer gently, uncovered, for 30 minutes. Strain.

MAKES APPROX 1.5 LITRES (2½ PINTS)

Wild Duck in a Red Wine Sauce with Blueberries

*breasts and legs of 2 wild ducks (mallards) (use
the livers to make a smooth pâté, a slice of
which can accompany the dish)
1 tablespoon each finely chopped carrot, onion
and celery
1 small clove of garlic, peeled and crushed
sunflower oil for frying
150 ml (¼ pint) game stock, or more if
necessary
150 ml (¼ pint) red wine
2 tablespoons sherry vinegar
25 g (1 oz) caster sugar
60 g (2 oz) cold unsalted butter, diced
60 g (2 oz) blueberries or bilberries*

Preheat the oven to 130°C/250°F/Gas ½.
Sweat the vegetables and garlic in a little
of the oil in a roasting pan over a low
flame. Place the four legs skin-side up on
the vegetables. Pour over a little of the
game stock, bring to simmering point and
place in the oven, uncovered, to cook for
approximately 2½ hours. Remove and
keep warm. Increase the temperature of
the oven to 230°C/450°F/Gas 8. Sauté the
breasts, skin on, in a little oil to seal them,
then roast in the hot oven in a second
roasting pan for approximately 7 minutes.
Remove the duck from the pan. Rest in a
warm place while you make the sauce.

Reduce the wine, vinegar and sugar to a
syrup in a small pan, add the remaining
stock and reduce again, whisking from
time to time. Finish by whisking in the
diced butter. Add the blueberries and
simmer for approximately 1 minute until
they are soft but still retain their shape.

To serve, divide the sauce between four
warm plates and place a mound of diced
vegetable and a roasted leg on top. Carve
each breast fillet into three thick slices and
fan out round the lower edge of the plate.
If you have had time to make the liver
pâté, place a thin slice on each plate.

Note: wild duck is cooked in this way
because the legs are thin and sinewy and
need long, slow cooking to tenderize
them and bring out their flavour. The
breasts on a plump bird can be treated in
the same way as those of a domestic duck.

FOR FOUR PEOPLE

Wild Duck in a Red Wine Sauce with Blueberries

Venison Liver in a Rich Wine Sauce

*450 g (1 lb) venison liver, thinly sliced
4 tablespoons peeled and finely chopped onion
sunflower oil for frying (David Wilson adds a
little groundnut oil as well)
1 tablespoon caster sugar
150 ml (¼ pint) red wine
1 tablespoon sherry vinegar
300 ml (½ pint) strong meat stock
60 g (2 oz) cold unsalted butter, diced
2 tablespoons peeled and diced potato
salt and pepper*

Sauté 2 tablespoons of the onion in a very
little oil, then add the sugar, red wine and
vinegar. Reduce until the liquid has
almost evaporated and then add the stock.
Reduce gently until the sauce has thickened, strain and then whisk in the diced
butter. Taste for seasoning and keep
warm.

Cook the potato and remaining onion
in oil until they are crisp and golden.
Drain on kitchen paper and keep warm.

At the last moment before serving
(always crucial with liver dishes), season
the sliced liver with salt and pepper. Heat
oil in a sauté pan and cook the slices
briefly on each side. They should be
browned evenly, but still rosy inside.
Drain on kitchen paper. To serve, run the
sauce round the edge of the heated plates.
Place the liver slices on the sauce, season
the potato and onion garnish and strew
over the liver. Serve immediately.

Note: for this dish David Wilson normally uses roe deer liver, now becoming
popular in England, but a long-time
prized delicacy in central Europe. The
liver of the red deer is more robust, but
can be treated in the same way.

FOR FOUR PEOPLE

Saddle of Venison in a Game Sauce with Port with Forfar Bridies

575g (1¼ lb) saddle of venison, boned and trimmed
4 tablespoons tawny port
85g (3 oz) shredded white cabbage
oil for frying

Forfar Bridies
120g (4 oz) venison trimmings
a little oil for sautéing
60g (2 oz) peeled and finely chopped onion
4 tablespoons venison or other game stock
60g (2 oz) peeled and finely diced potato
60g (2 oz) puff pastry dough
1 egg yolk, beaten
salt and pepper

Sauce
150 ml (¼ pint) red wine
1 tablespoon sherry vinegar
2 teaspoons redcurrant jelly
300 ml (½ pint) game stock
60g (2 oz) cold unsalted butter, diced
salt and pepper

Mince or chop the venison trimmings finely and sauté in a little oil over a brisk heat. Add the chopped onion, lower the heat and cook for a further 2 minutes. Add the stock, and simmer, covered, for another 15 minutes. Cook the diced potato briefly in salted water, refresh under cold water so that the heat in the potato does not 'work' on the pastry, drain and add to the venison and onion. Season with salt and pepper. Roll out the puff pastry as thinly as possible, and cut out four circles 10 cm (4 inches) in diameter. Brush the edges with a little cold water, spoon the venison mixture equally on to the four pastry circles and fold the pastry over to form half-moon shapes, sealing the edges firmly with your fingers. Make three small slashes in the top of each Bridie and brush with beaten egg yolk. The Bridies can be made a few hours in advance and cooked in the same oven as the venison (see below) until the pastry is golden, about 8 minutes.

To make the sauce, reduce the red wine, vinegar and redcurrant jelly until the liquid has almost evaporated, then stir in the stock and reduce again by about one third. Whisk in the cold diced butter and season with salt and pepper. Strain and keep hot.

To finish the dish, preheat the oven to 230°C/450°F/Gas 8. Heat a little oil in a sauté pan and brown and seal the venison saddle on all sides. Place in an oiled roasting pan and roast for 7 minutes. Remove and put in a warm place to rest for up to 20 minutes. Deglaze the roasting pan with the port and add the contents to the sauce. Stir-fry the shredded cabbage and arrange at the top of four heated plates with a Bridie on top. Slice the venison saddle into twelve equal pieces. Pour the hot sauce over the lower part of the plates and put three slices of venison on each. Serve immediately.

Note: Bridies are a pasty made in the Scottish county of Angus, in the town of Forfar. They are traditionally made with minced beef from the Aberdeen Angus breed, onion and suet, and wrapped in pastry. An early cook famous for the pastries was Mistress Margaret Bridie.

FOR FOUR PEOPLE

Caramelized Apple Pastry with a Caramel Sauce

4 Granny Smith or similar apples

Sauce
200g (7 oz) condensed milk
40g (1½ oz) unsalted butter
120g (4 oz) sugar
1 tablespoon golden syrup
1 teaspoon liquid glucose
a small piece of vanilla pod
300 ml (½ pint) almost boiling water

Syrup
1 tablespoon sugar
300 ml (½ pint) almost boiling water

Pastry
120g (4 oz) puff pastry dough
50g (2 oz) icing sugar

To make the sauce, which can be done in advance, put all the ingredients except the water into a heavy bottomed pan. Bring to the boil, stirring all the time, and then simmer for 20 minutes, still stirring. Remove from the heat and stir in the previously boiled water carefully. Strain into a bowl and keep warm.

Make the syrup with the sugar and water and let it reduce to a light caramel. Meanwhile peel and core the apples and cut them in 1.5 cm (½ inch) dice. Cook them in the syrup until they are golden – about 2–3 minutes.

Preheat the oven to 200°C/400°F/Gas 6. Roll out the puff pastry to no more than 3 mm (⅛ inch) thick. Have ready two baking sheets 35.5 × 30.5 cm (14 × 12 inches) in size and cut the pastry to fit one of these exactly. Place it on one sheet and cover with the other. Place kitchen weights or other heavy objects – about 1.8 kg (4 lb) in all – on the upper baking sheet. Bake in the hot oven for about 10 minutes or until the pastry is golden. Reduce the heat to 180°C/350°F/Gas 4 if you think there is a risk of the outer edges burning. Remove from the oven and cut into 8 oblong shapes, approximately 10 × 5 cm (4 × 2 inches). Dust four of the rectangles with icing sugar and decorate with a lattice pattern using a red-hot skewer.

To serve, pour the warm caramel sauce on to four hot plates (this is important as it will set solid on a cold plate). Put the four unsugared pastry rectangles on the plates, divide the caramelized apples between them and top with the latticed pastry rectangles. Serve immediately.

Note: if you make the pastry in advance, it should be warmed through very gently before serving.

FOR FOUR PEOPLE

HUNGARY

IMRE SPIELBERGER

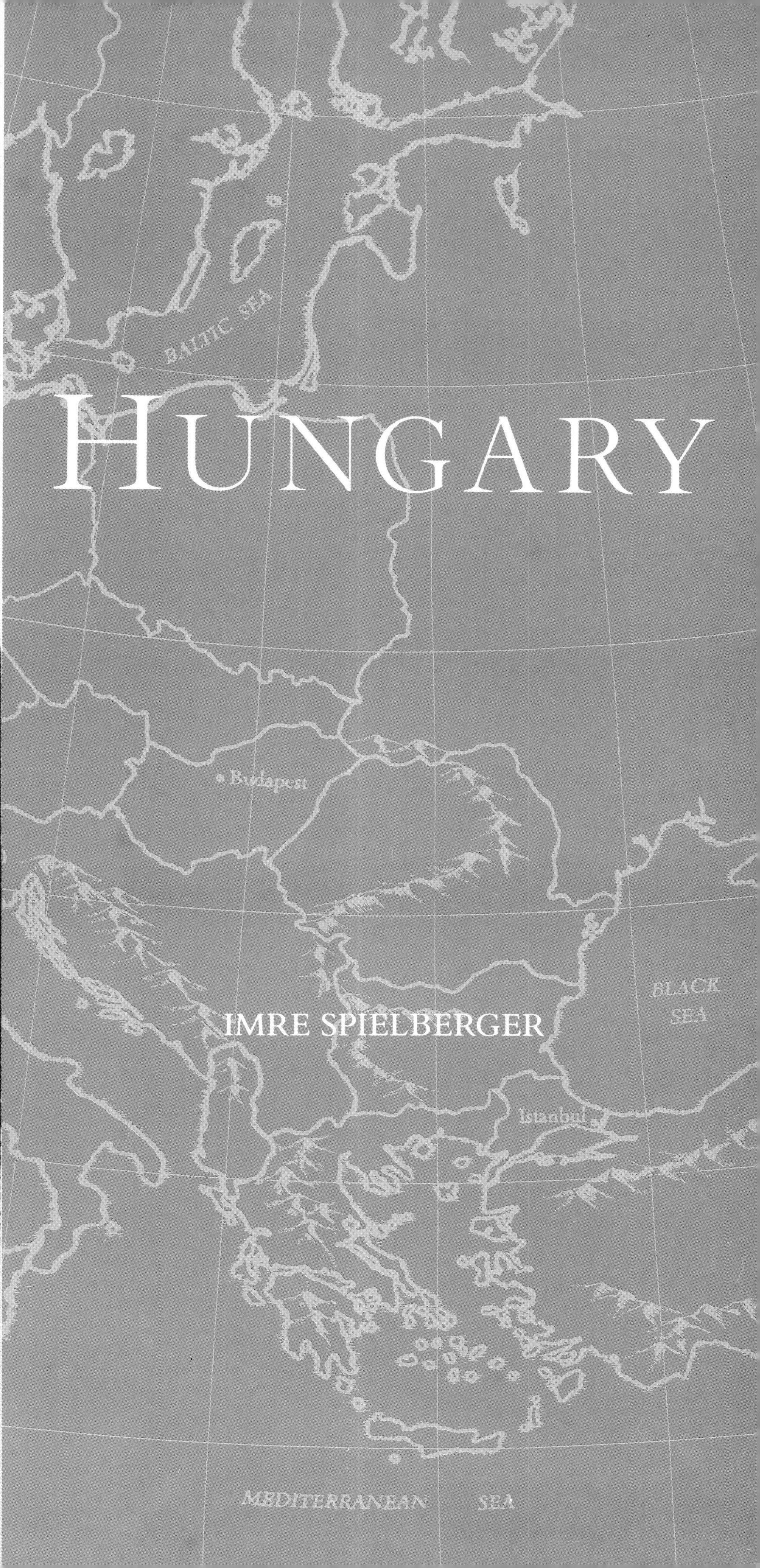

BALTIC SEA

BLACK SEA

• Budapest

Istanbul

MEDITERRANEAN SEA

IMRE SPIELBERGER

THE CAFÉ-RESTAURANT NEW YORK-HUNGARIA

Budapest

The Café-Restaurant New York-Hungaria is, if you like, Budapest's equivalent of the old Café Royal in London. The famous artists and writers of the late nineteenth and early twentieth centuries, whose caricatures and portraits line the walls, are long gone, but it still has the same raffish grandeur, and is probably the most atmospheric place in the city to dine – or to while away an hour drinking coffee and liqueurs with a succession of sticky cakes. It lies in the flat city of Pest; beyond lie the Danube and the hills, thermal springs and palaces of Buda. Until the construction of the Chain Bridge by British engineers in 1839–49, the two cities were united only by a bridge of boats, or in winter by precarious journeys over the Danube ice floes, and grew up as separate centres.

This Budapest institution was founded in 1894 as the Café-Restaurant New York. It occupies the ground floor of the grandiose building in Lenin Boulevard which, then as now, houses most of the most important publishing enterprises in Hungary, and it immediately became the principal meeting place of the literary and artistic intelligentsia. It fell on hard times before and after the Second World War, losing its name – at least officially, but now it has been painstakingly restored with gilt, paint and marble to its original form. It may even revert to its original name, the Hungaria label having been transferred to one of Hungarhotel's largest modern hotels. A recipe from the Grand Hotel Hungaria's head chef Zoltán Bara, one of the most senior in Hungary and a great teacher, appears on page 135.)

It is one of those places which make you feel slightly tipsy even before the first sip of Hungarian apricot brandy, a demure-seeming drink with the kick of a camel. Barley-sugar marble pillars, sub-Tiepolo ceilings, riots of gilding, mirrors everywhere: all this comes as a shock after the drabness of the streets outside. But no one could deny that it is fun – great fun. The upper balconies hum with the chat of people taking coffee and cakes and reading the daily papers, some of which are edited in the building. The lower, restaurant, area is known colloquially as 'The Deep Water', not just because it resembles a swimming

Chef Imre Spielberger

'The Deep Water'

In the extensive produce markets of Pest, the paprika merchant's stall is the most important and colourful, stocking every kind of sweet and hot pepper in a spectacular display. Other stalls sell everything from live carp to a vast range of sausages and, of course, vegetables, many of them produced by peasant co-operatives.

The atmospheric grandeur – and the rather raffish charm – of 'The Deep Water' is apparent in this formal buffet. The two tureens at either end of the table hold goulash.

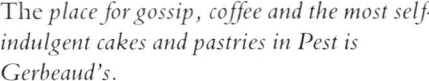

The *place for gossip, coffee and the most self-indulgent cakes and pastries in Pest is Gerbeaud's.*

pool let into the floor of the main room, but because it was where the 'sharks' of the late nineteenth-century world – the editors, publishers and agents – ate their expensive meals while the penniless writers drank their coffees on the balconies above. It is also where the modern diners, mainly tourists (because the food is expensive for Hungarians) eat, to the deafening accompaniment of zither players and other musicians. And they eat surprisingly well, considering the vagaries of supply and budgetary controls. For foreigners, Hungary is very cheap, except in the western-owned hotels like the Hilton (bizarrely constructed on the Buda ridge, in and around the ruins of a Dominican church), and in the Café New York a more-than-ample meal can be had for as little as £20 for two people. The recipes that follow indicate something of the wide range of Hungarian food (and for those who want to know more, George Lang's *The Cuisine of Hungary* (Penguin/Atheneum) is an indispensable guide). The food is totally different from anything else in this book, and may seem heavy, flour-rich and, above all, paprika-rich. Whatever the more progressive chefs may say, the revolution of the nouvelle cuisine movement has hardly dented Hungarian eating habits. Sunflower seed oil may have replaced lard as the cooking medium, more fresh vegetables are available to vary the winter diet of preserved cabbage and dried produce, but it is still an identifiable, authentic national cuisine based on a wealth of tradition and with regional specialities still bearing the names of towns no longer within Hungary's borders. Cooked with care, and with good ingredients, it can be outstanding. Its exuberance plays counterpoint to the atmosphere of Budapest, at once melancholic and triumphant, as suits a city so often overrun and reconstructed.

The Café-Restaurant has a relatively conservative menu: its clients, whether Hungarian or foreign, come to eat Hungarian food, and they will be offered soups and goulashes, veal and goose-liver dishes (it is worth remembering that many of the other restaurants described in this book get their goose liver from Hungary). Nearly all the dishes contain sour cream in some form; fresh cream aerated by a special machine appears as an ingredient or garnish in many others. Flour is used routinely as a thickener; paprikas, either fresh or in powder form, are used in every savoury dish. The New York's chef, Imre Spielberger, is larger than life, and looks to the inch like the William Orpen portrait of 'The Chef at the Hotel Chatham, Paris' in the Royal Academy, London. He trained in Budapest and has worked in Rhodes, as well as Yugoslavia, Bulgaria and other eastern bloc countries, and would like to travel again once his young family grows up. His kitchen staff of twenty-five is young and enthusiastic; their equipment is not exactly modern, but in some ways more practical than that of many smarter establishments.

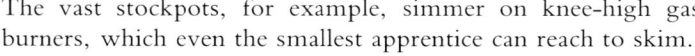

Gerbeaud's pastry-shop

The vast stockpots, for example, simmer on knee-high gas burners, which even the smallest apprentice can reach to skim.

The à la carte menu presented by the dozen or so formally suited waiters does not change, and the weekly menu changes only at the chef's discretion, according to the seasons and the availability of produce. A buffet for a formal reception or wedding will have great heated silver-plate tureens of goulash, plates of pan-fried goose liver, whole carp in aspic and many other set-pieces, both savoury and sweet.

Those ingredients which do not come from central supplies are bought from the produce markets of Pest, where live carp, whole carcases of veal (quite unlike the baby milk-fed veal that western Europeans are used to, and a great deal tastier, if chewier: the colour of the veal in the recipe on page 132 shows this), an enormous variety of sausage and other pork products and a good selection of seasonal and pickled vegetables – including cabbage – are all available. Everything on sale is grown in Hungary or in neighbouring Eastern bloc countries, much of it by peasant co-operatives. The most important, and certainly the most self-important stall, is the paprika merchant's. Festooned with every kind of sweet and hot pepper, it is a work of the window-dresser's art. Here are the extra-hot small round peppers, the milder long peppers, green and red, and ground paprika of every kind all being scrutinized and haggled over by expert Budapest housewives.

The Hungarians, like the Italians, at least until recently, do not think of restaurants as places to eat sweet things. It is true that in the Café New York there are puddings on the menu: recipes for two follow, and there are cakes and ices available to the balcony customer. But for the visitor to Budapest, there is only one place to eat cakes – Gerbeaud's, in the part of Pest nearest the Danube. It is a hubbub of people gossiping, drinking coffee, chocolate or sweet liqueurs and eating any one of the vast variety of cakes and pastries available. Specialities include the Dobos Torta, a marvellously sinful chocolate cake; every kind of hazelnut and walnut confection; and, of course, the Gerbeaud Szelet – the famed Gerbeaud Slice – made with eggs, butter and flour, with a walnut filling laced with apricot liqueur and chocolate.

Hungary, though now much reduced in area, has regions of great horticultural excellence. Her fruit is famous, and exported far beyond the borders of the Eastern bloc. The apricots of Kecskemét, in the area between the rivers Danube and Tisza known as the orchard of Hungary, are used to produce the famous Barackpálinka, which is used in the recipe on page 134. This apricot eau-de-vie comes in various strengths, and should be treated with caution, especially when used in unheated dishes served to guests who may not welcome alcohol, or to drivers.

Hungarian wines are famous, and vary from the sweetest Tokay to the full-bodied Bull's Blood (Egri Bikavér). Some of the best come from the northern shores of Lake Balaton where a pocket of volcanic soil produces excellent white wines. The range of distilled liqueurs ranges far beyond apricot brandy or eau-de-vie: every kind of fruit is put to use and the exact methods and proportions are jealously kept family or village secrets.

There are many reasons for visiting Budapest: the fine art gallery, the thermal baths, the pleasures of both Buda and Pest, the swirling (and definitely un-blue) Danube with its river steamers and majestic bridges. The sheer individuality and gusto of its inhabitants is also a powerful incentive.

Tárkonyos Bárányragu Leves

Tarragon Lamb Soup

750 g (1 lb 10 oz) lean lamb on the bone
40 g (1½ oz) peeled onion (the sweet purple kind if possible)
150 g (5 oz) chopped mixed vegetables (for example celery, carrot, etc)
25 g (1 oz) tarragon leaves in tarragon vinegar, or 2 tablespoons of chopped fresh tarragon leaves and 1 tablespoon of tarragon vinegar
80 g (3 oz) butter
40 g (1½ oz) flour
1 tablespoon lemon juice
150 ml (¼ pint) sour cream
a pinch of sugar
4 good sprigs parsley, chopped
50 ml (3½ tablespoons) single cream
1 small egg yolk
paprika
100 ml (3½ fl oz) sour cream (optional)
salt and pepper

Bone the lamb, and make a strongly flavoured stock with the bones. Strain and add the cubed meat and the whole peeled onion, the mixed vegetables, salt and pepper. Simmer until the meat is half cooked, then remove the onion and add the tarragon leaves.

Meanwhile, make a light roux with 30 g (1 oz) of the butter and 15 g (½ oz) of the flour and use this to thicken the soup, away from the heat. Add the lemon juice, sour cream, tarragon vinegar (if fresh tarragon leaves were used) and a pinch of sugar. Mix the remaining flour and butter with the parsley, season and form into tiny dumplings. Add them to the hot soup and simmer for 10 minutes. Before serving, mix the cream and egg yolk together thoroughly and stir in the hot, but not boiling, soup (gently, so as to avoid breaking up the dumplings). Serve in hot soup bowls, or a large tureen, with a sprinkling of paprika and a swirl of sour cream if you wish.

FOR FOUR PEOPLE

Tarragon Lamb Soup

Szász Pulykamellsaláta

Turkey Breast Salad with Peaches and Walnuts

150 g (5 oz) cold cooked turkey breast, cut in strips
1 hard-boiled egg, chopped
75 g (2¾ oz) fresh or canned peaches, peeled, stoned and sliced
50 g (2 oz) peeled and seeded grapes
50 g (2 oz) walnut pieces
1 lettuce heart, shredded
a few drops lemon juice
3 tablespoons mayonnaise
2 tablespoons aerated cream (see note)
2 tablespoons medium-dry white wine
1 orange, peeled and segmented
4 tomato wedges
4 lemon wedges
4 sprigs parsley
salt

Mix the first six ingredients gently in a bowl (reserving the outer leaves of the lettuce and four handsome walnut pieces for decoration), and season with salt and a few drops of lemon juice. Mix the mayonnaise, aerated cream and wine in a separate bowl and then fold in the first six ingredients.

To serve, line four glass or china bowls with the reserved lettuce leaves and divide the mixture evenly between them. Decorate each salad with a reserved walnut piece, two orange segments, one tomato wedge, a lemon wedge and a sprig of parsley.

Chill if not wanted immediately, but allow to return to room temperature before serving.

Note: when aerated cream is specified in this or in any of the following recipes, you can use whipping cream whipped in the normal way. However what Imre Spielberger at the Café New York-Hungaria and chefs at other Hungarian restaurants and pastry shops would use is cream prepared in a special mixer which incorporates compressed air at the same time as it whips. The result is uniquely light, airy froth, which is almost impossible to re-create at home. Cream whisked by hand with a balloon whisk provides the closest equivalent.

FOR FOUR PEOPLE

Turkey Breast Salad with Peaches and Walnuts

Dorozsma Pontyderék

Dorozsma Carp with Bacon in Mushroom Sauce

600 g (1¼ lb) middle cut of carp in four fillets,
with the skin on
75 g (2¾ oz) smoked fat bacon (speck) or
pork belly, thinly sliced
3 tablespoons sweet paprika
oil for frying
100 g (3½ oz) onion, peeled and finely
chopped
350 g (12 oz) button mushrooms, chopped
150 g (5 oz) seeded and diced green pepper
75 g (2¾ oz) peeled, sliced tomato
250 ml (8 fl oz) sour cream
30 g (1 oz) flour
100 g (3½ oz) dried sheet pasta (lasagne),
broken into irregular pieces
1 onion, peeled and sliced
a few small green peppers
a few small red cherry peppers
2 large tomatoes, sliced
2 tablespoons chopped parsley
salt and freshly ground black pepper

The prepared carp fillets should be placed, skin-side up, on a board and slashed diagonally at 3–4 cm (1–1½ inch) intervals with a sharp knife. A slice of *speck* or pork belly should be inserted into each slash. Sprinkle lightly with some of the paprika and set aside in a cool place.

The remainder of the *speck* or pork belly should be diced and fried in oil (or in a non-stick pan without fat if you prefer). Add the chopped onion and fry until translucent. Add the chopped mushrooms and the rest of the paprika and cook over a medium heat, watching that the paprika does not burn. Season with a little salt. When the mushroom juices have evaporated, add the diced green pepper and the peeled tomato slices. Moisten with any juices which have run out of the prepared carp fillets, or with a little cold water. Mix half the sour cream with the flour

and thicken the mushroom sauce with it.

Cook the broken pasta pieces in boiling salted water until they are *al dente*, and add to the mushroom sauce. Keep the sauce warm.

Place the carp fillets in a single layer in a lightly oiled ovenproof serving dish and strew onion rings, sliced green peppers and red cherry peppers and tomato slices over the top. (If you have the roes of the carp they can be added at this stage.) Cover the dish and bake the fish in the oven for 20 minutes at 150°C/300°F/Gas 2 until it is half cooked, then remove and pour over the mushroom sauce, sprinkle with the remaining sour cream and return to the oven, uncovered, to cook through and brown. Sprinkle with chopped parsley before serving.

FOR FOUR PEOPLE

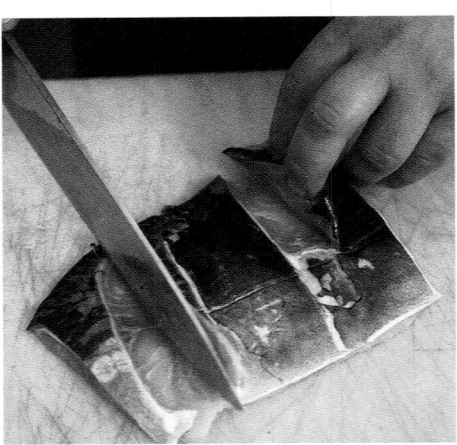

Slashing the carp

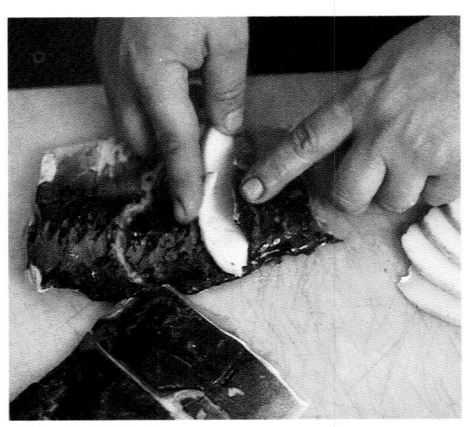

Inserting the slices of fat bacon

Carp with Bacon in Mushroom Sauce

Stuffed Cabbage with Pickled Cabbage, Pork and Sausage

Kolozsvári Töltött Káposzta

Kolozsvar Stuffed Cabbage with Pickled
Cabbage, Pork and Sausage

100 g (3½ oz) rice
800 g (1¾ lb) whole pickled cabbage leaves
(see note)
100 g (3½ oz) smoked fat bacon (speck),
cubed
150 g (5 oz) onion, peeled and chopped
2 fat garlic cloves, peeled and chopped
150 g (5 oz) lard
700 g (1½ lb) minced pork
a pinch of marjoram
50 g (2 oz) sweet paprika
1 egg
2 kg (4½ lb) shredded pickled cabbage
(sauerkraut)
500 g (1 lb) smoked sausage
600 ml (1 pint) sour cream
75 g (2¾ oz) flour
dill, finely chopped (optional)
oil for frying
600 g (1¼ lb) trimmed pork chops, on
the bone
150 g (5 oz) thickly cut fat bacon (speck)
salt and pepper

Boil the rice until just done, then drain. Remove and reserve the ribs from the pickled cabbage leaves and, if the flavour seems too vinegary, soak them for a while in water.

Fry the cubed bacon, half the chopped onion and the garlic in half the lard and add to the minced pork, together with the rice, marjoram, most of the paprika, a good pinch of pepper and the egg. Beat all the ingredients together until you have a doughy mass. Lay out the pickled cabbage leaves on a cloth and divide the mixture between them. Fold them up to make neat parcels, pleating the edges so that the filling cannot burst out.

Fry the remaining onion briefly in the remaining lard in a large flameproof dish, sprinkle with the remaining paprika and moisten with a little water. Add most of the shredded cabbage and stir to form a cooking base for the stuffed cabbage parcels. Arrange the parcels evenly in the

cooking dish on top of the cabbage. Slice the sausage coarsely and place the slices in and around the parcels. Place the remaining pickled cabbage in a layer over the top. Cover the dish with a lid or foil and bake in a medium oven (190°C/375°F/ Gas 5).

When the pork filling is cooked through (after about 50 minutes: undo a parcel to make sure), remove the parcels and the sausage slices to a warm place. Mix 500 ml (18 fl oz) the sour cream with 50 g (2 oz) of the flour to a smooth batter and use it to thicken the cabbage cooking base remaining in the flameproof dish. A little finely chopped dill added at this stage will improve the flavour. It is important not to overcook the pickled cabbage (which should retain some crispness) nor to make the sauce too thick, so care should be taken at this stage.

Dry the reserved cabbage ribs, flour them lightly with a little flour and fry in oil briefly. Beat out the meaty parts of the pork chops with a cutlet beater, season, flour them lightly with the remaining flour, then fry quickly in oil. The thickly sliced fat bacon (*speck*) should be cut into a cockscomb shape (see photograph) and fried very briefly.

To serve, make a base of the thickened pickled cabbage mixture in a heated serving dish and arrange the cabbage parcels and sausage slices on it. Prop up the fried pork and cabbage ribs against the parcels and sprinkle with the remaining sour cream. Top with the 'cockscomb' and serve.

Note: pickled cabbage of all kinds is readily available in Hungary. Elsewhere, you may have to make do with bottled or preserved sauerkraut. Fresh cabbage leaves, blanched in well salted and vinegared water, can be used instead of whole pickled cabbage leaves. The Hungarians, for whom this is almost a national dish with as many variants as there are cooks to dispute them, say that, once cooled, nothing (particularly love) is good warmed up again – except this stuffed cabbage.

FOR TEN PEOPLE

Veal Sautéed with Goose Liver

Borjújava Kedvessy

Veal Sautéed with Goose Liver

800 g (1¾ lb) boned leg of veal
200 g (7 oz) trimmed and prepared veal kidney
300 g (10½ oz) fat goose liver (foie gras)
150 g (5 oz) peeled and chopped onion
150 g (5 oz) butter
100 g (3½ oz) peeled, seeded and chopped
green pepper
1 tomato, peeled, seeded and chopped
1 bunch fresh dill, chopped
6 tablespoons veal stock
300 ml (½ pint) sour cream
150 ml (¼ pint) single cream
75 g (2¾ oz) flour
25 g (1 oz) melted butter
4 button mushrooms
250 g (9 oz) fresh or frozen green peas
1 small bunch fresh parsley, finely chopped
6 tablespoons oil
sweet paprika
salt and pepper

Lightly fry the chopped onion in 75 g (2¾ oz) of the butter and add the chopped green peppers, the chopped tomato and half the dill. Season and cook over a moderate heat until the liquid has evaporated. Moisten with the stock. Make a thin batter with 200 ml (7 fl oz) of the sour cream, the cream and 50 g (1¾ oz) of the flour, and add this to the vegetables and stock in the pan. Cook until you have a thinnish vegetable sauce. Sieve the sauce, or liquidize for a fuller flavour. Chop the remaining dill finely, heat through in 25 g (1 oz) of the butter and add to the sauce. Cover the sauce with a thin layer of melted butter and set aside in a warm place.

Divide the boned veal into four escalopes, and beat each flat. Slice the kidney and the goose liver into four equal pieces. Salt all the meats and the button mushrooms. Heat the peas in the remaining butter with the finely chopped parsley. Flour the veal, kidney and goose liver very lightly using the remaining flour and cook briefly in very hot oil in separate pans. Fry the mushrooms in whichever pan has most room for them.

To serve, take four heated plates and place a veal escalope on each, topped with first a slice of kidney, then a slice of goose liver and finally a button mushroom. Pour over the vegetable and dill sauce, and sprinkle with the remaining sour cream and a sprinkling of paprika. Add a small mound of the buttered green peas, and serve with deep-fried potato croquettes.

FOR FOUR PEOPLE

Hátszegi Túrós Palacsinta

Hatszeg Curd Cheese Pancakes in a Soufflé Sauce

Pancakes
175 (6¼ oz) flour
1 tablespoon fine sugar
pinch of salt
185 ml (6½ fl oz) full-cream milk
2 eggs
3 tablespoons oil

Filling
200 g (7 oz) sieved curd cheese or
soft cheese
2 eggs, separated (whites reserved for
soufflé sauce)
75 g (2¾ oz) fine sugar
1 teaspoon grated lemon zest
20 g (⅔ oz) seedless raisins

Soufflé sauce
3 eggs, separated
100 g (3½ oz) fine sugar
200 ml (7 fl oz) sour cream
50 g (2 oz) butter
1 tablespoon lemon juice
25 g (1 oz) vanilla sugar

To make the pancakes, put the flour, sugar and salt in a bowl and slowly pour in the milk, stirring constantly. Add the eggs and oil and beat to combine well. Fry the pancakes, then layer between sheets of greaseproof paper and cover until needed.

To make the filling, beat the cheese, egg yolks, sugar and lemon zest together until smooth and stir in the raisins. (Pancakes and filling can be made ahead.) Divide the filling between six pancakes, mounding it in the centre of each. Fold up the sides of each pancake like an envelope to make a rectangular package and place the pancakes, seam side down, in a buttered ovenproof baking dish several inches apart. Warm through in the bottom of a preheated hot oven (230°C, 450°F, Gas 8) while the soufflé sauce is being made.

Beat the egg yolks with half the fine sugar until pale and thick, about 3 to 4 minutes. Stir in the sour cream. Meanwhile, melt the butter with the lemon juice and a tablespoon of the remaining fine sugar. Whip the 5 egg whites until they form soft peaks, then gradually add the remaining fine sugar and the vanilla sugar, beating constantly until they form stiff peaks. Fold the egg yolk and sour cream mixture into the meringue gently. Cover the pancakes with the meringue and drizzle with the butter mixture. Return to the oven and bake about 12 minutes until puffed and browned. Serve immediately.

FOR SIX PEOPLE

Curd Cheese Pancakes in a Soufflé Sauce

Kecskemet Apricot Pudding

Kecskeméti Barackpuding

Kecskemet Apricot Pudding

Jelly
350 ml (12 fl oz) water
150 g (5 oz) sugar
a pinch each of cinnamon and powdered cloves
15 g (½ oz) leaf gelatine
4–6 syrup-poached apricot halves

Custard
10 g (¼ oz) leaf gelatine
150 ml (¼ pint) full-cream milk
4 tablespoons whipping cream
3 small egg yolks
50 g (2 oz) vanilla sugar
250 ml (8 fl oz) plus 6 tablespoons apricot
eau-de-vie (Barackpálinka)
125 g (4½ oz) full-fruit apricot jam
600 ml (1 pint) aerated cream (see note
on page 128)

Several hours in advance, put 4–6 metal dariole moulds in the freezer to chill. The jelly should be made first.

Mix the water with the sugar and warm until the sugar has dissolved. Add the cinnamon and cloves. Soak the gelatine in this water until it, too, has dissolved. Allow the jelly to cool until it is on the point of setting and then quickly remove the chilled moulds from the freezer one by one and swirl the jelly round inside to form a 2–3 mm (⅛ inch) coating over the inner surface. Place an apricot half on the bottom of each mould, rounded side down, and add enough jelly to cover. Return the moulds to the refrigerator while you make the custard.

Soften the gelatine in a little hot water, squeeze and then cook together with the milk, cream, egg yolks and sugar in a double boiler, whisking continuously. Cool to 30°C/85°F and add the 6 table-spoons apricot eau-de-vie. Pour the mixture into the prepared moulds and chill.

Mix the larger quantity of eau-de-vie with the jam to form a cold sauce. Turn out the moulded puddings on to serving plates and surround with the jam sauce and aerated cream.

Note: Barackpálinka is exceedingly potent. Because it is not heated in this recipe, do not serve to drivers.

FOR FOUR TO SIX PEOPLE

Töltött Sertés Fiakkeres-Módra

Stuffed Pork Fiaker-style with a Dumpling Roll

Zoltán Bara is one of Hungary's senior chefs, with vast experience of cooking in different restaurants in the Netherlands and Greece as well as in Hungary, and has trained many of the chefs now working in Hungary today. He is much influenced by the healthier principles of the nouvelle cuisine, some of which show themselves in his recipe (below), but as the executive chef of The Grand Hotel Hungaria, a spankingly modern hotel which opened on the site of the old Freedom Hotel in 1985, he is restricted by the need to supply meals for 400–500 tourists a day, to a strict budget. The thirty-two chefs and thirty apprentices in his sparkling kitchen

inevitably have to make use of modern aids to mass catering: vacuum packing and blast freezing of produce for example. The whole operation runs smoothly and punctually, with an endless flow of meals being taken out to the guests in the attractively decorated dining halls. Naturally, tourists expect to eat Hungarian dishes, but Chef Bara tries to offer as many salads and fresh vegetables as possible to offset the heavier dishes.

This recipe is the creation of Chef Zoltán Bara. We include it, and his portrait, as a tribute to the influence this enormously experienced chef has had on younger Hungarian chefs.

Zoltán Bara

300 g (12½ oz) boned pork loin
150 g (5 oz) shredded pickled cabbage
(sauerkraut)
2 eggs
200 g (7 oz) cooked rice
50 g (2 oz) shredded smoked streaky bacon
½ teaspoon dried basil, or 1 teaspoon shredded
fresh basil
250 g (9 oz) mixed root vegetables and
cauliflower florets, roughly chopped (optional)
200 g (7 oz) breadcrumbs, toasted
4 sprigs of parsley, chopped
½ teaspoon paprika
a little milk
a little flour
salt and pepper

Cut the pork loin so that it makes a flat single piece of meat, beating it if necessary and trimming off all sinew and fat. Mix the cabbage, one egg, the rice, bacon and basil together and season with salt and pepper. Spread this filling over the flattened pork fillet. Roll it up and truss or secure with skewers. Heat the oven to 200°C/400°F/Gas 6 and grease a roasting pan. Roast the stuffed loin for 50 minutes, then place the mixed vegetables and cauliflower florets (if using) around the pork loin and continue to roast for a further 40 minutes.

Meanwhile make the dumpling roll. Mix the remaining egg, the breadcrumbs and chopped parsley together and season with paprika, salt and pepper. Moisten

with a very little milk if necessary. Form into a roll, dust lightly with flour, and wrap in muslin. Cook in boiling water for about 20 minutes.

To serve, slice the pork loin and the dumpling neatly and arrange on the plate with the mixed vegetables and cauliflower

with which the meat was cooked, or, if preferred, with a selection of steamed vegetables. A sauce may be made with a reduction of the pan juices, seasoned with mustard.

FOR FOUR PEOPLE

Stuffed Pork with a Dumpling Roll

135

IRELAND

MYRTLE ALLEN

MYRTLE ALLEN

BALLYMALOE HOUSE

Shanagarry

The plane from London to Cork flies in over the mouth of Ballycotton Bay, where the Rooskagh and Bridog brooks join the Atlantic. If the sky is clear – as it often is, even in Ireland – the gastronomic pilgrim may catch a glimpse of the group of buildings, a few miles inland, which make up the remarkable Ballymaloe complex of hotel, restaurant, cooking school and kitchen gardens. Ballymaloe House is the most widely praised and visited of restaurants in Ireland, and its creator, Myrtle Allen, has won an international reputation for traditional, yet at the same time innovative, cooking. Her style has been called 'the best of Ireland', and the high praise Ballymaloe is accorded by guidebooks, and the comments of delighted – and regularly returning – guests, combine to prove the point. Unlike many of the other country restaurants in this book, Ballymaloe is essentially a holiday hotel, though a luxurious one. No one goes to Ballymaloe for pomp and elaborate service, though the J. B. Yeats paintings, the beauty of the surroundings and the friendly staff make it a memorable place to stop, whether for a weekend or several weeks. They go for the exceptional atmosphere.

Guests also come for the sheer quality and, above all, the freshness of the food. Nothing is cooked at Ballymaloe except the freshest ingredients, most of them local. The vegetables are almost all grown in the kitchen garden or in the glasshouse complex at Shanagarry nearby, while the carrageen moss for the famous pudding is gathered on the Cork coast. The smoked fish comes from the German Schwartau family a few miles away, the cheeses from local farm producers from several neighbouring counties. The beef and pork are purchased from a butcher who supervises his own slaughtering and can be trusted to hang the carcases to the point of perfection. The lamb is all home produced, and careful husbandry produces both baby lamb and yearling lamb, which has a much stronger taste, for a large part of the year. Chickens and turkeys run free, and are fed on a diet without additives; the latter are served, small, from April to November only.

The fresh fish, one of Ballymaloe's glories, is nearly all landed at Ballycotton, and the menus for dinner are not finalized until the afternoon's catch has been inspected and found perfect, by Myrtle herself if she can spare the time. If not, then her deputies Paddy Cullinane and Rory O'Connell, brother of daughter-in-law Darina, will do the job for her.

There is no formal lunch service, though a lavish buffet of salads, cold and smoked meats and fish, and a daily selection of hot dishes is provided for those guests who prefer to stay around

Myrtle Allen finalizing the day's menu

The gatehouse at Ballymaloe

Niall O'Flynn as baker – he now works at the Crawford Gallery outpost, which is managed by the youngest Allen daughter, Fern.

Ballycotton Harbour is the source of much of the extraordinary quality fish served at Ballymaloe. The menus for dinner are never finalized until the afternoon's catch has been scrutinized and pronounced satisfactory.

The dynamic Myrtle Allen, who manages to keep an eye on everything and everyone in the busy, buzzing kitchen at Ballymaloe, is here making Carrageen Moss Pudding. Her cooking has been described as typifying 'the best of Ireland'.

Ballycotton Harbour

the pool or gardens rather than exploring the coast or hinterland. But the kitchen is buzzing from early morning, especially in the baking area, where sixty or seventy loaves of the famous Ballymaloe yeast breads are baked every day by Niall O'Flynn, a precociously talented young cook from a nearby village who appeared in the office one day, announced he wanted to be a chef, was tried out for a week, and trained as the baker. These loaves go not just to the hotel, but also to the Crawford Gallery in Cork, managed by the youngest Allen daughter, Fern. Billy Motherway, one of Myrtle's two most experienced chefs (he has cooked in the Ferme Irlandaise in Paris) is making carrageen pudding and other desserts for the evening service, while other members of the fifteen-strong kitchen staff are packing up empty quiche cases, pâtés and salads for the Cork restaurant.

Almost everyone on the Ballymaloe staff is local, and most are young. All are enthusiastic, and their feeling that this is more than just a job is obvious in everything they do. Few have had any previous training, but Myrtle's talent-spotting ability – as in the case of Niall the baker – is legendary; many Ballymaloe graduates are now running their own kitchens in other Irish restaurants, or have gone on to gain experience in Europe.

In the kitchen, Myrtle is everywhere – Darina, who came as an apprentice, married the elder son and has stayed to create the internationally famous Ballymaloe cooking school, claims she has eyes in the back of her head. The dinner service is the high point of the day, and the emotional temperature rises in the kitchen and dining room as menus are finalized and place-settings checked. Fine white cloths replace the homelier blue and white ginghams which have served for breakfast and lunch. When the hotel is full, as it always is in season, there is a minimum of sixty houseguests to be served, and casual diners can increase the number to 120. The menu changes daily, and is likely to be made up, on a typical summer day, of two soups, one fish and one vegetable; two or three fish starters, which might be

an orange meringue; a choice of ice-creams served in Myrtle's famous ice bowl; and the Ballymaloe chocolates which Billy makes each morning.

Myrtle Allen was born near Cork in 1924 and worked in various jobs, including a spell in her father's architectural practice. Her early cooking training was at the Cork Technical College 'where they taught us to put soda in the vegetable water and to boil fish in vinegared water', but her early marriage to a local farmer, Ivan Allen, and her growing family opened her eyes to the immense superiority of genuine fresh produce and she became increasingly interested in cooking.

The Ballymaloe experience – and that is what most guests would call it – started when she and Ivan had the chance to extend their farm by buying the estate of an old friend and with it the substantial Irish Georgian Ballymaloe House, built round the tower of a medieval castle, with extensive farm buildings and grounds stretching down to the brook. For a while Myrtle and Ivan lived there raising their six children and farming. 'I then thought about opening a restaurant and decided that people could be persuaded to come, and to do it at Ballymaloe.' 'It' was the Yeats Room Restaurant, opened in 1964. Local people and knowledgeable tourists made up the first clientele, but the good news soon spread to the point where the Allens knew they could expand. Rooms were added, bathrooms contrived, and the public rooms brought up to the standard of a luxurious country house hotel. The cooking school was started at first as occasional lessons at slack times, but then as a full-blown venture close by at Shanagarry.

Since its earliest days Ballymaloe House has been praised continuously in the guidebooks; has been reviewed in virtually every food and travel magazine in the world; has, in short, become an institution. Myrtle is vice-president of the European Community of Chefs—Euro-Toque for short. She is much in demand at conferences and demonstrations everywhere, and was for a time the guiding spirit behind the phenomenally popular restaurant La Ferme Irlandaise in Paris, which had the Parisians queuing up for Ballymaloe specialities. She has also written *The Ballymaloe Cookbook*.

Her roots, however, are definitely here in Cork, and very specially in this place. She might not thank you for calling her a matriarch, but that is what she is: formidable and vigilant mistress of an enterprise which is essentially a family one. Her husband Ivan is the sheet anchor, calm and affable, fending off crises and supervising the bar and wine list with his senior son-in-law Jim Whelan and grandson Sacha Whelan. Of their six children, five are employed full or part-time in the Ballymaloe complex, and of their nineteen grandchildren, two are so far employed there.

It is hardly surprising that Myrtle's sense of place and history are intense. Her plan for retirement – something which appears inconceivable as she bustles indefatigably from stove to cold room and from quayside to kitchen garden – is to write another book. Meanwhile, as Smith's *History of Cork* points out, Ballymaloe is a place where 'several kinds of myrtle, thrive and flourish' exceedingly. So they do, so they do.

monkfish in red pepper sauce, fillets of plaice stuffed with lobster, a gratinée of mussels and clams or a simple salmon dish; and a herb terrine. The main courses also feature fish: the choice might be between plaice with herb butter; mussels stuffed with a delicious creamy hollandaise; brill with herbs; hot buttered lobster; or turbot. The meat dishes could include lamb with wild garlic gathered locally, roast guinea fowl or fillet of pork *en croûte*. Vegetables, served hot and buttery, are seasonal and include asparagus, peas, beans, artichokes, courgettes, baby turnips and carrots. The Irish don't on the whole like waxy potatoes, which they call 'soapy', so Ballymaloe spuds are hearty and floury. The selection of cheeses, all Irish, includes Cashel Blue, an extraordinarily good blue cheese from Tipperary; Milleens and Gubbeens, both from County Cork; Gigginstown from County Navan and Saint Killian from County Wexford. The puddings are simple and refreshing: seasonal fruits, sometimes served just as they have been picked, sometimes macerated or in a compôte; a soothing carrageen moss pudding;

Poached Salmon and Salmon Soup

This soup requires salmon cooking water and a salmon carcase; the salmon flesh can be used for another dish.

900 g (2 lb) salmon – fresh, in one piece
salt

To poach the salmon, first choose a saucepan that the piece fits snugly into. Cover the fish with water, then pour off, measure and reserve. Remove the salmon. Put the water back in the saucepan and add 1 teaspoon of salt per 600 ml (1 pint) of water. Bring the water to the boil and put in the fish. Gently simmer until cooked, about 20 minutes. Reserve the poaching water for the soup. The fish can be eaten hot or cold as desired, but keep back 100–120 g (3½–4 oz) of flesh.

Prepare the soup by adding to the reserved poaching water a salmon stock, béchamel sauce and vegetable base, blended together. Finally, stir in an enrichment. (See the following instructions.)

Stock
1 salmon carcase
bouquet garni
1 carrot
1 onion, peeled

Make sure the salmon head is thoroughly cleaned. Put it into a saucepan with the tail, the spine cut into pieces, the bouquet garni and vegetables. Cover with cold water, bring to the boil and simmer for 30 minutes. Strain and reduce to 500 ml (18 fl oz).

Béchamel sauce
300 ml (½ pint) milk
bouquet garni
half a carrot
half an onion, peeled
roux

Simmer the milk with the bouquet garni and vegetables very gently for 20 minutes. Strain and thicken with a previously prepared roux to make a light sauce, barely of coating consistency. Do not salt.

Vegetable base
2 carrots
2 onions, peeled
3 ripe tomatoes
1 tablespoon oil
1 clove garlic

Slice the carrots and onions. Peel and slice the tomatoes. Heat the oil in a saucepan, add the vegetables and garlic and cover with a butter wrapper and a tight fitting lid. Cook very gently for about 15 minutes. When completely soft, sieve them or reduce to a smooth purée in a blender.

To make the soup
salt and pepper
lemon juice

Gradually blend the stock, the salmon cooking water, the béchamel sauce and the vegetable base in a saucepan. Finally add salt, pepper and lemon juice to taste.

Enrichment
reserved 100–120 g (3½–4 oz) cooked salmon
50 g (2 oz) butter, softened
2 tablespoon whipped cream
2 teaspoons finely chopped chives
2 teaspoons finely chopped parsley
salt

Put the butter and salmon into a blender and make into a smooth paste. Add the whipped cream, herbs and salt to taste. Put a generous teaspoonful of this mixture on top of each soup plate and allow to melt to a foam on top.

FOR FOUR TO SIX PEOPLE

A freshly caught salmon at Ballycotton quay

Tomato Rings with Avocado Mousse

For this dish you will need tomatoes that are over-ripe, very dark red and soft. Tomatoes lose about a fifth of their weight when peeled. You will also need eight 10 cm (4 inch) ring moulds.

Tomato rings
*450 g (1 lb) peeled, roughly chopped ripe
tomatoes*
*1 spring onion with some of the green stem, or 1
slice onion (5 cm/2 inches diameter, 7 mm/
¼ inch thick)*
2 teaspoons white wine vinegar
1 teaspoon sugar
1 teaspoon salt
a few grinds of black pepper
1 large stem of basil
15 g (½ oz) gelatine

Mix all the ingredients together except the majority of the basil leaves (include 2 or 3) and the gelatine, and blend to a purée. Pass the mixture through a sieve to remove pips and then add the rest of the basil leaves, chopped finely. Measure the purée and if necessary add a drop of water to make up to 450 ml (¾ pint). Dissolve the gelatine in 2 tablespoons of water over a gentle heat, blend carefully with the purée and test for a set by dropping a spoonful into a saucer of iced water before pouring the remainder into the ring moulds. Chill for 1 hour before turning out on to chilled serving plates.

Avocado mousse
2 very ripe avocados
juice of 2 limes
4 tablespoons whipped cream
salt
cayenne or paprika pepper (optional)

Peel and stone the avocados and rub their flesh through a sieve. Add the lime juice and salt to taste, seasoning further with cayenne or paprika if liked. Fold in the whipped cream. Pipe into the centre of the rings and serve at once.

MAKES EIGHT FILLED RINGS

Tomato Rings with Avocado Mousse

Cucumber, Lettuce and Mint soup

This is a good way of using the outer leaves of a head of lettuce or heads that are beginning to wilt or shoot and that could not otherwise be used.

60 g (2½ oz) butter
*140 g (5 oz) potatoes, peeled and roughly cut
into 2.5 cm (1 inch) dice*
*110 g (3¾ oz) onions or spring onions, peeled
and chopped*
170 g (6 oz) cucumber, diced but not peeled
1 litre (2 pints) chicken stock
*85 g (3 oz) lettuce leaves, shredded and cut across
again roughly into 2.5 cm (1 inch) squares*
salt and pepper to taste
chopped mint
cream (optional)

Melt the butter in a heavy saucepan. When it foams, add the potatoes and onions and turn them in the butter until they are well coated. Sprinkle with salt and pepper. Cover and sweat on a gentle heat for 10 minutes. Add the cucumber and stock. Bring to the boil gradually, then simmer until the cucumber is almost soft. Add the lettuce and simmer the mixture for another minute. Do not overcook or the vegetables will lose their flavour.

Liquidize, sieve or put through a food mill to make a smooth, even texture. Adjust seasoning. Add chopped mint and a little cream if you wish.

FOR FOUR TO SIX PEOPLE

Brill with Summer Herbs

1 fillet of brill of approximately 225g (8oz)
25g (1oz) butter
4 tablespoons finely chopped parsley
2 tablespoons finely chopped spring onion
4 tablespoons finely chopped watercress
salt and pepper

Preheat the oven to 190°C/375°F/Gas 5. Cut a rectangle of doubled greaseproof paper large enough to wrap the fish in, with both ends sealed. Season the fish top and bottom and smear it with the butter. Seal the parcel and place in the preheated oven. Cook for 15–20 minutes.

Remove from oven, open the parcel and drain out all the buttery juices. Stir the remaining ingredients into the juices and serve with the brill fillet.

You can adapt this simple recipe for other kinds of fish. Other herbs – tarragon, chives, basil – can be added to vary the taste.

FOR ONE PERSON

Plaice in Herb Butter

This attractive recipe could be used for other flat fish, but Myrtle Allen prefers making it with the exquisite 20–25 cm (8–10 inch) plaice caught in abundance in Ballycotton Bay. Taken in a small trawl net by the local inshore fishermen, the fish are not bruised as they would be by the sheer weight of fish in a large trawl. And their freshness is beyond question.

1 plaice
salt and pepper
15–30g (½–1oz) salted butter
1 teaspoon finely chopped mixed fresh parsley, chives, fennel and thyme

Preheat the oven to 200°C/400°F/Gas 6. Clean and wash the fish, removing the head. Lay it flat on a firm board and with a very sharp pointed knife cut round the upper skin approximately 15 mm (½ inch) from the edge, just inside the radiating fringe of small bones. Take care to cut right through the skin, and make sure the cut is continuous across the backbone at the tail. Sprinkle with salt and pepper and place in 7 mm (¼ inch) of water in a baking tin just large enough to hold the fish. Bake in the preheated oven for 20–30 minutes according to size and thickness. The water should have evaporated by the time the fish is cooked, but check, and add a few tablespoons of hot water if necessary.

While the fish is cooking, melt the butter in a heavy pan and add the herbs.

Just before serving, free the central skin with a spatula or blunt knife and lift off carefully, leaving a beautiful white plaice surrounded by a frill of darker skin. Spoon over the herb butter to create a marbled green effect and serve at once on a heated dish.

Note: It is fascinating to see that this simple and attractive treatment is coincidentally repeated with turbot by Roger Vergé.

FOR ONE PERSON

Brill with Summer Herbs

Calves' Liver Flamed in Irish Whiskey

Summer Turkey with Marjoram

3.6–4.5 kg (8–10 lb) turkey
2 tablespoons chopped fresh marjoram
115 g (4 oz) salted butter
200 ml (7 fl oz) cream

Preheat the oven to 180°C/350°F/Gas 4. Mash half the marjoram into the butter and smear it over the turkey breast.

Bake the turkey for approximately 1½–2 hours in a covered casserole until almost cooked. Remove the lid from the pot and roast uncovered for another 30 minutes or so until golden brown.

Meanwhile make the sauce. Skim the fat from the pot juices, then reduce until slightly thickened. Add the cream and remaining marjoram.

FOR 8 PEOPLE

Calves' Liver Flamed in Irish Whiskey

110–170 g (3¾–6 oz) thinly sliced calves' liver
flour seasoned with salt and pepper
7 g (¼ oz) salted butter
1 tablespoon Irish whiskey
120 ml (3½ fl oz) reduced stock
garlic to taste, peeled and finely chopped
1 teaspoon chopped fresh tarragon
1 tablespoon double cream

Heat the butter in a heavy cast-iron pan until it sizzles. While the butter is heating, toss the liver slices in seasoned flour – a plastic bag is useful for this in the home kitchen. Fry the liver quickly on both sides, then push the slices to one side of the pan.

Pour in the whiskey, and light either with a match or by tilting the pan so that the gas jet just catches the spirit fumes. When the flames have died down, add the stock, garlic and tarragon and reduce until syrupy.

Stir in the cream, check seasoning and serve as soon as possible on a heated serving dish or individual plate.

FOR ONE PERSON

Lamb Braised with Wild Garlic, Spring Onions and Potatoes

Lamb Braised with Wild Garlic, Spring Onions and Potatoes

The wild garlic *Allium ursinum* has a brief and pungent season and is found in woods all over the British Isles. Except in May and June, you will have to be content with the bulbs, together with fresh herbs, such as thyme or marjoram, to replace the green garlic leaves. Make certain you do not confuse garlic bulbs with bluebell bulbs, which they resemble. A rapid taste should be enough to establish which bulb you have found. Mark the position of the plants during the flowering season to help you locate the bulbs later.

leg of young lamb
oil, butter or lamb fat
3–6 wild garlic plants picked preferably just
before they flower, or bulbs and fresh herbs
450 g (1 lb) spring onions, trimmed
450 g (1 lb) small potatoes, peeled
salt and freshly ground black pepper

Preheat the oven to 180°C/350°F/Gas 4. Brown the lamb in a little oil, butter or lamb fat. Season with salt and freshly ground black pepper. Chop up the garlic plants or the cloves with herbs and press into the skin.

Sauté the spring onions and potatoes in the same oil, butter or lamb fat and then put them round the meat with more chopped herbs if wished, in a heavy, cast-iron casserole with a tight-fitting lid.

Cook for 1½–2 hours or to taste in the preheated oven. When the lamb is cooked, strain off and skim the juices. Serve them separately as a gravy. A little good stock may be added if not enough cooking juices are left in the pot to serve as gravy. More chopped fresh herbs can be added to the gravy to enhance the flavour.

FOR SIX PEOPLE

Carrageen Moss Pudding

This is a Ballymaloe speciality, and its creamy, marine flavour is a welcome alternative to the richer ice-creams and meringues on the menu. The carrageen moss, a seaweed rich in natural gelatines and minerals, comes from the small seaside hamlet of Ballyandreen, where it is harvested from the rocks at the lowest tide mark. Once dried and bleached in the sun on the clifftop grass, it is ready to be used, sparingly, in this pudding.

7g (¼oz) (a small fistful) dried and cleaned
carrageen
925 ml (1½ pints) full cream milk
1 small vanilla pod or ½ teaspoon good vanilla
essence
2 tablespoons sugar
1 egg, separated

Soak the carrageen in tepid water for 10 minutes. Drain it and then transfer it to a saucepan with the milk and the vanilla pod (if using vanilla essence, do not add it until later – see below). Bring to the boil and simmer very gently for 20 minutes. Remove the vanilla pod and rub the carrageen through a fine strainer into a mixing bowl – the carrageen will be swollen and exuding jelly.

Beat in the sugar, egg yolk and vanilla essence if using. Test a teaspoonful of the mixture on a cold saucer to make sure the pudding will set. Meanwhile whisk the egg white stiffly. Fold in the egg white gently, and pour the whole pudding mixture into a serving dish. It will set to a soft jelly with an attractive fluffy top. Serve with a fruit compôte, or caramel or Irish coffee sauce.

A delicious chocolate carrageen pudding can be made by adding several level tablespoons of cocoa to the recipe above. This is better made the previous day to allow the flavour to develop, and the amount of carrageen should be increased by half again.

FOR FOUR TO SIX PEOPLE

Irish Brown Soda Bread

The correct amount of bread soda (bicarbonate of soda) and proper handling are the most important factors in making this bread successfully. Too much soda will spoil the flavour; too little means that it will not rise. Kneading in the normal sense will give a heavy flat loaf. The dough should be wet enough to fold and bend easily. If you have no sour milk (not heat-treated milk which has gone bad, but properly soured unpasteurized milk) use buttermilk, whey or fresh milk and baking powder instead.

620g (1 lb 6 oz) wholemeal flour
140g (5 oz) plain white flour
55g (2 oz) oatmeal
1 teaspoon bicarbonate of soda
1 teaspoon salt
470–720 ml (16 fl oz – 1 pint 3 fl oz) sour milk

Preheat the oven to 200°C/400°/Gas 6. Mix the dry ingredients thoroughly together, and moisten with the sour milk until you have a pliable dough. Gather it together on a floured board, flatten out and fold over once or twice with the tips of your fingers very lightly to give a smooth coherent consistency. This is not kneading as one kneads yeast bread.

Form into a flattish round on a greased baking tray, mark with a cross, and bake in the preheated oven for 30–35 minutes.

FOR ONE LARGE LOAF

Gooseberry and Elderflower Compôte

570 ml (19½ fl oz) cold water
450g (1 lb) sugar
flowers from one large elderflower spray
680g (1½ lb) gooseberries

Put the water, sugar and the elderflowers into a saucepan and gently bring to the boil. Add the gooseberries and cook them until they just begin to lose their shape. Chill.

FOR FOUR TO SIX PEOPLE

Carrageen Moss Pudding with a purée of summer fruits

The spectacular Ballymaloe Ice Bowl with scoops of chocolate ice-cream

Ballymaloe Chocolates

55 g (2 oz) plain chocolate, partly melted
12–14 small hulled sliced strawberries or peeled
and seeded grapes
6 tablespoons stock syrup, made by boiling 450 g
(1 lb) sugar with 600 ml (1 pint) water
for 2 minutes
6 tablespoons kirsch

Take small paper petit-four cases and smear the insides lavishly with partly melted chocolate. Chill, then peel off the paper carefully when the chocolate has set. (Keep some more melted chocolate on one side, to patch any imperfect examples.)

While the chocolate is hardening, macerate the fruit in the syrup and kirsch for 10 minutes.

Spoon the fruit into the chocolate cases and add enough syrup to cover. Store in the refrigerator until a few minutes before serving. Ideally, these chocolates should be eaten no more than two hours after you have made them but they can be made up to six hours in advance.

TO MAKE 12–14 CHOCOLATES

Ballymaloe Chocolates

46
BRUNELLO DI MONTALCINO
RISERVA
IL·GREPPO
FRANCO BIONDI SANTI

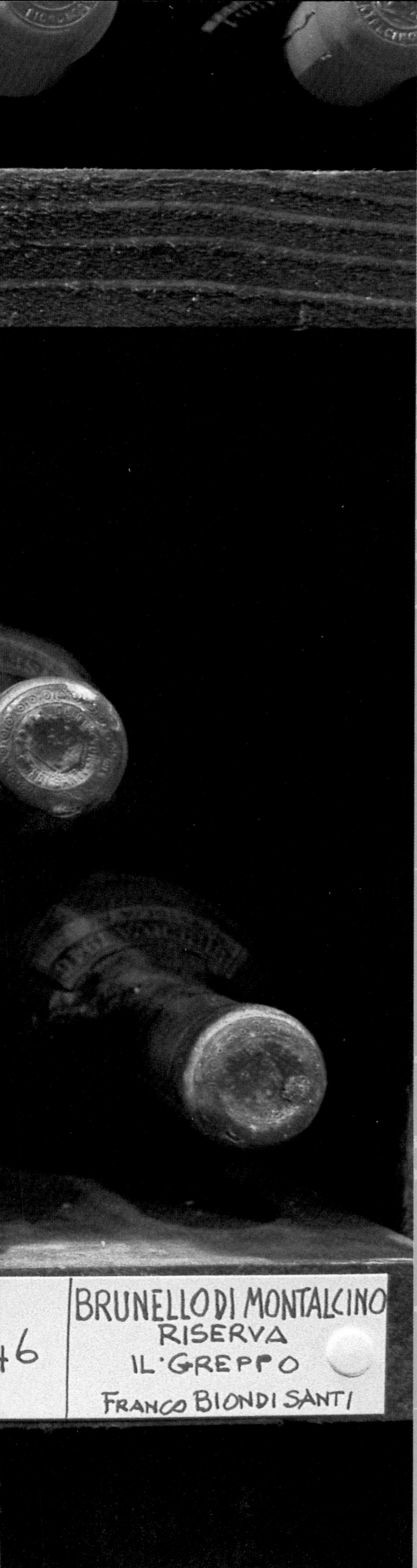

ITALY

ANNIE FEOLDÉ
GIANLUIGI MORINI &
VALENTINO MARCATTILII

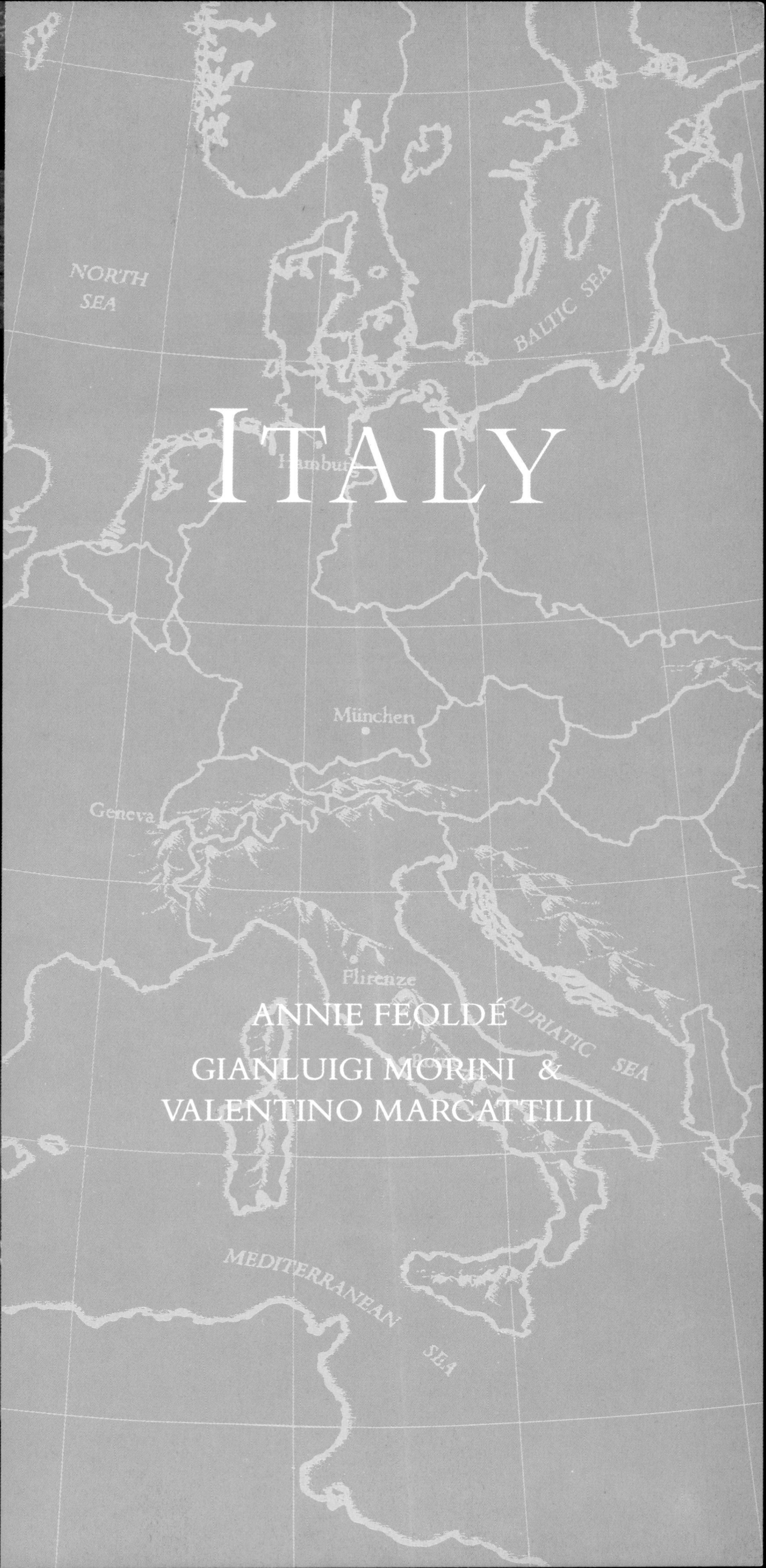

NORTH SEA
BALTIC SEA
Hamburg
München
Geneva
Firenze
ADRIATIC SEA
MEDITERRANEAN SEA

ANNIE FEOLDÉ

RISTORANTE-ENOTECA PINCHIORRI

Florence

The narrow, noisy Via Ghibellina, just north of Santa Croce, is not one of the most chic Florence streets – no designer clothes or smart art galleries here – but at no. 87 it houses arguably Florence's best restaurant and without question one of the most remarkable wine cellars in the world. *Enoteca* means literally 'wine library', more informally 'wine-bar', while Pinchiorri is the family name of Giorgio Pinchiorri, who started the establishment in 1975 as the Enoteca Nazionale, with nine partners, partly to indulge the passion for wine he acquired as a sommelier in Florentine restaurants, and also to provide a showcase for his Tuscan partners' wines and other produce.

Clients, private and professional, came to taste and learn about wines, so it seemed sensible to provide food as well. Annie Feoldé came to cook, first snacks, then, almost reluctantly, to serve full meals. She and Signor Pinchiorri bought out the original co-partners in 1979, and established a full-scale luxury restaurant renamed the Ristorante-Enoteca Pinchiorri. The result has been an exceedingly fruitful gastronomic partnership.

Annie Feoldé is chic and vivacious in a peculiarly French way as she whisks around the Enoteca shadowed by her two poodles Coco and Bandi, exuding energy and charm. Born in 1945 in Nice, where her family was in the hotel and restaurant business, she first learned to cook from her grandmother, a noted Provençal chef, but never thought of cooking professionally, preferring a civil service job in Paris. This palled, and she travelled, first to England, and then to Italy where she hoped to improve her Italian. She found work in a pizzeria, then met Giorgio Pinchiorri and started to prepare snacks for his wine tastings. Once absorbed into the cooking world, she set about learning her trade single-mindedly, spending brief periods in many of the major kitchens of Europe, and applying her sparky intelligence to the re-creation and adaptation of traditional Tuscan cooking. Her versions of Scottiglia, Pappardelle sulla Lepre and Cibreo are examples of this, and her cooking, while it shows the influence of the French nouvelle cuisine, is most definitely Tuscan, and could be found nowhere but south of the Apennines. Parmesan, for example, and other cheeses play little part in her kitchen, and cream and béchamel sauces are rare. The kitchen – if a little cavernous because of its lofty ceiling – is lively and individual, like her predominantly young staff of twelve. If,

Ristorante-Enoteca Pinchiorri

Annie Feoldé

Florence from the Piazzale Michelangelo.

Pecorino cheeses at a country fair near Florence.

Annie Feoldé takes an energetic part in everything, although the usual kitchen routines are managed by the sous-chef. Apart from preparation, cooking and tasting, she spends time discussing food and wine with the guests and loves to experiment with new combinations of flavour and texture and is constantly trying out new, or newly discovered, recipes.

like one young chef we saw, someone chooses to peel onions in motorcycle goggles, that's acceptable – provided the onions are perfectly peeled. If her young chef-pâtissière grumbles (only half-jokingly) that if she had her way she would start a restaurant which served the puddings first, the excellence of her work more than excuses the complaint. (It is a sad fact that in most good restaurants, petits fours, made freshly and lovingly each day, end up in the dustbin, and that many clients find themselves too sated for the puddings. But such things are expected on the menu of any first-class restaurant, and must be provided. The same, of course, applies to cheeses, which only remain in prime condition for a short time, and are as expensive to buy as good meat. An experienced restaurateur will learn to judge the likely demand for dishes cooked to order and can market accordingly, keeping waste to an absolute minimum.)

The Enoteca occupies the ground floor of a large seventeenth-century town house, once the home of the family, whose bearings still appear on a shield in the hallway. The palazzo is built round an open courtyard, full of statuary and leafy with potted lemon trees, oleanders and palms. On summer evenings this serves as an additional dining room, though the cognoscenti always sit inside. The interior is intimate, with widely spaced tables for eighty diners, some on a raised balcony. The furniture is antique and glows with careful polishing, and the menu reproduces the modern version of Raphael's 'La Fornarina' (now in the Palazzo Barberini, Rome) which hangs in the entrance.

Pasta is obviously all-important and comes in all kinds – with squid ink, with chocolate, with spinach, with tomato, all made fresh twice daily and rolled out with a small electric machine for each order: in sheets for the filled pastas and pappardelle, in strips for the tagliatelle and taglierini. A Japanese stagiaire deals with the fish; an English boy, who is going on to Roger Vergé's Moulin de Mougins next, prepares the vegetables. Almost nothing is frozen; nothing is vacuum-packed; nothing is microwaved. Even if Annie approved of such things, they are unnecessary in a restaurant within walking distance of some of the finest markets in Europe and with a network of producers in the Tuscan countryside, and beyond. She goes every two or three weeks to

dining-room and the entire staff of the restaurant appeared as if drawn to a magnet, so powerful, almost erotic, was the aroma. Those people, and they are many, who say that the (almost never cooked) white truffle is infinitely superior to the (always cooked) black truffle have a strong case. Shaved over a risotto or dish of pasta, or better still, a salad of raw wild mushrooms, the white truffle is incomparably delicious.

The same attention to quality is paid to all ingredients. The beef comes from the famous Val di Chiana farms, the lamb from France, goose liver from the Landes, the chocolate from Belgium and the all-important olive oil from Carmignano near Leonardo's birthplace at Vinci, between Florence and the sea.

Nearer home, the liqueurs for flavouring sorbets come from the workshops of the monks of Santa Maria Novella, established in the fourteenth century, and the bread, some of it flavoured with olives, herbs or raisins, is all baked on the premises.

The food at the Enoteca is original, based on freshness and *sapore* (flavour) and the recipes which follow give a fair example of what you would enjoy there. There is an à la carte menu, but except for the high tourist season most of the Enoteca's clients have sufficient trust in the kitchen to choose either the set 'Cucina Creativa' or the 'Cucina Toscana Ritrovata' daily menu, or even to leave the choice entirely up to Annie or the head waiter Marco Nesi. The 'Cucina Creativa' menu reflects both seasonal availability of produce and Annie's instincts on that day, while the 'Cucina Toscana Ritrovata' menu offers more traditional dishes, like Torta Manfreda con Fegatini and Carne Secca, red mullet with a red wine sauce with clams and fresh parsley, pappardelle with ortolan sauce, *arrosto morto* of rabbit, a sorbet made with the monks' Mediceo herbal liqueur, served in one of the same exquisite silver mounted glasses which hold the tiny bouquets of flowers, and a rich semi-freddo pudding.

Nice to see her family and to buy fresh herbs and exotic fruit (chervil and limes, for example, are not available in Italy), and to bring back supplies of the French butter which she prefers to Italian butter (with cream it is the other way round). The usual kitchen routines are managed by Fabio Martinuzzi, the sous-chef, but Annie Feoldé herself takes part in everything – preparation, cooking, tasting. During the actual service, usually light at lunchtime and crammed to capacity in the evenings, she prefers to move around, taking orders, discussing the choice of wine and food with her guests and checking every dish as it passes through the servery. She herself enjoys working most with fish and meat, and leaves the pastries and puddings to her young *pâtissière* and her mother. She loves to create new combinations of flavour and texture and to try newly-discovered traditional recipes. The result is a constant ferment of new ideas. Even as we left, late for our flight, Annie Feoldé rushed out of the kitchen to ask us to taste a new idea: deep-fried fresh sage crumbled over gnocchi.

It was, in fact, the white truffle season, and a wooden box such as expensive cigars are packed in had been delivered earlier that morning from the truffle capital of Alba. Fabio opened it in the

But no one ever forgets that the original reason for the Enoteca's existence is its wine cellar, described by one leading guide recently as 'the best, the most considered, the most unbeatable,' and the reluctance which the owners felt in opening a restaurant was that the food might relegate the wine to second place. Happily this has not happened, and thanks to the great care taken with seasonings in the kitchen, the one, to an extraordinary degree, complements the other. Guests, if they recognize their good fortune, do not consult the wine list, they consult the sommeliers Gianni Fortunati and Antonio Rosolino, or the owners and accept their recommendations. Wine is poured in glasses to suit the diner's choice of food, so one bottle may be shared among tables, to be followed by others. For a full menu the guests might expect to taste two white wines, one or two reds and a dessert wine. All will be of the first quality – nothing else ever enters the house, even for cooking – and if the diners are lucky, they may pick the night when an exceptional bottle is opened. Below the restaurant is a Tutankhamen's tomb of wine, spirits and liqueurs in a vast vaulted cellar. As Martin Brigdale describes overleaf, the wines are not binned as in a conventional cellar but either laid casually on tables or piled in perilous pyramids on the floor. The value of the wines is quite enormous, and one's heart leaps as Annie Feoldé's boisterous poodles race

A 'family' of d'Yquem

The glorious treasures of the Ristorante-Enoteca Pinchiorri feature such rarities as this extraordinary pile of bottles (top right) of old Pétrus, Latour, Lafite and artist-labelled Mouton-Rothschild. The names on the bottles are the finest, but it is not until one notices the dates on them that one realizes what treasures they truly are.

Pyramids of Chateau d'Yquem of all years are characteristically stored in one room devoted to Sauternes (bottom right). The novelty side of the collection is shown by a range of bottles of different sizes of d'Yquem displayed beneath a painting that catches your eye as you enter the dining room.

There are all sorts of beautiful wine-related objects, collected over the years and placed around the restaurant, including many fine decanters (right).

The cellar at the Enoteca

around them. Bottles are brought up for service in the restaurant to suit both Giorgio's whims and Annie's choice of menu, and they make it a personal rule to drink and discuss a bottle of the finest wine every day, to keep their palates in training. The worrying, or perhaps exciting, fantasy is that if and when the Arno floods again with little warning, as all realistic Florentines know it will, and the low-lying parts of Florence are soaked in a mixture of polluted water and central-heating fuel as they were in 1966, then the Enoteca cellar will flood, the labels will float off, and the greatest oenological lottery of all time will follow.

Meanwhile, Giorgio Pinchiorri and Annie Feoldé's restaurant remains one of the most civilized and pleasant places to eat in one of Europe's most beautiful cities. It is an expensive restaurant in a country where the fortunate and knowledgeable can eat excellent food at reasonable prices. But the ambience, the sheer quality of the food, and the endless variety and unexpectedness of the wines make any meal at the Enoteca something quite out of the ordinary.

The Cellar at Enoteca Pinchiorri   *by Martin Brigdale*

Two glass cabinets stand on either side of the cellar's entrance. One contains a fascinating collection of wine memorabilia; the other contains bottles of fine, dated Bas-Armagnac stretching back to the nineteenth century. These two cabinets, with their eclectic and near-priceless contents, set the tone for the Enoteca's entire collection.

The layout of the cellar is unusual. Wooden bins along the walls do not surprise, but the tables piled with apparently unsorted bottles of fine wine, and the high pyramids of Bordeaux Premiers Crus which dominate the floor space will take the ordinary collector's breath away.

Separate rooms house specific collections: one of Tuscan wines, generally young but of the best quality (Tignanello and Brunello di Montalcino are much in evidence, for restaurant consumption; one of fine white burgundy, like Montrachet from the Marquis de Laguiche; one of red burgundy – again, the best growers' names, like Comte Georges de Vogüé, stand out; and a room of white wines from growers more generally noted for their reds, with Château Margaux's Pavillon Blanc well represented. A side room for dessert wines dazzles with its golden pyramids of Château d'Yquem.

Most staggering of all is the 'Collectors' Room', where only the finest and rarest bottles are stored. Complete sets of Mouton-Rothschild's artist labels – and their wine – and magnums and larger of Romanée-Conti are balanced somewhat precariously on a large table in the middle of the room. Boxes of Krug champagne, Pétrus of many vintages and a bin of Latour '61 seem almost commonplace in this company. The cellar has been, until recently, both warm and dry: ideal for humans, less so for wines. Temperature and humidity controls are being installed next year.

Only the most favoured guests and visitors are led down to the cellar. In the light of the collection's value this is hardly surprising. For those with no entrée, or who cannot visit the Enoteca, the photographs reveal some of the casual splendours to be found there.

Prawns in a Piquant Sauce

Gnocchi di Ricottae Spinaci con Salsa Pomodoro e Basilico

Ricotta and Spinach Gnocchi with Tomato and Basil Sauce

Gnocchi
300 g (10½ oz) very fresh, well-drained
ricotta
300 g (10½ oz) fresh spinach, well washed
and with stems removed
2 whole eggs
90 g (3 oz) flour
50 g (1¾ oz) grated parmesan
a generous grating of nutmeg
1 litre (1¾ pints) light meat stock for boiling
the gnocchi
salt and pepper

Sauce
1 kg (2¼ lb) ripe tomatoes, peeled, seeded and
finely chopped
1 onion, peeled and chopped
2 cloves of garlic, peeled and chopped
2 tablespoons olive oil
10 basil leaves, shredded
salt and pepper

Cook the spinach with no more water than remains on the leaves after washing. When the leaves have wilted, squeeze them to remove all moisture and process or sieve to make a fine purée. Mix this thoroughly with the drained ricotta, the eggs, flour, cheese and nutmeg. Season and chill in the refrigerator.

Meanwhile, make the sauce. Soften and lightly brown the onion and garlic in the oil and add the chopped tomato. Season with salt and pepper, stir and cook on a low heat for 1 hour. Cool a little, then liquidize. Add the basil leaves.

To serve, bring the meat stock to the boil while you form the chilled dough into little balls between the palms of your hands (or by using two teaspoons). Cook the gnocchi in the boiling stock in batches, removing them with a slotted spoon as soon as they float to the top of the liquid. When all the gnocchi are cooked, add them to the hot sauce, and mix gently but thoroughly over the heat for a further 2–3 minutes. Divide between four very hot plates and serve immediately.

FOR FOUR PEOPLE

Gamberoni in Dolce Forte

Prawns in a Piquant Sauce

1 kg (2¼ lb) large uncooked prawns
200 g (7 oz) celery, trimmed and cut in strips
50 g (1¾ oz) unsalted butter
20 g (⅔ oz) sugar
5 tablespoons olive oil
1 scant teaspoon powdered cinnamon
juice of 1 lemon
100 g (3½ oz) sultanas, soaked and well
drained
a wineglass of fish stock
salt and pepper

Cook the celery strips in enough water to cover, adding the butter, sugar and a little salt and pepper. When the liquid has become a syrupy sauce, remove from the heat and keep warm.

Shell and de-vein the prawns and colour them in the oil over a high flame. When they have turned bright pink, lower the heat and season with salt, pepper and the powdered cinnamon. Add the lemon juice and the drained sultanas. Continue cooking on a low heat for 2 minutes to allow the flavours to amalgamate, moistening with fish stock. Serve with the celery on hot plates.

FOR FOUR PEOPLE

Ricotta and Spinach Gnocchi with Tomato and Basil Sauce

Il Cibreo

Chicken Giblets with Egg and Lemon

This dish is now seldom found on menus because it is not easy to obtain the necessary ingredients, unless you have an obliging poultry dealer who is prepared to keep the 'spare parts' for you. It is, however, a much appreciated speciality on the Enoteca's menu.

200 g (7 oz) mixed cocks' crests and combs
80–100 g (2½–3½ oz) cocks' testicles
4 very fresh chicken livers
1 onion, peeled and chopped
50 g (1¾ oz) unsalted butter
7 tablespoons chicken stock
8 small carrots, trimmed and turned
8 small courgettes, halved
8 small potatoes, trimmed and turned
2 cooked chopped artichoke hearts
1 hot chilli
2 egg yolks
juice of ½ a lemon
salt and pepper

Boil the crests and combs in salted water for 30 minutes, drain, cool and skin. Cook with the chopped onion in the butter until they are lightly browned. Add stock to cover, then add the carrot, courgette and potato, the chopped cooked artichoke and the hot chilli. Salt and pepper lightly.

Cook over a medium heat for 15 minutes and then add the testicles and livers, all thoroughly cleaned and freed of tough sinews and membranes. After 10 minutes further cooking, remove and discard the chilli. Add the egg yolks beaten with the lemon juice, and stir briskly off the heat for 2 minutes. Test seasoning and serve immediately.

Note: the artichoke hearts can be replaced with fresh ceps (*funghi porcini*) or with freshly cooked green beans.

FOR FOUR PEOPLE

Chicken Giblets with Egg and Lemon

Pappardelle sulla Lepre

Pasta with Hare Sauce

1 young hare, skinned and gutted, with its
liver, heart, lungs and blood
2 medium carrots, chopped
1 onion, peeled and chopped
1 celery stick, chopped
1 sprig parsley, chopped
1 clove garlic, peeled and chopped
6 tablespoons olive oil
500 ml (18 fl oz) good red wine
360 g (12¾ oz) fresh pappardelle (see below)
salt and pepper

Only the saddle of the hare is used for this dish, with the innards. The rest of the animal can be roasted or stewed.

Soften the chopped vegetables, parsley and garlic in the olive oil. Meanwhile, separate the saddle from the hare, and break up into pieces. Do this with your hands or with a very sharp cleaver in order to avoid any splinters of bone ending up in the sauce. Finely chop the heart and lungs of the hare.

Add the hare pieces to the vegetables and cook for 10 minutes, stirring all the time. Season with salt and pepper, add the prepared heart and lungs, stir again and pour in the wine and about 3 tablespoons of the blood, diluted with a little hot water. Simmer for approximately 1 hour, adding a little warm water if the sauce becomes too thick. Meanwhile, make the pasta.

Pappardelle
200 g (7 oz) white flour
100 g (3½ oz) chestnut flour
1 whole egg and 1 yolk
water
a pinch of salt

If you are using a food processor, process all the ingredients to a smooth dough; otherwise mix them together with your hands to create a homogeneous mass. Wrap in clingfilm and refrigerate for 30 minutes. Then divide the dough into two equal parts, re-wrap one, and pass the other through a hand-cranked or electric pasta machine until you have a very fine sheet. Spread on a floured surface, sprinkle with flour and cut into pappardelle – rectangles 8 cm x 2 cm (3 inches x

¾ inch). Repeat with the remaining dough and set aside until you are ready to cook the pasta.

Take the pieces of hare out of the saucepan and remove all the bones. Chop up the meat with the liver of the hare and return to the pan. Stir, check seasoning, and reheat while you cook the pasta in boiling salted water. This will take approximately 3 minutes. Drain the pasta thoroughly and mix with the hot hare sauce. Serve with grated parmesan cheese or grated white truffle.

FOR FOUR PEOPLE

La Scottiglia

Tuscan Mixed Meat Stew

Scottiglia is a peasant dish of mixed meats which Tuscan country people make with whatever they have to hand. This might be pork, veal or beef as well as, or instead of, the game and poultry which Annie Feoldé prefers for their greater delicacy of flavour and shorter cooking time.

1 pigeon
1 saddle of rabbit
2 duck breasts
1 breast of guinea-fowl
2 carrots, 2 celery sticks, 1 onion and herbs to make a stock
3 tablespoons oil
300 ml (½ pint) red wine
200 g (7 oz) ceps (funghi porcini), cleaned and sliced
2 tablespoons olive oil
1 clove of garlic, peeled and chopped
100 g (3½ oz) little onions, peeled
50 g (1¾ oz) unsalted butter
2 teaspoons sugar
polenta made with 80 g (2¾ oz) maize meal and 200 ml (7 fl oz) water
olive oil for frying
1 dessertspoon chopped parsley
200 g (7 oz) ripe tomatoes, peeled, seeded and diced
salt and pepper

Bone the pigeon, keeping the breasts and thighs for the Scottiglia. Bone the saddle of rabbit and cut the fillets into large cubes. Do the same with the duck and guinea-fowl breasts and pigeon breasts and thighs and put all the meats on one side.

Tuscan Mixed Meat Stew

Brown the stock vegetables in a pan with 3 tablespoons of oil, the pigeon carcase and rabbit bones. When they begin to brown add the wine and herbs and simmer for 30 minutes. Pour the stock through a fine sieve and reduce until you have 2 tablespoons of sauce. Add a very little salt.

Fry the ceps briskly in 2 tablespoons of hot oil with 1 chopped clove of garlic for 3–5 minutes. Drain and keep warm. Stew the onions in 6-7 tablespoons of water with the butter, sugar and a little salt until most of the liquid has evaporated.

Make the polenta by pouring the maize meal in a fine stream into the boiling water and stirring continuously until it thickens. Salt, and pour on to a wooden board, cover, and cool.

To finish, brown all the meats together in olive oil over a brisk heat. Salt, and when they have coloured nicely, add the reduced stock, the little onions and ceps and mix well. Finally add the chopped parsley and the raw tomato dice. Check for seasoning and serve immediately on hot plates accompanied by a plate of polenta slices.

FOR FOUR PEOPLE

Breast of Guinea-Fowl roasted with Bacon, Rosemary and Sage

Petto di Faraona con Pancetta, Rosmarino e Salvia

Breast of Guinea-Fowl roasted with Bacon, Rosemary and Sage

4 guinea-fowl breasts, boned, with their skin
4 handsome sage leaves, chopped
the leaves from a sprig of rosemary
50 g (1¾ oz) unsalted butter, softened
4–8 thin slices of smoked pancetta (or smoked
streaky bacon), sufficient to cover almost the
whole surface of the guinea-fowl breasts
pork caul fat sufficient to wrap each breast
completely
1 tablespoon olive oil
1 tablespoon melted butter
salt and pepper

Mix the chopped herbs very gently with the softened butter and a little salt and pepper. Loosen the skin of each breast and push the flavoured butter between the skin and the flesh. Salt the breasts lightly all over, cover with *pancetta* slices and wrap up in caul fat, pinching the edges or securing with toothpicks so that the parcels do not unwrap themselves when they are cooked. This can be done well in advance.

Before serving, cook the breasts in a mixture of oil and butter for 10 minutes, turning them every two minutes so that they cook evenly. Serve with the pan juices and seasonal vegetables.

FOR FOUR PEOPLE

Rotolo di Castagne al Cioccolato, Salsa al Pistacchio

Chestnut Roulade Stuffed with Chocolate Cream with a Pistachio Sauce

2 kg (4½ lb) good chestnuts, peeled
350 g (12 oz) sugar
300 ml (½ pint) single cream
600 g (1¼ lb) good cooking chocolate, melted
150 g (5¼ oz) shelled and peeled unsalted
pistachio nuts
6 egg yolks
500 ml (18 fl oz) full-cream milk

Cook the chestnuts in water until they are tender. Drain well and process or push through a fine sieve. Add 200 g (7 oz) of the sugar and one third of the cream and blend to a smooth paste.

Add the remaining cream to the melted chocolate and stir thoroughly. Allow to cool but not to solidify. Spread out a sheet of cling film and spoon the chestnut paste on to it. Cover with a second sheet of film and roll out the paste to an even thickness of 2 cm (¾ inch). Remove the second sheet of film and cover the chestnut rectangle with the chocolate cream. Roll up the paste like a Swiss roll, leaving the bottom sheet of film behind. Place the roll on a flat serving dish and chill in the refrigerator.

Meanwhile, make the pistachio cream. Boil the pistachios, then work or process to a smooth purée. Blend the remaining sugar with the egg yolks and add to the hot milk in the top of a double boiler. Cook for 5–8 minutes until it thickens, then add the pistachio purée.

Slice the chestnut roulade and serve with the pistachio cream. It should be eaten on the day it is made.

FOR TWELVE PEOPLE

Biscotto Friabile Farcito di Mousse alla Banana

Banana Mousse in a Delicate Tartlet

200 g (7 oz) flour
80 g (2¾ oz) fine sugar
1 very small or ½ a large egg
100 g (3½ oz) unsalted butter, softened

Banana mousse
300 g (10½ oz) cream whipped with
40 g (1¼ oz) sugar
2 very ripe small bananas
juice of ½ a lemon
500 ml (18 fl oz) strawberry or raspberry
purée
6 whole strawberries or 18 whole
raspberries

Preheat the oven to 180°C/350°F/Gas 4. Mix the flour, fine sugar, egg and butter together very thoroughly. Roll out this dough very finely and use it to line six 10 cm (4 inch) rum baba moulds. Prick the dough with a fork and bake in the pre-heated oven for 10 minutes. Ease the cooked shells out of the moulds and set aside to cool.

Whip the cream, adding the sugar gradually as it becomes thick. Peel the bananas and liquidize or mash them finely with the lemon juice. Mix gently but thoroughly with the cream. Fill each tartlet shell and place it, filled side down, on a plate. Fill the hollow centres with more banana mousse. Serve with a purée of strawberries or raspberries, sweetened if necessary, and top with a whole strawberry or three raspberries. Mint leaves are a pleasant addition.

FOR SIX PEOPLE

Banana Mousse in a Delicate Tartlet

GIANLUIGI MORINI
& VALENTINO MARCATTILII

SAN DOMENICO

Imola

The small city of Imola, thirty-three kilometres to the east of Bologna down the Via Emilia, is known to the sporting world as the home of the famous Imola circuit, where the San Marino Grand Prix is held every spring. For a brief period the international motor-racing circus descends on the town and engines roar night and day. The city then returns to its usual provincial daily life. There is a pleasant *rocca* (small castle commanding the town) dating from the thirteenth and fifteenth centuries, and some elegant squares and streets. To the north lies the Po valley, with its chessboard poplar plantations, sluggish waterways and endless fields of sunflowers. Fruit orchards and isolated red brick farmhouses stretch away to the horizon. Immediately to the south are the Apennine foothills, their valleys planted with vines and persimmons, rising sharply to the chestnut-clad slopes of the mountains themselves.

There is, in fact, a very good reason for visiting Imola at any time of the year as discerning food-lovers, both Italian and foreign, have long known. In the low building which housed guests, the factor and his family and the stores of wine, oil and grain brought in from the countryside by peasant tenants of the fifteenth-century Convent of San Domenico, there is a remarkable restaurant, with a cuisine based on the best of the old and new in Italian cooking, and with an unusual history.

San Domenico is the creation of Gianluigi Morini, born in 1935 in one of rooms above the present restaurant, where his family had lived since the turn of the century, running a prosperous butchery business based on their cattle farm outside the city. It was here that the young Gianluigi learned from his father and grandfather the art of choosing wine, of knowing the best cuts of meat for preserving, and the secrets of the best regional dishes – in fact acquired a lifelong love of good food.

His father intended him for a banker but, cinema-struck, he set off for Rome with a letter of introduction to Federico Fellini. His cinematic career was interrupted when family illness called him, as the only son, back to Imola. He somewhat reluctantly entered the Cassa di Risparmio Bank in 1956, escaping from Imola to the festivals and concerts of Bologna and Venice as often as he could. He married, and set up house with his wife Renza nearby in

Gianluigi Morini and Valentino and Natale Marcattilii

The intimate dining room has a club-like atmosphere.

The staff of San Domenico

In the front row, seated from left to right, are Valentino Marcattilii, Renza and Gianluigi Morini, and Natale Marcattilii.

Nino Bergese was the 'founding father' of San Domenico's cuisine. It took Morini two years to persuade him to come out of retirement in Liguria for six or seven months a year to teach the secrets of his cuisine to young chefs (among them at one time, Valentino Marcattilii, a favourite pupil).

Gianluigi Morini and Valentino Marcattilii in the vast wine cellars under the restaurant.

Imola, where their two daughters were born. He became a passionate cook, delighting in entertaining friends. His wife and father urged him to put his talents as a host to more serious use. And so San Domenico was born, on 7 March, 1970.

Widely read in the classics of Italian cooking and gastronomy, Morini decided to recreate in his restaurant the authentic cooking of pre-war Italy, especially as it had been practised in the well-to-do, noble and even royal households of the day. Accordingly, he sought out one of the great heroes of Italian cooking, Nino Bergese, born in 1904, whose list of employers included kings, nobles and great industrial barons. Bergese, who also had had his own celebrated restaurant in Genoa, was by now living in retirement in Liguria, and it took Morini two years to persuade him to come to Imola for six or seven months a year – not to cook, but to teach young chefs the secrets of his cuisine. Among them was a young cook from the Abruzzi region, east of Rome, Valentino Marcattilii, who with his maître d'hôtel elder brother Natale, now owns the restaurant jointly with Morini. Valentino,

who had entered San Domenico as an apprentice in 1970, when he was only sixteen, says that he recognized very soon that Bergese was a teacher of genius, whose great talent must be handed down, as he himself passes it on to the present-day apprentices of San Domenico. Bergese allowed no machines in his kitchen: everything was chopped, sliced, mixed, sieved and kneaded by hand. His menus were made up and agreed in the evening and the necessary ingredients – only the necessary ingredients – bought fresh the following morning. It was truly a 'cuisine of the market'. Bergese at once formed an unusual rapport with Valentino, and sent him off to work stages with the great chefs of France, so that he might broaden his experience and learn from the ideas of the nouvelle cuisine.

On his return Valentino set about using his experience of other kitchens to forge an efficient working team of specialist chefs for the various departments, with a chief pastry chef Diego Genna, from Sicily. There are now fifteen cooks when the kitchen is working at high-season capacity, and among them there are

cheeses and polenta with white truffles brought to the table, like succeeding courses, on a flower-decked silver tray. The pasta course might be ricotta and parsley ravioli briefly browned in a sage-flavoured béchamel. A variety of breads is served: plain rolls, glazed sweet brioche and the house speciality of grissini bread sticks flavoured with heavily browned onion shreds. Lobster in a black truffle sauce might be followed by a guinea-fowl braised in marsala or a saddle of veal. Salads, and vegetables served separately, play little part in the meal: it is assumed that they are eaten at home as part of lighter meals, but vegetable garnishes are often, and imaginatively, used to set off the main ingredient on the plate. And of course, in season, the ceps brought in by trusted collectors and the white truffles from the Alba region dominate the menu, just as the smell of the truffle dominates the kitchen.

The desserts are varied between simple fruit sorbets in various combinations and much more elaborate confections involving dark and white chocolates and Italian meringue. Flour is used to thicken some sauces – and naturally in pasta and pastries – but most of the sauces are reductions of stocks and juices in the modern manner. The menu has moved on from that taught by Bergese, but some of his most famous dishes remain; the ravioli with egg and the Lamb Cutlets Villeroi. Another legacy is his practice – not new, but closely associated with his name – of adding a small glass of wine in place of one egg when making dough for stuffed pastas, to give extra rigidity and strength.

The wine cellar of San Domenico, Gianluigi Morini's special pride and care, occupies the ancient *cantina* of the building, the same cellar which housed whole families of refugees during the bombardment of Imola in the Second World War. Built of red brick, its vaulted tunnels are a treasurehouse of wines, many of them collector's items, though Morini says indignantly that he collects only empty bottles, not full ones. There are forty sparkling white wines, including champagnes, 180 white wines and 320 red wines, plus a fabulous assemblage of malt whiskies, of eaux-de-vie made specially for every year of the proprietor's life, and a vast range of locally produced fruit liqueurs.

always apprentices from the regional catering schools and young foreign chefs. The dining rooms themselves are intimate and somewhat old-fashioned, with leather upholstered chairs and banquettes, raspberry pink cloths, small serving tables and ice-bucket stands. Signor Morini and his wife are Anglophiles and the ceilings are papered with the same William Morris 'chrysanthemum' print as covers the hanging table lamps. The ornate and heavy candelabra and other silverware all date from a massive buying expedition to the London silver vaults. Together with the comfortable salon where clients can enjoy an apéritif before and coffee after their meal, and the numerous separate rooms, which can be brought into use for private functions or during Grand Prix week (when up to two hundred diners have been served in a single evening) the dining rooms give San Domenico a comfortable, club-like air.

San Domenico's food is not for the faint-hearted, and certainly not for every day. A typical menu might start with the recently introduced Morbidelle: a deliciously rich confection of various

San Domenico is in one sense a celebration of the past, but the future is very much in the partners' minds. This year, the aging and somewhat inconvenient kitchen will be resited with new equipment in the present pasta-making room, and the old kitchen will then become a small dining room looking out on a courtyard garden formed from the present goods-receiving area. At some time in the future, a few suites for clients of the restaurant will be created upstairs. Meanwhile, Gianluigi Morini, the Marcattilii brothers and their senior staff have formed a cooperative to re-vitalize what was once Bologna's most famous restaurant: Il Pappagallo. A franchise has also been granted for a San Domenico restaurant in New York.

Both Marcattilii brothers and their ebullient co-proprietor are still relatively young men, firmly rooted in the traditions of San Domenico and in the city of Imola itself, so it is reasonable to predict that this unusual and outstanding restaurant, at once grand and welcoming, will continue to attract food-lovers from all over the world.

Morbidelle di Formaggi con Polenta e Fonduta al Tartufo
Chilled Cream Cheese with a Hot Polenta and Truffle Sauce

150g (5¼ oz) robiola
100g (3½ oz) caprino, or other fresh goats'
milk cheese
150g (5¼ oz) ricotta
400g (14¾ oz) fontina cheese
500ml (18 fl oz) full-cream milk
40g (1½ oz) butter
4 egg yolks
1 tablespoon extra virgin olive oil
450–500g (1–1¼ lb) maize meal
1 fresh white truffle
salt and pepper

Mix the three soft cheeses together and form into small ovals, allowing three ovals for each person. Refrigerate.

Cut the fontina into fine dice and melt in the milk for two hours in the upper part of a double boiler, stirring frequently. Add the butter, egg yolks and a little salt and keep hot.

Meanwhile, make the polenta by bringing 1 litre (1¾ pints) of lightly salted water, with the tablespoon of olive oil, to the boil and trickling in the meal in a fine stream. Stir continuously with a wooden spoon for 1½ hours until a smooth coating consistency is achieved.

Put three cold cream cheese ovals on each cold plate, pour over the hot polenta and then the fontina sauce. Finally grate the white truffle liberally over each plate and serve immediately.

Notes: maize meal varies in consistency and water content and therefore exact quantities cannot be specified. The cook must use his or her discretion.

This is an extraordinarily rich and delicious dish which is well worth the effort its preparation requires. At the San Domenico polenta is made in the traditional way described above of which the best description can be found in Gabriele d'Annunzio's *I Promessi Sposi*. It is a soothing but very time-consuming activity, and shorter, though less authentic, methods can be found in modern Italian cookery books.

FOR FOUR PEOPLE

Chilled Cream Cheese with a Hot Polenta and Truffle Sauce

Tortellini alla Crema di Fegato

Stuffed Pasta with Liver Sauce

200 g (7 oz) unsalted butter
a bay leaf
100 g (3½ oz) chicken livers, cleaned and
trimmed
3 tablespoons cognac
tortellini stuffed with meat
chicken stock for cooking the tortellini
50 g (1¾ oz) fresh goose liver, sliced
7 tablespoons single cream
a grating of nutmeg
50 g (1¾ oz) grated parmesan
salt and pepper

Melt 50 g (1¾ oz) butter in a sauté pan with the bay leaf and cook the chicken livers briefly. They should still be pink inside. Remove the bay leaf, pour off and reserve the cooking fat and flame the livers with the cognac. Allow to cool, then liquidize with the remaining butter, melted, to a smooth paste, seasoning with salt and pepper. Rub through a fine sieve.

Cook the tortellini in the boiling stock. Cook the goose liver in the reserved cooking fat as before. Meanwhile put the cream, the liver mousse, the nutmeg and parmesan in a large pan and heat through, stirring, without allowing the mixture to boil. Drain the cooked tortellini and toss them in the sauce. Add the cooked goose liver. Serve at once on heated plates.

FOR FOUR PEOPLE

Stuffed Pasta with Liver Sauce

Insalata Tiepida di Funghi Porcini con il suo Burro

Warm Salad of *Porcini* Mushrooms

600 g (1¼ lb) small ceps (funghi porcini)
1 tablespoon extra virgin olive oil
1 peeled clove of garlic
250 g (9 oz) unsalted butter
1 tablespoon each of chopped chervil
and parsley
salt

Brush off the earth and trim 500 g (1 lb) of the ceps. Slice them thinly and arrange them on a serving plate in an attractive fan pattern (see photograph). Warm up the oil with the garlic clove in a deep sauté pan, then discard the garlic. Chop the remaining cep or ceps very finely and add them to the oil with a pinch of salt. Cover the pan and cook for a few minutes until their juices have run. Liquidize the contents of the pan (or use a hand-held liquidizer) and, over a moderate heat, beat in the butter piece by piece, without boiling. When the sauce is hot and frothy, add the chopped chervil and parsley. Briefly warm the mushrooms in a very cool oven, pour over the sauce and serve.

FOR FOUR PEOPLE

Warm Salad of Porcini *Mushrooms*

Uova ai Tartufi

Truffled Eggs in Pasta

50 g (1¾ oz) washed, cooked and chopped
spinach
50 (1¾ oz) drained ricotta
100 g (3½ oz) grated parmesan
5 eggs
nutmeg
8 thin discs of fresh pasta 15 cm (6 inches) in
diameter
100 g (3½ oz) unsalted butter
50 g (1¾ oz) fresh white truffles, sliced
salt and pepper

Mix the spinach with the ricotta, half the grated parmesan, 1 egg, a grating of nutmeg, salt and pepper until you have a homogeneous mass. Place four of the pasta discs on a sheet of oiled paper or foil. Divide the spinach mixture into four and spoon or pipe into a hollow ring on each disc. Put 1 egg yolk into each of the 'wells' and season. Brush the edges of the pasta discs with cold water and imprison the spinach and egg mound by placing the remaining pasta discs over the top and pressing the edges down firmly, eliminating as much air from the interior as possible while you do so.

Bring a large pan of salted water to the boil and cook the pasta parcels for about 2 minutes each. Meanwhile, cook the butter to a fine nut-brown colour. Have ready four heated soup plates and place a drained pasta parcel in each. Strew with the sliced truffles and the remaining grated parmesan, and pour round the browned butter. Serve at once.

Note: step-by-step photographs show Valentino Marcattilii making this dish. The recipe above has been slightly adapted for the home cook in several respects. In particular, it will be seen that Valentino Marcattilii uses green and white striped pasta, but ordinary pasta gives just as delicious, if not so spectacular, a result.

FOR FOUR PEOPLE

Branzino al Basilico

Sea Bass with Basil

1 sea bass of about 1.5 kg (3¼ lb) gutted and
scaled, but with the head and tail still attached
3 firm tomatoes, peeled, seeded and coarsely
chopped
1 tablespoon of finely chopped basil
3 shallots, peeled and finely chopped
200 g (7 oz) unsalted butter
1 wine glass each of dry white wine and fish
stock
salt and pepper

Preheat the oven to 170°C/325°F/Gas 3. Fit the cleaned bass snugly in an oven-proof dish 10 cm (4 inches) deep. Add the chopped tomato, the chopped basil, the chopped shallots, 50 g (1¾ oz) of the butter, the wine and the stock. Season with salt and pepper, cover with foil and bake for about 15 minutes in the pre-heated oven.

When you are sure the fish has cooked through, carefully remove it from the cooking dish with a fish slice and place it on a work surface. Remove the skin from the fish body, but not from the head and tail, with a small sharp knife. Keep the fish warm on a heated serving dish.

Strain the cooking juices into a small pan and reduce briskly to half the original quantity. Lower the heat and whisk in the remaining butter, cut into a cubes, adding a few at a time. (A few cubes of diced, peeled and chopped tomato, and some chopped fresh herbs, make an attractive addition to the sauce.) Season again with more salt and pepper. Pour a little of this sauce over the bass and serve the rest in a sauceboat. Decorate according to taste. Take to the table on the serving dish, divide between four heated plates and add the sauce lavishly.

FOR FOUR PEOPLE

Truffled Eggs in Pasta

1 A strip of green and yellow pasta is rolled thin.

5 A little white truffle is grated over each yolk.

7 carefully moulded round the spinach mounds,

2 Spinach and ricotta 'rings' are piped on.

3 The eggs are separated.

4 A yolk is poured into each 'ring'.

6 The pasta is folded back over the spinach rings,

8 cut into rounds and the edges crimped.

At last!

Lobster with Chambord Sauce (normally served halved)

Faraona alle Verze con Funghi Porcini

Guinea-fowl with Cabbage and and Ceps

1 cleaned and trussed guinea-fowl of about
1.5 kg (3¼ lb)
50 g (1¾ oz) unsalted butter
50 ml (3½ tablespoons) extra virgin olive oil
5 peeled cloves of garlic
a sprig of fresh rosemary
300 g (10½ oz) small ceps (funghi porcini),
cleaned and cut into quarters
2 small Savoy cabbages, leaves separated and
the central stalk of each leaf removed
1 litre (1¾ pints) meat stock
salt and freshly ground pepper

Preheat the oven to 180°C/350°F/Gas 4. Season the guinea-fowl inside and out and place in a deep roasting pan with the butter and 2 tablespoons of the olive oil. Roast in the oven for approximately 1 hour, turning and basting frequently.

Heat the remaining olive oil in a cast-iron or stainless-steel pan with the garlic and rosemary, taking care not to brown the garlic. Remove the pan from the heat, cool and discard the garlic and herb. Return the pan to the stove, turn up the heat and put in the quartered ceps. Cook briskly for about 2 minutes, then add the prepared cabbage leaves. Add the stock and cook slowly for about 30 minutes. Season with salt and pepper.

When the guinea-fowl is cooked, remove from the oven, pour off the fat from the pan, surround with the drained cabbage and ceps and return all to the oven for a further 10 minutes. Then slice the guinea-fowl and arrange on four heated plates, decorating with the cabbage and ceps.

Note: At the San Domenico the cooked guinea-fowl is normally brought to the table whole, with its cep and cabbage garnish, and carved by the waiter in front of the guests. It is later brought back for second helpings.

FOR FOUR PEOPLE

Astaco in Salsa Chambord

Lobster with Chambord Sauce

2 live lobsters of about 400 g (15 oz) each
50 g (1¾ oz) sliced white truffles
225 g (8 oz) tinned tomatoes, puréed and
strained
a pinch of paprika
500 ml (18 fl oz) whipping cream
1 liqueur glass of cognac
30 g (1 oz) very finely chopped parsley
salt and freshly ground pepper

Preheat the oven to 150°C/300°F/Gas 2. Kill the lobsters and chop them in half lengthwise with a cleaver. Remove the intestine, but do not wash the lobsters. Place the four halves flesh-side down in a large metal oven dish in a single layer. Season with salt and pepper and add all the other ingredients except the parsley. Cover the dish and bring to the boil on the top of the stove. Simmer for 10 minutes, then place in the oven for about 5 minutes.

Remove the pan from the oven and place one half lobster on each of four heated plates. Season again with salt, pepper and paprika if necessary, and sprinkle with parsley and the sieved pan juices. Accompany with a rice pilaff or steamed potatoes, and serve immediately.

FOR FOUR PEOPLE

Guinea-fowl with Cabbage and Ceps

Lamb Cutlets Villeroi

Crespella Calda alla Mele

Hot Apple Pancakes

Pancakes
2 eggs
100 g (3½ oz) flour
20 g (⅔ oz) butter
250 ml (8 fl oz) milk
a pinch of salt

Stuffing
3 sweet dessert apples, cored, peeled and diced
(reserve the peel)
75 g (2½ oz) unsalted butter
100 g (3½ oz) sugar

Candied apple
1 sweet dessert apple, cored, peeled and cut into
12 segments (reserve the peel)
600 g (1¼ lb) sugar
100 g (3½ oz) unsalted butter, softened
100 g (3½ oz) finely ground almonds
2 eggs

For the sauce
reserved apple peel
500 ml (18 fl oz) cider
2 tablespoons calvados
100 g (3½ oz) sugar
300 g (12 oz) butter

Costolette d'Agnello alla Villeroi

Lamb Cutlets Villeroi

12 lamb cutlets from the central part of the
saddle, trimmed carefully, seasoned and lightly
floured
1 tablespoon extra virgin olive oil
50 g (1¾ oz) butter
a few bay leaves
500 ml (18 fl oz) thick béchamel sauce
50 g (1¾ oz) grated parmesan
100 g (3½ oz) finely chopped black truffles
200 g (7 oz) fine breadcrumbs
2 eggs, beaten
flour
oil for frying
salt and freshly ground pepper

Heat the olive oil, butter and a few bay leaves in a cast-iron or stainless-steel sauté pan. When it begins to sizzle, remove the bay leaves and put in the prepared cutlets. Cook them for one minute on each side. Set them aside to drain on absorbent paper.

Mix the hot béchamel sauce with the grated parmesan and the finely chopped truffles and dip the cutlets in the mixture, holding them by the bone so that the flesh is completely submerged in the sauce. Place them individually on a chilled baking sheet and refrigerate for 1 hour.

When they are thoroughly chilled and the sauce coating is firm, dip each cutlet first in the breadcrumbs, then in beaten egg and finally in flour. Heat the oil in a deep saucepan until it smokes. Fry the breaded cutlets until golden brown (this takes approximately 2 minutes). Drain the cutlets thoroughly on absorbent paper and put three cutlets on each of four heated plates. Garnish the cutlets with potato lattices and suitable seasonal vegetables. Serve immediately.

FOR FOUR PEOPLE

Combine all the ingredients for the pancake batter, make the pancakes in the usual way, and set aside until needed in a warm place. Mix the diced apple with the butter and sugar and heat under the grill until the apple is nicely browned. Keep warm.

To make the candied apple, first make a syrup with 1 litre (1¾ pints) water and 500 g (1 lb) of the sugar. Bring the syrup to the boil and cook the 12 apple segments in it for 5 minutes. Remove them and pat dry. Reserve the syrup. Separately, mix the remaining sugar with the softened butter, the ground almonds and the eggs and beat vigorously for 5 minutes. Cover the candied apple slices with this and set aside.

To make the sauce, poach the apple skins in the reserved syrup until the liquid has reduced by half, strain out the skins and stir in the cider, calvados, sugar and butter. Keep hot.

Stuff the pancakes with the grilled apples and divide them between 4 hot plates. Place the candied apple mixture under a hot grill or salamander until the top is golden brown. Serve the pancakes and the candied apple slices in a pool of the hot apple sauce, and decorate according to taste (see photograph). Here the pancke is decorated with mint leaves and a *tuile* filled with a créole ice-cream with grapes soaked in marsala and lemon. At the San Domenico this dish is served with a Moscato di Asti.

FOR FOUR PEOPLE

Cassata alla Frutta Secca di Bosco con Salsa di Lamponi

Cassata of Woodland Fruits and Nuts with Raspberry Sauce

300 ml (½ pint) double cream
100 g (3½ oz) sugar
1 large egg white
70 g (2½ oz) candied fruits, finely diced
30 g (1 oz) shelled fresh pistachio nuts, blanched and skinned
50 g (1¾ oz) toasted hazelnuts
500 g (1 lb) fresh raspberries

Whip the cream until stiff, then refrigerate. Cook the sugar in a little water until a half a teaspoonful dropped into a saucer of iced water forms a semi-solid layer. Whip the egg white and add to the hot syrup, whisking continuously (preferably using an electric whisk), until the whole mixture is cold. Add the candied fruit and nuts, fold in the chilled whipped cream and freeze in a cassata mould (or a chilled basin) for 3 hours.

Make the raspberry sauce by liquidizing the fruit and pushing it through a fine sieve. Serve the cassata in slices on a layer of sauce, decorated according to taste.

FOR FOUR PEOPLE

Hot Apple Pancakes

SPAIN

VICTORIA ROQUE
PEDRO SUBIJANA

VICTORIA ROQUE

AZULETE

Barcelona

Barcelona, Spain's second city and the capital of Catalonia, has seen a renaissance in recent years. As restrictions on regional autonomy and on the use of the Catalan language were lifted, new economic and cultural strength returned to the city of Picasso and Gaudi. The Barcelonans walked with new assurance and the Ramblas seemed fuller of colour and animation than ever before. For many people, especially young artists and designers, it became one of Europe's most exciting places to visit, and if the pace has perhaps become a little less frenetic recently, there is always the 1992 Olympic Games to look forward to . . . The city has always had good restaurants, with the cosmopolitan flavour appropriate to a major seaport, but the style and range of cooking and ambience has widened dramatically of late. Nowhere is all this seen to better advantage than in the Restaurante Azulete, the remarkable creation of Victoria Roque. Her dazzling glass palace is the most pleasant place in Barcelona to dine, and the food is some of the most original in Spain.

Victoria Roque was born here, the youngest of three daughters of a prosperous middle-class family. Her sisters both became interior designers: she married young, and with her first husband José Sanglas, opened a small restaurant in 1973 near the family's summer house at Bagur on the Costa Brava. The local people there had nicknamed the young Victoria 'the canary' because of her inordinate fondness for eating raw greenery – not then or now a highly valued part of the Spanish diet – and so El Canario was the obvious name for the restaurant. She had always been fascinated by cooking, and as a child used to run home from school to help in the kitchen. The Roque family ate both Spanish and French food, so at El Canario 'I went on cooking exactly what we ate at home'. In spite of her family's initial horror at their daughter's choice of work, it was a success, and she began to think seriously about cooking as a long-term career. Her parents were frequent visitors to Roger Vergé's Moulin de Mougins, and they arranged for her to work briefly for him. It was her first experience of a big professional kitchen – 'Roger Vergé and his staff opened my eyes to the realities and possibilities of cooking'. She was to return many times to the Moulin, but she also spent time with Georges Blanc at Vonnas, and with Jacques Maximin at the Negresco in Nice. In Italy she worked with Gualtiero Marchesi in Milan and at San Domenico in Imola, and in Munich with Heinz Winkler. These were mainly short visits, not *stages* in the normal sense of the word, as she now had a small daughter, Andrea, at home, but they exposed her to a whole range of culinary experience. Roger Vergé may

The painted screen at the entrance to Azulete

176

Victoria Roque and her senior staff in the dining room at Azulete

The cheese selection includes many Spanish regional varieties of cow, sheep and goat cheeses as well as French ones.

Victoria Roque is a slim and elegant figure. In her baggy black trousers and neat white coat she looks younger than her years. But there is no question of who rules the kitchen, where she constantly experiments with new ideas and also supervises the presentation of every dish.

have been the first and most important influence on Victoria Roque, but the time she spent in Taiwan in 1986 made an enormous impression on her, particularly the quality of cooking attained there with the most basic ingredients and equipment. Traces of Chinese influence can be seen on her menus today, for example in Lambs' Brains in the Peking Style.

Perhaps because her family and upbringing was cosmopolitan by the standards of the time, she feels herself to be Mediterranean rather than Spanish, and Spanish rather than Catalan. She has been little influenced by the current fashion for regional Spanish cooking, and for that reason, and because she has always shunned the media, she has received far less recognition inside Spain than she has abroad. Foreign journalists usually ask her whether she has found it difficult to make a career as a woman restaurateur – especially those looking for signs of prejudice and expecting to find it rampant in Spain. In fact, in the local family restaurants of Spain, cooks have usually been women, and her first venture, though resisted by her family, was regarded as no more than a cheerful eccentricity on the part of a middle-class young woman. Azulete, a smart city restaurant, was a different matter, but by this time she had established her reputation as a cook through the friends she made outside Spain. 'I was very lucky, the other chefs were very, very kind to me. I suppose I could even say I was spoiled by them.' She was also by now married to her second husband, the internationally-known designer Oscar Tusquet, who devised the present restaurant and whose friends and business connections came to eat. 'When we started, people said, we must go because the chef is a woman; then they said the place is beautiful and the food is good, and now it does not matter whether or not I am a woman.'

Azulete, Victoria's second restaurant of that name in Barcelona – the first was in Calle Camp – is in the Via Augusta, a pink turn-of-the-century town house set back from the street. When she found it, the house had been a nursery school and was showing its age. With great skill it has been refurbished without losing its slightly melancholy atmosphere, with plain linen covers on the easy chairs and sofas, and chandeliers elegantly swathed in dust-covers. 'We wanted it to feel like a town house which has been shut up for the summer.' This might seem eccentric, but it is the perfect counterpoint to the ultra-modern cocktail bar, where young Barcelonans can choose from a choice of fifty cocktails and 'fantasias' – and even more so to the fairyland beyond. As at Marc Meneau's L'Espérance, the main dining-room is a conservatory, built out from the back of the house; an elegant glass and metal structure supported by cast-iron corinthian columns and hung with slightly raffish striped internal awnings. It almost fills the large rear garden, and at night the guests look out on a floodlit fringe of greenery, palms, mulberries and every kind of climbing plant. An ancient bay tree even protrudes into the restaurant itself; a central fountain splashes among trailing plants, and a period marble fireplace holds a log fire in winter. The furniture is cast-iron, painted dark green, and the tablecloths pink, with plain white plates and simple glassware. Azulete is essentially an evening place of unique charm, for the beautiful people, who arrive late and stay late, though not as late as they would in Madrid.

The kitchen is in the lower part of the house, reached through glass swing-doors so heavy that the waiters' stamina must be severely tested by the end of a long evening. As at Dominique Nahmias's Olympe, the kitchen is small and storage limited – a licence to extend under the front garden is held up because the Barcelona Metro runs (conveniently and inaudibly) under the street outside. Efficiency and routine are therefore all-important, and Victoria is lucky to have enjoyed exceptional continuity in her kitchen *brigade* and waiting staff. Her sous-chef, José Jimenez, has been with her from the beginning and takes complete charge during her absence, and many of the other chefs have spent most of their working lives with her. This is partly because opportunities, and therefore temptations, for talented young chefs are far fewer in Spain than they would be in France or Britain, and partly because her personal style has attracted the kind of chef who is happy doing a prestigious job well, and who does not yearn for independence. She takes a personal interest in everyone who works for her – attending their weddings and family celebrations, even turning a blind eye to the television set tuned at slack moments to important football matches. The result is a loyal and immaculately trained staff. The financial side is looked after by her first husband. 'No one can understand why we all get on so well, but we do.'

In her kitchen she is undisputed queen, sitting cross-legged on the stainless steel *passe* in her baggy black trousers and neat white coat while she discusses this or that dish for the next service, or grabs a quick bowl of soup. She drinks only Coca-Cola, having decided that if she did not want to drink wine she should find a substitute available everywhere, and smokes (unlike her clients) only a few cigarettes a day. Her daily work-out in a local gymnasium and her natural dynamism have kept her slim and elegant at forty, and with her dark hair drawn back in a silver-clasped pigtail, she sometimes looks almost oriental.

Her cooking is eclectic in the extreme, drawing on the nouvelle cuisine, on Spanish cooking, on anything which fires her imagination. If she eats a dish in a restaurant abroad she may copy it, with acknowledgment: a terrine based on one of Raymond Blanc's, for instance, or an idea for a potato confection from Georges Blanc. She is also constantly experimenting with new ideas, always seeing them as complete dishes, with their garnishes and as they will appear to the client. Her attitude to ingredients is practical and no-nonsense, and although she uses agents in the huge Boqueria wholesale market, she often shops in the local Mercado Galvany for extra kitchen supplies and to keep up with developments. The fish must be the freshest and the vegetables the best. The five different kinds of bread are bought in, and excellent Spanish truffles are bottled on the premises for use throughout the year. Because the restaurant can rely on over ninety-five per cent bookings every evening, and because the basic menu changes only three times a year, there is little waste and no need for freezers or *sous-vide* machines.

Many guests choose the Menú de Degustatión (the staff pray fervently that it won't be too many, as the menu involves small portions of many different courses and makes a great deal of extra work). This menu changes from time to time, but typically it might start with *amuse-gueules* – deep-fried chicken and foie gras croquettes, beignets of salt cod and a Catalan speciality of toast spread with tomato, duck ham, oil and garlic. An Ajo Blanco – a delicate creamy garlic soup – follows, then a salad of cold marinated chicken breast. After red mullet in a rosemary cream sauce with couscous comes a grapefruit sorbet made with

a dash of dry vermouth. Lamb cutlets wrapped in spinach and encased in puff pastry are the last of the main courses. A selection of cheeses is then offered, including Spanish cow, sheep and goat cheeses, followed by a choice between three different desserts: the Corona de Naranja, a vanilla crème brûlée and a house speciality of fresh figs served with honey and raspberry sauce. The à la carte menu has a broad spectrum that includes expensive 'standards' like smoked salmon, caviar, salmon and steak for less adventurous diners, and original dishes like the rabbit stuffed with black pudding and the fresh sardine fillets rolled round an egg-cream stuffing and served on a bed of salad leaves. The olive oil is a pungent green Spanish variety, but nut oils are used for more delicate vinaigrettes.

The wine list is sound but limited in scope, partly because there is not yet room for a proper cellar, although the customers certainly seem satisfied with the good-quality Spanish and French wines and house champagne. This fact would certainly deny her the second Michelin star her cooking and the ambience of Azulete deserve, but in reality she does not seek further recognition. She has achieved what she set out to do, and does not want the pressures which a new star would bring. Her kitchen works as she wants it, her restaurant is full every night with appreciative customers and she still has time to spend at home with her daughter, husband and friends, and time for holidays in England visiting Lutyens houses and famous country gardens. Her self-knowledge and composure is the key to Azulete's success and is perfectly expressed in the screen at the entrance to Azulete, where she stands, painted with her beagle Pok, looking serenely into the distance into the mirrors over the cocktail bar.

Azulete – a dazzling glass palace

Ajo Blanco

Cold Garlic Soup

325 ml (11 fl oz) olive oil
1 egg
500 g (1 lb 2 oz) ripe tomatoes, peeled and
seeded
200 g (7 oz) cucumber, peeled
1 clove of garlic, peeled
chopped parsley
wine vinegar
salt and white pepper

Make a mayonnaise with the oil and the whole egg, but do not season at this stage. Liquidize the tomatoes, cucumber and garlic together. Mix this vegetable purée with the mayonnaise gradually, stirring with a wooden spoon. Add water until you have a thinnish white/pink soup, and season with salt and pepper. Add vinegar a few drops at a time, tasting constantly. Chill the soup.

Serve very cold, decorated with a little chopped parsley. This is a most delicate and subtle soup, ideal for a hot evening.

FOR SIX PEOPLE

Ensalada Templada de Sardinas

Warm Sardine Salad

1 head of curly endive
15 fresh sardines – about 750 g (1½ lb) in all
9 egg yolks
200 ml (7 fl oz) milk
15 g (½ oz) cornflour
6 large ripe tomatoes, peeled and seeded
olive oil
4 tablespoons vinaigrette
salt and pepper

Wash the endive and separate it into sprigs. Drain well and dry in a cloth.

Wash the sardines and remove heads and intestines. Lift the fillets off the back-bone, leaving the skin on. Rinse and pat dry. Roll each fillet up, leaving a cavity in the middle, and set aside on a lightly oiled baking tray.

Preheat the oven to 180°C/350°F/Gas 4. Beat the yolks, milk and cornflour together thoroughly. Cook very gently over a low flame or in the upper part of a double boiler, stirring constantly, until the mixture thickens. Season with salt and pepper. Using a forcing-bag with a medium nozzle, fill the cavity of each rolled sardine fillet with this mixture.

Liquidize or process the tomatoes, season and add a little good olive oil.

Bake the sardines for 5 minutes. Meanwhile have ready six warm plates and divide the tomato purée between them. Place a mound of endive on each plate and sprinkle with vinaigrette. Remove the sardines from the baking tray with a spatula and arrange round the endive.

FOR SIX PEOPLE

Escalopa de Lubina a las Aceitunas Negras

Sea Bass with Black Olives

2 kg (4½ lb) sea bass
500 g (1 lb 2 oz) black olives preserved in
brine
3 tablespoons olive oil
Swiss chard to make 250 g (9 oz) after de-stalking
500 ml (18 fl oz) single cream
small tomatoes, whole stoned black olives and
small boiled potatoes to decorate
salt and pepper

Lift off the two fillets of the sea bass, removing the skin and as many bones as possible. Cut into six equal fillets, making them as rectangular as you can. Wash, pat dry and season with salt and pepper.

Stone the olives and process them with the oil to make a very smooth paste. Pass it through a fine sieve and smear a layer on the upper side of each escalope.

Boil the de-stalked chard leaves in water for 7 minutes. Drain and add the cream. Liquidize or mix with a hand-held liquidizer. Sieve and season lightly, and set aside in a warm place. Steam the fish for about 5 minutes over boiling water. Divide the hot sauce between six heated plates, lift the fillets carefully out of the steamer with a slotted spoon and place one, olive side up, in the centre of each plate. Decorate with a few tiny tomatoes, a few whole stoned black olives and small cooked new potatoes.

FOR SIX PEOPLE

Cold Garlic Soup

Warm Sardine Salad

Sea Bass with Black Olives

Saddle of Rabbit Stuffed in the Catalan Style

Preparing the mullet

Scaling the mullet

Lifting the fillets off the backbone

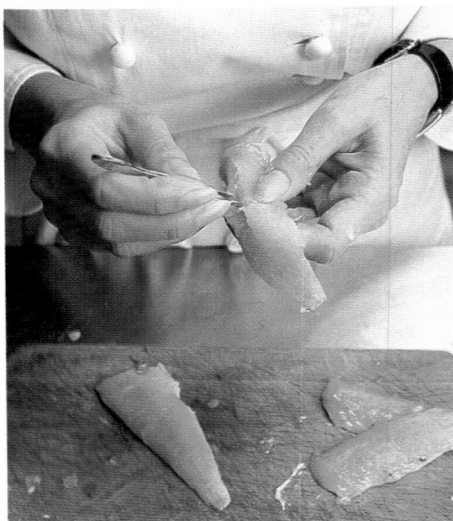

The small bones are removed with tweezers.

Deep diagonal cuts are made in each fillet.

A mint leaf is inserted in each cut.

An earthenware dish is brushed with butter.

Filetes de Salmonetes a la Hierbabuena

Red Mullet with Fresh Mint and a Mint Vinaigrette

6 very fresh mullet, 250g (8¾oz) each
a bunch of fresh mint
2 tablespoons unsalted butter
18 artichoke hearts
lemon juice
300 ml (½ pint) olive oil
5 medium-sized ripe tomatoes, peeled, seeded and diced
salt and white pepper

This is one of Victoria Roque's favourite first courses but, because she also likes to cook red mullet in a rosemary cream sauce, she alternates the two recipes on her menu. The mullet must be both small and very fresh. Because the skin is an essential part of the dish, every scale must be removed with a sharp knife or a special fish-scaler like the one Victoria Roque is using in the photograph.

Lift the fillets off the backbones and discard the heads and tails. Skin side uppermost, make three deep cuts in each fillet without severing them completely. Season each fillet well with salt and white pepper, rubbing them in with the tips of the fingers. Select enough handsome mint leaves and insert one in each cut (two if they are small). Butter a shallow earthenware dish large enough to hold the fillets in a single layer. Carefully lay the fillets in the dish, brush them with a spoonful of water and softened butter and cover with foil.

Bring a pan of salted water, acidulated with lemon juice, to the boil and cook the artichoke hearts for 4 minutes. Drain and keep warm.

Preheat the oven to 200°C/400°F/Gas 6 and cook the mullet for 6 minutes. Remove and let them cool to room temperature while you make the mint vinaigrette with the olive oil, lemon juice, 15 mint leaves and salt and pepper to taste. The sauce should be liquidized.

Arrange the cooled mullet fillets on plates, each surrounded by three warm artichoke hearts filled with diced tomato, and pour the liquidized vinaigrette over the vegetables.

FOR SIX PEOPLE

Cooking the mullet

The fillets fit snugly in a single layer.

They are brushed with butter.

Six minutes in a medium oven are sufficient.

Garnishing and serving

Warm artichoke hearts are arranged.

The liquidized vinaigrette is poured around.

The finished dish

Lambs' Brains in the Peking Style

Silla de Conejo Relleno a la Catalana

Saddle of Rabbit Stuffed in the Catalan Style

*the saddles from three domesticated rabbits,
with their bones in*
*400 g (14 oz) minced pork neck or breast meat,
seasoned*
*300 g (10½ oz) dark blood sausage (butifarra
negra)*
1.5 litres (2½ pints) chicken stock

Sauce
*200 g (7 oz) each of finely chopped carrot,
onion and leek*
*a bay leaf and a sprig each of parsley and
thyme*
150 ml (¼ pint) dry sherry
1.25 litres (2¼ pints) chicken stock
1.25 litres (2¼ pints) veal stock

Bean purée
*500 g (1 lb 2 oz) dried haricot beans, soaked,
cooked and drained*
milk
75 g (3 oz) unsalted butter
salt and pepper

Remove and set aside the bones from the three saddles. Trim, but retain the flaps of skin on either side. Put the stock to heat in a flameproof roasting pan large enough to hold it and the saddles, and preheat the oven to 180°C/350°F/Gas 4. Place a saddle flat on a working surface and cover with a third of the minced pork. Place a third of the blood sausage, in one piece, lengthwise on the pork and roll up the saddle so that the skin flaps overlap. Repeat with the other two saddles. Wrap each in muslin, and tie with string. Simmer in the stock for 20 minutes.

Meanwhile, make the sauce. Chop the saddle bones coarsely and brown them with a very little oil in the oven. Add the chopped vegetables and herbs and cook them without letting them brown. Remove the roasting pan from the oven and add the sherry. Reduce to half over a moderate heat, then pour over the chicken and veal stocks. Reduce slowly by half, strain into a pan, season and keep hot. Remove the saddles from the poaching water, unwrap them and cut each into 8 slices. Put four slices on to each of six

heated plates and pipe a little bean purée (see below) in an attractive mound in the centre. Pour the hot sauce over the saddles and the uncovered part of the plate, and serve immediately.

The purée of dried beans can be made in advance and kept warm. Heat the cooked beans in a little milk over a low flame and when they are very soft, push them through a fine sieve, or liquidize and sieve. Stir in the butter and season.

Note: if you have no home-made stocks, good stock cubes can be used.

FOR SIX PEOPLE

Sesos de Cordero al Estilo de Pekin

Lambs' Brains in the Peking Style

6 sets of lamb's brains
100 g (3½ oz) flour
100 g (3½ oz) butter
salt and pepper

Sauce
35 g (generous ounce) sugar
2 teaspoons white wine vinegar
2 tablespoons dry sherry
2 tablespoons Worcestershire Sauce
2 tablespoons soy sauce
2 tablespoons hoi-sin sauce
1 teaspoon salt
1 teaspoon sunflower oil
650 ml (1 pint 2 fl oz) chicken stock
1 teaspoon cornflour, moistened with water

Soak the brains in cold water for 1 hour and rinse away the blood. Pat dry, season and coat with flour. Heat the butter in a heavy frying-pan and fry the brains till they are golden – about 10 minutes over a low flame, turning them once. Remove them carefully from the pan with a slotted spoon and drain on kitchen paper.

Make the sauce by mixing all the ingredients except the cornflour in a saucepan. Heat over a low flame, stirring all the time. When the mixture is hot but not boiling, add the moistened cornflour and continue stirring until the sauce has thickened slightly.

Put one set of brains on each of six heated plates and pour the sauce over them. Accompany with salad, or perhaps with boiled baby corn cobs, boiled pickling onions and braised leeks or celery.

FOR SIX PEOPLE

An Azulete waiter about to serve amuse-gueules

Grapes in a Cream Pastry

Corona de Naranja
Fría y Caliente

Cold and Hot Orange Crown

Crown
8 eggs
250 g (8¾ oz) sugar
250 ml (8 fl oz) single cream
250 ml (8 fl oz) fresh strained orange juice

Ice-cream
85 ml (6 tablespoons) single cream
85 ml (6 tablespoons) milk
3 egg yolks
85 g (3 oz) sugar
75 ml (5½ tablespoons) fresh strained
orange juice

Candied orange peel
the peel of two oranges, cut in matchsticks
125 g (4½ oz) sugar
250 ml (8 fl oz) water
mint leaves and orange segments to decorate

Hojaldrina de Uvas

Grapes in a Cream Pastry

Pastry
30 g (1 oz) melted unsalted butter
30 g (1 oz) icing sugar
30 g (1 oz) honey
30 g (1 oz) flour
1 egg white

Caramel
200 g (7 oz) sugar
25 ml (1¾ tablespoons) water

Cream
375 ml (13 fl oz) milk
150 ml (¼ pint) single cream
100 g (3½ oz) sugar
25 g (1 oz) cornflour
3 egg yolks, beaten
125 ml (4 fl oz) grape juice
125 ml (4 fl oz) sweet white wine
2 tablespoons double cream, whipped
54 peeled and seeded white grapes

Process all the ingredients for the pastry and allow to stand for an hour. Preheat the oven to 200°C/400°F/Gas 6. Lightly butter a baking tray and spoon on the pastry in little circles, taking care that they do not touch. Bake until golden brown (about 3 minutes). Remove with a spatula and leave to cool on a flat surface.

To make the caramel, first boil the water. Then melt the sugar in a separate heavy-bottomed pan, stirring all the time until it starts to caramelize. Add the hot water and mix well. Pour the cooling caramel on to a lightly greased sheet of aluminium foil, and before it sets, cut out six circles of the same diameter as the pastry circles. Let them cool and then loosen them carefully with a spatula.

For the cream, bring half the milk with 2½ tablespoons single cream and all the sugar to almost boiling point. Meanwhile mix the rest of the milk and another 2½ tablespoons cream with the cornflour, add the yolks and beat the mixture thoroughly. Fold into the hot milk mixture and whisk over a low flame until it thickens. Let it cool, then divide in half. Add to one part 5 tablespoons of grape juice, 5 tablespoons of white wine and the remaining single cream, beat well and strain. This is the sauce. Mix the remaining custard cream with the remaining grape juice and wine and fold in 2 tablespoons of whipped cream to make the filling.

Have ready six dessert plates and pour a layer of sauce on each. Place a pastry disc in the centre of each, with 3 grapes on each disc. Cover them with the filling, using a forcing bag, and repeat with two more layers of pastry and filling. Top with a caramel disc, decorate and serve.

FOR SIX PEOPLE

To make the crown, preheat the oven to 150°C/300°F/Gas 2. Beat the eggs with the sugar, add the cream, beat again and then add the orange juice. Lightly butter six 10 cm (4 inch) ring moulds and divide the mixture between them. Place the moulds in a bain-marie with enough hot water to come half way up the sides of the moulds, cover lightly with a sheet of aluminium foil and bake for approximately 1 hour. Leave to cool for a while and then turn out.

To make the ice-cream, bring the milk and cream almost to boiling point. Beat the egg yolks with the sugar until the mixture is pale and forms a ribbon when dropped from the spoon. Add the slightly cooled milk and cream mixture to the egg yolks and beat together. Add the orange juice, beat again and allow to cool. Freeze.

To make the candied peel, boil the sugar and water together, add the orange julienne and reduce over a low flame until nearly all the water has evaporated. Allow to dry out slightly on a rack.

To serve, warm the crowns through thoroughly, put a scoop of ice cream in the middle of each, decorate with candied orange peel, orange segments and mint leaves and serve as soon as possible.

FOR SIX PEOPLE

Cold and Hot Orange Crown

PEDRO SUBIJANA

RESTAURANTE AKELAŔE & EL BODEGON

San Sebastián & Madrid

There has recently been a great revival of interest in Spanish regional cooking, both inside and outside Spain. The long distances and the relative neglect of some areas by foreign tourists, together with innate regional pride, have preserved much of the individuality of the different cuisines, and the chefs of Galicia, Valencia and the Basque country are rapidly coming into their own. As non-package tourism increases and Spanish Government organizations, like Wines and Food from Spain, export their star chefs to demonstrate in other countries, Spanish food is beginning to be appreciated and understood on an ever-increasing scale. There is no Gault-Millau guide to Spanish restaurants at the moment and they are somewhat cavalierly treated by Michelin, but it can only be a matter of time before more of these talented cooks achieve the recognition they deserve – culinary masters on a par with many of their rosetted colleagues in the rest of Europe.

One of the most interesting chefs working today – who does have two Michelin stars – is Pedro Subijana from the Basque town of San Sebastián, where his Restaurante Akelaŕe is highly regarded. His cooking can also be sampled in Madrid, where he supervises the menu, trains the chefs and cooks for one or two days a week at El Bodegon, one of the capital's most elegant restaurants. (The photographs for this chapter were taken there.)

He hesitated for some time before agreeing to work outside Akelaŕe, 'but one day they came and persuaded me that they were serious and could offer me all the advantages'.

Any chef working on the Atlantic coast of Spain has the advantage of sublime seafood, and when Subijana flies into Madrid each week he brings fern-lined refrigerated containers full of live lobsters, oysters and spider crabs and superb sea-bass, tuna, hake, monkfish, sole, grouper and squid, and sometimes tiny elvers for a delicious dish served so hot that it is eaten with special wooden forks to prevent the diner burning his mouth or fingers. Good fish has long been a speciality of Madrid, in spite of its distance from the sea, but it is the glory of Pedro Subijana's cuisine. Other specialities include snails in puff pastry, spinach ravioli, hearty vegetable soups, roast pigeon with semolina gnocchi, salt cod in various guises, lamb with mushroom sauce and stuffed aubergines, and a fine selection of pastries and creams. These last, being egg and sugar heavy, tend to be less popular with northern Europeans, but they do include feathery *hojaldre* (puff pastry) confections with greengages or other fruit and some fruit sorbets. Also typical of the Basque country, but prepared with inimitable style, are the beef dishes – mainly in the

El Bodegon – the interior

Pedro Subijana

An earthenware dish of tiny elvers is a house speciality. (Indeed, these tiny, silvery baby eels are a Basque speciality.) They are served so hot that guests are provided with a small wooden fork to prevent them burning their mouths or fingers.

Fish is the crowning glory of El Bodegon's cuisine. Fresh fish and live shellfish are air-freighted to Madrid in fern-lined refrigerated containers. Here, Pedro Subijana (left) and one of the chefs inspect the morning's delivery.

form of sauced grilled or pan-fried cuts of sirloin or steaks. Game, which he particularly enjoys cooking because it is a challenge to the cook, is also much used in season, and includes wild quail, woodcock, boar, venison and hare, as well as the partridges so beloved of Spanish sportsmen. He likes to use his local white wine, Txacolí, with sole and with hake cheeks.

Pedro Subijana describes the menu as a mixture of traditional and modern. 'It's the same cooking here as at San Sebastián, though I don't do some of the more specialized dishes. In principle it's a Basque restaurant, but it is also quite special to me, and not exactly what people expect when they go to a Basque restaurant elsewhere. It's a personal cuisine.' The *Abanico* of fishes is modern, derived from his contacts with the nouvelle cuisine, for example, while the *chipironcitos* (tiny squid known as *dedales* or thimbles), stuffed with their chopped tentacles and stewed in their own ink, are traditional. He enjoys puns, and the *Endivia* of fish becomes by a simple transposition of letters an 'envidia' or jealousy, with each of the different types of fish vying for supremacy. Vegetables are seasonal and local, mainly from Madrid's excellent markets, and include the Spanish truffles, once almost exclusively exported to France, but now used once more in Spanish cooking. For salads he uses a Jaén or Córdoba oil from the olive regions of southern Spain, but for cooking he prefers a light olive oil. Cider vinegar, a Basque speciality, is much used, as are the various nut oils. The mainly Spanish cheeses include many sheep's varieties, perhaps because Pedro Subijana acts as chief judge at the annual September Basque fair where animals, vegetables and dairy products made by local

farmers are judged, and half the winning cheese auctioned for huge sums to help local charities.

The wine list is very largely made up of Spanish wines – Valladolids, Catalan wines and Riojas, all reasonably priced, with a token choice of French and German wines and French champagnes. Subijana takes a keen interest in the choice of wine, feeling strongly that prices should not be too high. He also thinks that people are too conservative and hopes to educate them into trying lesser known regional wines.

Pedro Subijana, moustachioed and handsome like so many of his fellow Basques, has an imposing presence and an infectious laugh – also the occasional bark to reprove an erring apprentice. Born on 5 November, 1948, in San Sebastián, he came from a family with gastronomic connections. His grandfather sold high-quality produce in Bayonne and his grandmother, though not professional, cooked for a succession of lodgers. His father was a successful pâtissier, but left the profession for a business career, confining his cooking to Christmas and family celebrations, when according to Basque custom 'the women got out of the kitchen and left it all to me and my father and uncle'. There was never any real doubt in the family about young Pedro's career; even when he joined a local boy scout troop he instantly became their cook. When he finished high school he obtained a place to study medicine at Pamplona, which his family urged him to take up. Instead, he went off at seventeen to the catering school in Madrid and, after completing the first diploma, returned to a

Restaurante Akelaŕe

hotel near San Sebastián. There he was the only pupil, in which he counted himself lucky, and happy to be back among his friends. After a four-year course, he turned teacher for two years, only starting his career in earnest in 1970, at the Hotel Marie Christina in San Sebastián. He married, and in due course became chef-de-cuisine of the Mesón de Idiáquez at Tolosa, not far from San Sebastián.

This period saw the beginning of the *nueva cocina vasca*, and with others he founded a group of eleven chefs whose interest matched his, including Arzac, Arguiñano, Castillo, Chomin and Roteta. They are now dispersed but still keep in touch, holding dinners which, he says, are not only highly enjoyable and a showcase for Basque cuisine, but help iron out any little feuds or jealousies. Paul Bocuse and the Troisgros brothers both visited San Sebastián, and as a result Subijana worked brief *stages* at both Collonges au Mont d'Or and Roanne at various times. Briefly, he and his wife had their own restaurant at Hernani, but when Zalacaín opened in Madrid he joined their *brigade* for 1972–3. In 1975 the opportunity came for him to return to San Sebastián to set up in partnership at Akelaŕe, and there he has stayed, earning his first Michelin rosette in 1978 and his second in 1983. He is now sole owner, and has been awarded the National Gastronomy prize for the best chef in Spain and named as the best Spanish chef by the Club des Gourmets.

Akelaŕe sits high above the sea, all whitewashed walls and flowers, and could hardly be in greater contrast to the suave city restaurant which is El Bodegon. In a residential quarter to the north of Madrid, well away from the noisy streets of the centre,

it is entirely modern, occupying the ground floor of a large building, and backing on to one of Madrid's leading restaurants, Zalacaín. The lights are discreet – unusual for a Spanish restaurant – and the walls are lined with muted red and beige velours. The main restaurant seats 60 and there is a luxurious private room decorated with hunting scenes. At lunch the guests are almost all men; in the evening the restaurant becomes more of a fashionable place for smart Madrid couples.

The kitchen has eleven cooks, supervised by Pedro Subijana. He does not mix much with the El Bogedon clients – quite the opposite to the situation at Akelaŕe, where he knows many of his customers of old and likes to vary dishes according to their tastes. He hates uniformity of taste and also the more extreme forms of nouvelle cuisine where flavour is subordinated to the picture on the plate. Everything he cooks must have its own integrity and taste of its individual ingredients. He delights in the variations between the different regions of Spain and is fascinated by the fact that one dish – for instance, gazpacho – can turn up in a dozen different ways. His work is genuinely his life, broken only by his December holiday which he spends in his house in the country and where he and his wife entertain their extended family (she has eight brothers, so there may be as many as 45 people), and he enjoys walking in the mountains and tending his herb garden. This is the break which enables him to continue working what seems like a punishing schedule. But for Pedro Subijana, cooking is a passion.

Ensalada Templada con Bonito Fresco

Warm Salad of Fresh Tuna Fish

170 g (6 oz) skinned fillet of fresh tuna, thinly sliced
4 tablespoons vinaigrette
140 g (5 oz) attractive mixed salad leaves
4 tablespoons diced mixed peppers which have been roasted and peeled
half a clove of garlic, very finely chopped

Arrange the tuna fillets in a single layer in a rectangular baking dish and pour over the vinaigrette. Cook briefly under the grill, turning the fillets once. Remove and set aside while you arrange the salad. Have ready four plates and arrange the salad leaves decoratively on them, with half a tablespoon of diced peppers mixed with a pinch of finely chopped garlic on each side. Divide the tuna fillets between the plates and pour over the warm vinaigrette from the baking dish.

FOR FOUR PEOPLE

Kokotxas de Merluza en Salsa al Pil-Pil

Hake Cheeks 'Pil-Pil'

150–200 g (5–7 oz) hake cheeks (see note)
3 tablespoons good olive oil
1 clove of garlic, very finely chopped
1 small hot red chilli, seeded and chopped
1 tablespoon chopped flat-leaved parsley
salt

Heat the oil in a shallow earthenware flameproof cooking dish (if possible the traditional round brown *cazuela*). Put in the garlic, and the chilli if you want a fiery result, and cook without browning, shaking the dish all the time. Remove from the heat and allow the juices of the garlic to settle a little. Then season the hake cheeks and add them to the dish, skin side uppermost. Cover and leave on the lowest possible flame for 5–10 minutes, shaking the dish with a rotary motion from time to time, using both hands in the traditional manner.

Raise the heat slightly, remove the lid and twirl the dish continuously to amalgamate the gelatinous sauce. When the sauce is bubbling gently, in the way which gives it the name 'pil-pil', add the chilli (if you have not done so earlier) and sprinkle with chopped parsley. Taste for seasoning and serve immediately.

Note: this celebrated dish, although it seems simplicity itself, is in fact quite tricky to do. The temperature and the constant swirling must be just right if the sauce is to acquire its famous gelatinous texture. It is also very expensive as at least one dozen large hake are needed to provide the cheeks for a single small dish.

If you prefer a thinner sauce, then you can add a little water, fish stock or, like Pedro Subijana, a dry white wine like his own local Txacolí. Some people also add a few drops of milk.

FOR ONE PERSON

Cutting the hake

The hake cheek

Hake Cheeks 'Pil-Pil'

Chipironcitos de Anzuelo en su Tinta

Stuffed BabySquid in Their Own Ink

60 baby squid
500 ml (1 pint) olive oil
6 large onions, chopped
1 small head of garlic, halved
3 green peppers, seeded and chopped
7 tablespoons white wine
3 tomatoes, thinly sliced
7 tablespoons red wine
salt and pepper

Clean the squid, one by one, by gently pulling the insides out. Carefully reserve the ink sacs in a bowl of water. Carefully scrape the suckers to remove the rings from the tentacles and gently remove and discard the beak from in between the small tentacles. Turn the cleaned body sac the right way out and stuff it with the tentacles and the fleshy parts of the squid.

Season the squid and sauté in a little olive oil in a covered pan (to avoid spattering) until lightly browned. Set them aside while you make the sauce.

Gently cook the onion in a pan of olive oil over a low heat. Add the garlic and green peppers and sweat the mixture thoroughly. Add the tomatoes.

Process the ink in a blender with the water in which the sacs were reserved and with the white wine. Pour all this into the sauce. Transfer the sauce to the blender. Coat the squid in the deposit remaining on the bottom of the pan and transfer them to a heatproof earthenware casserole. Loosen the caramelized deposit with the red wine and 7 tablespoons of water. Add this to the sauce. Purée the sauce in a blender and then rub it through a fine wire sieve.

Pour the sauce over the squid and simmer gently for one hour. Remove from the heat and set aside. When required, bring back to the boil.

Note: Squid are available almost all year round on Spain's North Atlantic coast, but the very tiny ones ('thimbles') are only available in the height of summer, from August to September.

FOR SIX PEOPLE

Stuffed Baby Squid in Their Own Ink

Lubina a la Pimienta Verde

Sea Bass with Green Peppercorns

4 fillets of sea bass weighing 200 g (7 oz) each,
skin on
1 tablespoon unsalted butter
3 tablespoons olive oil
1 shallot, peeled and finely chopped
50 g (1¾ oz) green peppercorns
3 tablespoons brandy
200 ml (7 fl oz) single cream

Preheat the oven to 220°C/425°F/Gas 7. Put the butter, oil and shallot in a flameproof baking dish and let the shallot soften a little. Place the sea bass fillets, skin side up, on top. Add the peppercorns, and flame with the brandy. Add the cream, and cook in the hot oven for 7 minutes, uncovered.

Remove the fish to four warmed plates and keep hot. Reduce the sauce a little, taste for seasoning and pour over the fish. If you like, decorate with a little fish made out of puff pastry.

FOR FOUR PEOPLE

Patridge with Chickpea Purée

Perdix con Pure de Garbanzos

Partridge with Chickpea Purée

4 young partridges, plucked and cleaned
450g (1 lb) cooked chickpeas
approximately 225g (8oz) mixed carrots,
turnips, courgettes and potatoes, all peeled,
sliced and cooked in a little oil
bouquet garni
a little flour
olive oil
225g (8oz) diced leeks, carrots and onions
a bay leaf, sprig thyme and a peeled and
crushed clove of garlic
1 teaspoon wine vinegar
2 tablespoons brandy
6 tablespoons white wine
2 ripe tomatoes, peeled, seeded and chopped
1 teaspoon unsweetened cocoa powder
150g (5½oz) white cabbage, chopped
85g (3oz) streaky bacon, finely chopped
salt and pepper

Begin by making the chickpea purée. Warm through the chickpeas with the cooked vegetables, bouquet garni and seasoning. Remove the bouquet, liquidize and sieve.

Bone out the partridges, and set the boned birds to one side. Season the bones and dredge with flour. Brown in a little hot oil. Meanwhile take a heavy bottomed pan and brown the mixed diced vegetables, herbs and garlic gently. Add the bones, sprinkle with a few drops of wine vinegar and flame with the brandy. Add the white wine, the chopped tomatoes and the cocoa. Add water to cover and cook very gently for 1–1¼ hours. Season with salt, remove the bay leaf and pass first through a coarse sieve and then through a fine sieve.

Preheat the oven to 200°C/400°C/Gas 6. Truss the partridges and roast them for 25 minutes. They should be pink inside with a golden brown skin. While the partridges are roasting, blanch the chopped cabbage, drain and sauté gently with the chopped bacon. Reheat the sauce and the chickpea purée.

To serve, place the chickpea purée in a mound in the centre of a heated serving dish and arrange the roasted partridges round it. Put the cabbage and bacon on one side and a selection of simply cooked vegetables, for example halved carrots and young turnips with potato croquettes, on the other. Pour the sauce over the partridges.

FOR FOUR PEOPLE

Filete de Cordero 'en croûte' al Aroma de Tomillo y Limón

Fillet of Lamb 'en croûte' flavoured with Thyme and Lemon

450 g (1 lb) best lamb fillet, boned and cut into chunks
400 g (14½ oz) shortcrust or flaky pastry
4 tablespoons each chopped aubergine and mushrooms, lightly cooked in oil and seasoned
1 egg, beaten
grated rind of 1 small lemon
a good pinch of fresh thyme leaves

Preheat the oven to 200°C/400°F/Gas 6. Divide the pastry dough into four, and roll out into large circles. Mix the lamb chunks with the cooked and seasoned vegetables and pile on the pastry circles. Fold over as if you were making Cornish pasties. Seal well and brush with beaten egg. Place in a lightly oiled baking dish and cook for 20 minutes in the preheated oven, or a little longer if you prefer your lamb well-done. Keep the lamb parcels warm on four heated plates while you pour off the juices which have escaped and let them infuse briefly with the lemon and thyme. Check seasoning, pour round the lamb parcels and serve immediately.

FOR FOUR PEOPLE

Cream Cornucopias with other pastries

Canutillos Fritos con Crema

Cream Cornucopias

6 tablespoons olive oil
200 ml (7 fl oz) full-cream milk
1 teaspoon wine vinegar
a pinch of salt
500 g (1 lb 2 oz) flour
corn or sunflower oil for frying
400 ml (¾ pint) crème pâtissière
icing sugar

Mix the oil, milk and vinegar with a little salt in a large china or glass bowl. Sift in the flour gradually, stirring all the time until you have a smooth but not hard mixture. Cover and chill for 30 minutes.

Roll out the dough with an oiled rolling-pin, and have ready 12 oiled cream-horn moulds (hollow conical metal shapes approximately 10 cm (4 inches) long). Cut the pastry into strips 2 cm (¾ inch) wide and 20 cm (8 inches) long and wind them in a spiral round the outside of the cones, starting from the pointed end. Deep fry in clean hot corn or sunflower oil, and drain on kitchen paper. Allow to cool and slide out the moulds. Pipe in the *crème pâtissière* and sprinkle with icing sugar. Serve three to each guest.

Note: these canutillos are served in memory of a famous regional cook, Joxepa of San Esteban in Navarre.

To make the *crème pâtissière*, mix 65 g (2½ oz) flour, 250 g (8¾ oz) caster sugar, and 6 egg yolks in a heavy pan. Stir in 500 ml (18 fl oz) vanilla-flavoured milk and bring to the boil, stirring. Continue boiling and stirring until the *crème* has thickened. Set aside to cool.

FOR FOUR PEOPLE

A last-minute check for the cheese selection

SWITZERLAND

ANDRÉ JAEGER

ANDRÉ JAEGER

RHEINHOTEL FISCHERZUNFT

Schaffhausen

The Rhine at Schaffhausen is a bright, clean river, full of undulating weeds, waterfowl and fish. Upstream is the inland sea of Lake Constance; downstream lie the great Rhine Falls so beloved of Victorian tourists, and the busy polluted waterway which links Basle with the North Sea. The small town straddles the river, its two halves joined by road and railway bridges, and on the northern side it climbs steeply up the vine-clad slopes of the castle hill. Just below, in a tree-lined square, is the Rheinhotel Fischerzunft, formerly the headquarters of the fishermen's guild, whose rolls of honour and family bearings still decorate the walls. The river is perhaps ten yards away, across a pleasant path: from the windows it seems almost part of the building. All this makes for an air of dreamy tranquillity, which is borne out by the present purpose of the building. For this is one of the most remarkable restaurants in Europe, created by André Jaeger and his wife Doreen Soong.

The fishermen's guild sold the building in 1898. It became and remained a traditional restaurant until only a few years ago. André Jaeger's father and mother ran it from 1957 while their children were brought up by grandparents some distance away down the Rhine, and they continued to do so later while André travelled the world gaining wide experience in the hotel business. He was managing the food and wine side of Hong Kong's most famous hotel, the Peninsula, and already married to Doreen, herself in the hotel business at the Hong Kong Hilton, when his father decided to retire. As a result, the couple resolved to come home to Switzerland to take over the restaurant at Schaffhausen.

To begin with, they continued as before, living on the upper floors of the building and serving only simple traditional dishes to the people of the town and passing travellers. André Jaeger, whose training had been a classic kitchen apprenticeship at the Beau Rivage Palace, Lausanne, and a management course at the Lausanne Hotel School, ran the dining room; the cooking was in the hands of Andrea Tognini who had worked with Jaeger senior and still works as deputy chef at the now transformed Fischerzunft. The Jaegers found this life unchallenging and unsatisfying. They missed the tastes and subtleties of oriental cooking, and could not easily satisfy their longings as there were virtually no ethnic restaurants in Switzerland and ingredients

were impossible to obtain. Using ingredients brought back from visits to Hong Kong or sent by Doreen's family, they started to cook for themselves. Their success in using Chinese techniques and flavours in conjunction with local ingredients grew, and gradually they decided to introduce a few dishes based on their discoveries into the standard menu. Sources of supply were found for spices, herbs and vegetables, and André Jaeger took over the kitchens.

From the beginning, the 'new' cooking was extraordinary: a blend of oriental themes with European ingredients. At first it met with a mixed reception: the local people looked on the dishes with suspicion – reasonably so, as in land-locked Schaffhausen few had met anything like them before. Gradually, however, the European restaurant press and then the world became aware that something extraordinary was happening, and now the Fischerzunft is a place of pilgrimage, where the menu retains only a few of the old traditional dishes such as plain grilled trout with steamed potatoes, kept for the irredeemably conservative or nostalgic customer. There are still a few taboos: shark's fin and *bêche de mer* are not served, soy sauce is treated with caution, and more revolutionary new dishes are introduced only after extensive trials. Although 'East meets West' has become almost a cliché these days, André Jaeger can rightly claim to have invented the style and to have practised it more inventively and successfully than any other chef.

A tall imposing man, André Jaeger conveys extraordinary tranquillity and calmness: in his kitchen no voices are raised, but his own soft tones invariably command instant attention. (This is partly because a period of illness some years ago has imposed on him a calmer life style than one would expect from the man who organized the catered celebration for 3,000 people when the Hong Kong-Kowloon tunnel was opened. The party was in the tunnel and the brass band must have been audible all the way to Macao.) This orderly manner extends to his immaculate clothes – his white kitchen jacket is merely a replacement for the jacket of his suit – and to his passionate love of the discipline of dressage, his main leisure activity. He and Doreen now live some twenty minutes away from the Fischerzunft, farther up the Rhine, but most of their time is spent at the hotel, which is open

André and Doreen Jaeger-Soong

An enormous tub of flowers, renewed daily, greets guests at the entrance to the main dining room. The flowers are bought from the wholesale market in Zurich and, together with all the rest of the day-to-day management of the restaurant, are Doreen's responsibility.

The dining room of the Rheinhotel Fischerzunft was formally the meeting place of the Schaffhausen fishermen's guild.

seven days a week. She is in charge of the eleven more-than-sumptuous rooms, situated in the upper part of the house, individually decorated and fitted out with every imaginable comfort. Like so many chef's wives, she is also in charge of the day-to-day management of the restaurant. Her speciality is the decor – a marvellous, eclectic mixture of old Schaffhausen prints, antique cooking equipment, Hong Kong views and Chinese porcelain – and above all, the flowers, bought from the wholesale market in Zurich, together with the vegetables and other produce. André Jaeger says proudly that his is the only restaurant in the world which spends more on flowers than on animal fats.

He warns visitors that they must not expect a Chinese kitchen, and indeed, apart from the Japanese cleavers which he alone uses, there is nothing typically oriental. His kitchen resembles other top-class European restaurant kitchens, with a *brigade* of four cooks, three apprentices, two trainees from hotel school and himself. He does not use Chinese cooks. Even though he greatly admires Hong Kong chefs, he feels they would be homesick in a town without a Chinese community, and in any case Swiss regulations would forbid it. The only foreigners he is allowed to

employ are a Portuguese dishwasher and a boy, also Portuguese, who helps Doreen with the flowers and generally runs errands. He is also at a disadvantage compared to other European chefs because all his male staff over twenty-one (and he himself until his illness) are called away to compulsory military service, on full pay, for three weeks every year. With all this, plus the difficulties of getting reliable meat and dairy products in a country which is adopting industrialized food production faster than any other, it is hardly surprising that he occasionally finds his lot hard, and almost a miracle that he manages to overcome his difficulties so successfully. Without Doreen it would be impossible. She is always at his side, and runs the dining room – with its twenty regular places extending to forty-five on gala nights – with perfect efficiency. She claims to have been unable to boil an egg or drive a car before she married; now she is expert in both fields. In addition to her perfect English, acquired at college in California, she speaks excellent German and enough of most other European languages to make customers feel immediately at home. Her six waiting staff are exceptionally well drilled in explaining to the clients exactly what each dish includes and what wine they should drink with it. Every new dish is analysed in detail with the waiting staff before it appears on the menu.

The Rheinhotel Fischerzunft

André Jaeger in his wine cellar under the castle hill

The cooking is extraordinarily meticulous. André Jaeger says that he cooks every dish 'in his head' many times before he even discusses it with Doreen and later tries it, first in the kitchen, then on the menu. Each recipe is filed, with a Polaroid photograph. Each regular client is also allocated an index card indicating his likes and dislikes, and what dishes he has eaten on previous occasions, in order that he may be coaxed to try something new. The execution is careful, and meticulously timed, based on the freshest and best ingredients that can be obtained, whether locally, or from Rungis, Brittany, Scotland, Norway, even Maine – or from the Rhine fishermen who regularly call at André Jaeger's door. His policy is always to buy local fish, for cash, even at times of glut, to ensure that he always gets first choice. If there is a surplus, live fish are put in the fish tanks at the back of the kitchen, and extra fish dishes are added to the daily menu. He also pays the local meat suppliers promptly and without questioning prices, unless they send him sub-standard meat, at which point they lose his extremely valuable account. Everything which can be made on the premises is, although some of the breads are bought in half-baked and then finished in the Fischerzunft ovens. Smoking is a particular speciality – especially of fish and duck – and is carried out once or twice a week. (See pages 204–5 for the Fischerzunft speciality – Marinated Tea-Smoked Salmon.) Ice-creams and pastas are both made every day in small quantities.

The Fischerzunft's food also happens to be exceptionally healthy, and André Jaeger always has calorific values and nutritional balance at the back of his mind when planning menus. He wants his customers to leave the table satisfied but not sated, having eaten a meal which is nutritious as well as delicious. Fish and vegetables are the staples: meat appears in small portions enlivened with unusual combinations of vegetables and spices. The oils used are mainly polyunsaturated, and butter is used sparingly. (Interestingly, the Fischerzunft serves salted butter with its excellent bread as an appetizing touch at the beginning of the meal.) Some form of starch is always included, whether it be pasta, polenta, rice, pastry or potatoes. André Jaeger deliberately has no cheeseboard, as he feels it is out of keeping with his style of cooking, and too heavy for the end of a meal. He also feels passionately that many cheeses ruin good wines. Cheese does play a part in his cooking, however, always as a dish in its own right: one starter is a piece of cold unpasteurized Boursault studded with toasted pine kernels and served with a lamb's lettuce salad.

The recipes which follow give a broad impression of André Jaeger's style, but it would be impossible to reproduce a repertoire so diverse and constantly in motion. The basic techniques are established and fully mastered by his highly competent *brigade*; the actual dishes change according to the produce available and whatever André Jaeger has dreamt up for that day. The rare grayling caviar might feature, for example, as might a cream of curry soup with coriander sprigs and two spring rolls to dip in it; a salmon trout with five Chinese spices lightly grilled with a beurre blanc sauce, and snow peas; dim sum (Chinese ravioli) with shiitake mushrooms and white fish in chilli tomato sauce; a chocolate sorbet with a warm blackberry sauce; or a gingerbread parfait with spiced apple sauce and a fig cut in a fan-shape. The desserts are often served on glass plates backed with decorative flower-strewn mirrors (the flowers used actually to be strewn directly on the plates, until the customers started to eat them).

The Rheinhotel Fischerzunft has now become an important focal point for both Swiss and international travellers wanting a luxury stop-over not far from Basle or Zürich. But it is also a local centre for good eating, whether the customers are Zürichers out for the day or businessmen. Its riverside setting, with swans sailing past at the diner's eye level, and its celebrated cellar across a perilous main road, where tastings are given to regular clients, make it a thoroughly pleasing spot. In the square, where diners can sit outside on a flowery terrace in the summer, there is a Tree of Heaven: this is entirely appropriate to the mood and feel of the place. The façade has recently been re-designed. Two white vertical banners, bearing the Fischerzunft's motif of two fishes intertwined to form the Yin-Yang emblem, float gently in the river breeze – over the legend 'Ma Cuisine du Bonheur.'

Four Chinese Delicacies in a Lacquer Box

Vier Chinesische Köstlichkeiten

Four Chinese Delicacies in a Lacquer Box

Gefüllte Shitake Pilz mit Rehtartar

Shiitake Mushrooms Stuffed with Venison Tartare

*4 whole fresh or dried shiitake mushrooms
(soaked overnight if dried)
100 g (3½ oz) good quality cut of roe deer
1 egg yolk
1 teaspoon chopped chives
salt and cumin powder, to taste*

If you are using dried mushrooms, drain and boil them in salted water for ten minutes. Chop the venison very finely and mix with the other ingredients. Remove the mushroom stems and stuff the caps with the venison tartare.

Grillierter, Marinierter Lachs

Grilled Marinated Salmon

*100 g (3½ oz) salmon, marinated in a
tablespoon of light soy sauce, seasoned with
salt and sugar to taste, for approximately
2 hours
a handful each of lamb's lettuce and chopped
Chinese cabbage
a sesame dressing made from the following:
1 teaspoonful each of light soy sauce, sesame
oil, sweet sake, white sesame seeds and black
(toasted) sesame seeds, 1 tablespoon chicken
stock, salt and sugar to taste*

Dress the salad, making sure it is not too sloppy and arrange in piles on each plate (or in each lacquer box). Heat either a grill or a non-stick pan to a temperature fierce enough to sear the salmon on both sides – it should be raw inside. Arrange on the salad.

Chinesische Ravioli mit Koriander und Ingwer

Dim Sum with Green Coriander and Ginger

*6 large prawns, raw if possible, peeled and
de-veined
¼ teaspoon bone marrow or lard
a pinch of finely chopped fresh ginger
a pinch of finely chopped green coriander
4 won ton sheets (available frozen from
Chinese supermarkets)
4 small lettuce leaves
4 green coriander leaves
salt and pepper*

Chop the prawns finely with the bone marrow or lard and add the ginger, coriander, salt and pepper. Divide the mixture between the won ton sheets and seal them tightly into little pouches. Steam over boiling water for about six minutes, covered, or until they are firm to the touch. Serve on a small lettuce leaf, topped with a coriander leaf.

Kleine Chinesische Ravioli mit Chili-Tomatensauce

Little Dim Sum with Chilli Tomato Sauce

*100 g (3½ oz) minced pork
1 fresh or dried shiitake mushroom (soaked
overnight if dried), chopped
20 g (⅔ oz) beansprouts
1 teaspoon hoi-sin (Chinese plum) sauce
4 won ton sheets (see opposite)
oil for deep frying
a small bunch of watercress, washed and
picked over
sauce made from ½ a peeled and seeded
tomato, 1 teaspoon ketchup, 1 small red chilli,
about 3 drops of sesame oil and salt and sugar,
liquidized together
salt and pepper to taste*

Mix the first four ingredients and season to taste. Make the dim sum as described opposite but deep fry in oil instead of steaming. Serve on a bed of watercress with a spoonful of the chilli tomato sauce.

FOR FOUR PEOPLE

Wine tastings are given to regular clients in the celebrated wine cellar.

Preparing the salmon

The salmon is boned and filleted.

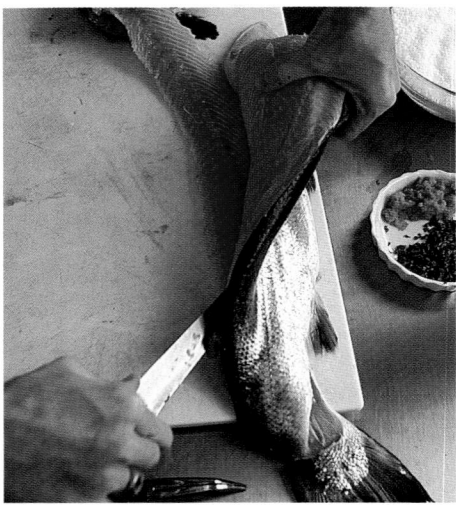

A razor-sharp Japanese knife is used.

The salmon fillet is ready for marinating.

Marinierter, Tee-Geräuchter Lachs mit Broccoli und Fritierten Broccoli Blättern mit Honig-Senf Sauce

Marinated Tea-Smoked Salmon with Broccoli and Deep-Fried Broccoli Leaves

300 g (10½ oz) salmon fillet
rock or sea salt, grated ginger, chopped herbs
and sugar, to marinate
2 handfuls of tea leaves (Earl Grey is usually
used but variety does not matter)

Sauce
1 tablespoon dry mustard powder
1 tablespoon honey
2 tablespoons white wine vinegar
2 tablespoons chicken stock
200 ml (7 fl oz) good quality olive oil
salt to taste
a large head of broccoli, with its leaves
oil for deep frying
a little dried scallop powder

Begin the recipe twenty-four hours in advance.

The quantities given above are sufficient for four people, but it is obviously more convenient and economical for a restaurant to smoke as large a quantity as possible at any one time. In the accompanying photographs André Jaeger is smoking a whole side of salmon, and the method is described in the captions and in the following text.

Remove all the small bones from the fish, and dry-marinate the fish with the salt, ginger, herbs and sugar for 24 hours in the refrigerator before smoking. The smoking process itself takes about 15 minutes, and at Schaffhausen is carried out in a an old oven in the back yard. The home cook can get as good a result with a lidded wok with an internal rack. Put the tea-leaves in the wok over a high flame and put the salmon on the rack. Cover tightly and when the first wisps of smoke appear remove from the heat, so that the salmon does not cook. Leave, covered, for about 15 minutes, then remove and cool. Slice the salmon thinly.

Mix the sauce ingredients to a thin mayonnaise-like consistency.

Separate the broccoli florets and blanch them for 1 minute in boiling salted water. Drain on a cloth. Cut the washed leaves into thin strips and deep fry in very hot oil. Remove, drain and sprinkle the crisp strips with a little dried scallop powder. Arrange the drained florets on four plates, and drape slices of the tea-smoked salmon over them. Pour a little sauce over the end of each fish slice and top with some deep-fried broccoli leaves.

FOR FOUR PEOPLE

The marinade ingredients are sprinkled on.

The fillets should be completely coated.

Smoking the salmon

Tea is sprinkled over the embers of a wood fire.

The pan of embers is put in the old oven.

The salmon is smoked for about 15 minutes.

Just before serving, the salmon is sliced so thinly that it is translucent.

Shitakecrèmesuppe mit Marinierter, Grillierter Jacobsmuschel

Shiitake Cream Soup with a Marinated Grilled Scallop

8 dried shiitake mushrooms, soaked overnight
300 ml (½ pint) chicken stock
700 ml (1 pint 3 fl oz) single cream
50 g (1¾ oz) unsalted butter
4 large fresh scallops, seasoned and
marinated for 1 hour in 2 teaspoons light
soy sauce
salt, pepper and sugar

Drain the soaked shiitake mushrooms and cook in the chicken stock for 15 minutes. Remove and set aside the mushrooms. Add the cream to the stock and boil for a further 15 minutes. Season with salt, pepper and sugar to taste and then add the butter, cut in pieces, stirring well. Slice the shiitake caps thinly (discarding the stems) and return them to the soup. Heat a heavy frying pan, and in a very little oil, sauté the drained scallops for 30–45 seconds on each side until warmed through but still translucent. Serve one with each bowl – or shell – of soup.

FOR FOUR PEOPLE

Shiitake Cream Soup, served in a seashell

Gänseleber mit Sesam Paniert auf Salat von Grünen Spargel

Breaded Goose Liver with Sesame Seeds and Fresh Asparagus Salad

2 tablespoons fresh white breadcrumbs
1 tablespoon each of white and black
sesame seeds
4 slices fresh goose liver (foie gras) about
1.5 cm (¾ inch) thick
8 spears of green asparagus
1 tablespoon sunflower or arachide oil
for frying
1 tablespoon Chinese black vinegar
1 tablespoon soy sauce
1 tablespoon sunflower or arachide oil
1 teaspoon grated fresh ginger
salt and pepper

Mix the breadcrumbs with the sesame seeds in a soup plate. Season the slices of goose liver with salt and pepper and press them into the breadcrumb-sesame mixture so that each one is firmly coated. Keep cool. Trim and peel the asparagus spears and slice them very finely. Fry them briefly in a little hot oil. Remove to a warm place, add more oil to the pan if necessary, and increase the heat. Sauté the goose liver slices quickly, so that the coating becomes crisp and the centres remain succulent. Mix the Chinese vinegar, soy sauce, the second tablespoon of oil and the grated ginger with the asparagus, divide between four heated plates and place a piece of goose liver on each. Serve immediately.

Note: André Jaeger gets his goose liver from the Landes. Although he would prefer to use duck liver as he feels it is less fatty and tastier, the quality – of prime importance to such a perfectionist – is not always consistent. Here, as in all his recipes, soy sauce is used with caution.

FOR FOUR PEOPLE

Lobster Sautéed with Chinese Cabbage, Black Beans and Chanterelles

Hummer mit Chinakohl, Fermentierte Sojabohnen und Pfifferlingen

Lobster Sautéed with Chinese Cabbage, Black Beans and Chanterelles

a lobster of 700 g–1 kg (1½–2¼ lb)
1 tablespoon arachide oil
half a medium Chinese cabbage, cut in 2 cm
(¾ inch) strips
100 g (3½ oz) fresh chanterelles (girolles),
cleaned
2 teaspoons preserved black beans
1 tablespoon oyster sauce (from Chinese
supermarkets)
2 tablespoons chicken stock
2 tablespoons olive oil
1 teaspoon chopped fresh green coriander
salt and pepper

Kill the lobster and cook in boiling water for just 2 minutes, then plunge in cold water. Shell it as soon as it is cool enough to handle: the meat should still be translucent and almost raw. Cut in chunks.

Heat the arachide oil in a heavy pan and sauté the cabbage and chanterelles for about 2 minutes. Add the black beans and stir-fry quickly for 5–10 seconds. Remove from heat and stir in the oyster sauce and chicken stock. Keep warm over hot water or on the corner of the stove.

Heat the olive oil in a separate pan. When it is hot, throw in the lobster chunks, the coriander and salt and pepper and sauté together for about 30 seconds, or until warm through. Add the entire contents of this second pan to the first, stir well and serve.

FOR FOUR PEOPLE

Langustine in Thailändischen Nudeln Gebacken auf Süss-Sauren Linsensprossen

Langoustines in Crispy Thai Noodles with Sweet-and-Sour Lentil Sprouts

4 langoustines, shelled and de-veined
200 g (7 oz) lentil sprouts
2 tablespoons Chinese red vinegar
2 tablespoons arachide oil
a pinch of freshly grated ginger root
200 g (7 oz) uncooked fresh noodles,
preferably Thai
oil for deep frying
salt, pepper and sugar to taste

Mix the vinegar, oil, ginger and seasonings to make a sweet-and-sour sauce and let the lentil sprouts soak in it for at least half an hour. Spread the noodles out flat. Roll each langoustine up tightly in the noodles (they will open out during cooking). Divide the lentil sprouts in their sauce between four heated plates while you heat the frying oil. When it is very hot, plunge in the noodle-wrapped langoustines for about 10 seconds. The noodles should be crisp and brown. Drain and place on the lentil base and serve immediately. You can use a large lettuce leaf as a base for the lentil sprouts if you wish.

FOR FOUR PEOPLE

Rehrückenfilet mit Fünf Chinesischen Gewürzen auf Linsenkompott mit Polenta-Küchlein mit Tomatensauce

Saddle of Venison with Five Chinese Spices, a Lentil Compote and Polenta Cake with Tomato Sauce

400 g (14 oz) boned saddle of roe deer
100 g (3½ oz) small green lentils, soaked
2 tomatoes, peeled, seeded and diced
1 small aubergine, diced
1 small courgette, diced
1 small red pepper, peeled, seeded and diced
100 g (3½ oz) unsalted butter
Chinese five-spice powder (contains star anise,
fennel, cinnamon, clove and cardamom)
2 tablespoons unsalted butter for frying
salt, pepper and nutmeg

Polenta cake
150 g (5¼ oz) maize meal
4 egg yolks
100 g (3½ oz) unsalted butter
4 teaspoons very thick tomato sauce or
carefully seasoned tomato purée
a little grated parmesan and butter (optional)

Begin by making the polenta cake. Mix the maize meal with 500 ml (18 fl oz) cold water and bring to the boil, stirring. Season with salt, pepper and nutmeg to taste. Boil until the maize meal is cooked (approximately 10 minutes), then remove from the heat, allow to cool slightly and stir in the egg yolks and unsalted butter, cut in pieces, until you have a firm dough. Roll or press out to approximately 1–1.5 cm (½–¾ inch) thick and cut out eight 5 cm (2 inch) rounds with a biscuit cutter. Place four of the rounds on a buttered baking tray and top with a spoonful of tomato sauce. Place a second round of dough on top to form your 'polenta' cake and sprinkle with melted butter and parmesan if wished. Set aside.

Drain the lentils and boil in salted water until *al dente*. Drain and add the diced vegetables and 100 g (3½ oz) butter. Season and reheat to simmering point. Keep warm.

Season the venison (still in a single piece) generously with salt, pepper and the five-spice powder, and pan-fry in 2 tablespoons of hot butter for approximately 5 minutes on each side until it is medium rare. Let it rest on a covered dish for 5–10 minutes, before slicing. Cook the polenta cakes for 5 minutes in a 180°C/350°F/Gas 4 oven.

To serve, divide the lentil compôte between four heated plates, arrange the meat on it and add a polenta cake.

FOR FOUR PEOPLE

Soufflé von Bananen und Aprikosen mit Vanille Eis und Lebkuchensauce

Soufflé of Banana and Apricot with Vanilla Ice-Cream and Gingerbread Sauce

1 banana, peeled and sliced
4 apricots, poached in syrup or tinned in syrup,
stoned, skinned and sliced
a little icing sugar and butter for preparing
the ramekins
200 ml (7 fl oz) full-cream milk
6–7 tablespoons double cream
1 tablespoon commercial gingerbread spices or
pulverized pain d'épice
300 g (10½ oz) plain chocolate, broken into
small pieces
8 eggs, separated
80 g (2¾ oz) sugar
160 g (5½ oz) Quark, or other low-fat
soft cheese
4 heaped tablespoons or scoops vanilla
ice-cream

Butter four large individual soufflé ramekins and dust with icing sugar. Divide the sliced banana between them and follow with the sliced apricot, forming a fruit layer on the bottom of each ramekin. Preheat the oven to 200°C/400°F/Gas 6.

Heat the milk and cream together to simmering point, but do not boil. Add the spices or *pain d'épice* and then the chocolate. Remove from heat and stir until the chocolate had completely melted. Allow to cool a little and divide the mixture between the ramekins, pouring it over the fruit.

Make the soufflé mixture by beating the egg yolks, sugar and Quark in a bowl over hot but not boiling water until the mixture is nearly hand-warm. Whisk the egg whites until stiff and fold carefully into the warm yolk mixture. Quickly place a scoop of ice-cream in each ramekin and pour over the soufflé mixture. Tap each ramekin on a hard surface to eliminate air pockets and add more soufflé mixture if necessary. Put immediately into the preheated oven for 7–10 minutes, until the top is puffed and golden. Dust the top with a little more icing sugar and serve immediately.

FOR FOUR PEOPLE

Saddle of Venison with Five Chinese Spices

Langoustines in Crispy Thai Noodles

Soufflé of Banana and Apricot

209

TURKEY

ADNAN ASLAN

ADNAN ASLAN

DIVAN HOTEL

Istanbul

Text by Jeremy Round

When a Turk thinks of pudding, he or she conjures up one or other of an extraordinary range of traditional dishes, little known in the West, whereas we tend to imagine sticky pastries such as *baklava* are the whole story. The most basic of these dishes are little more than flour or dry semolina fried in butter with a few pine kernels, then plumped up with sugar syrup (*ün* or *irmik helvası*). More delicate – as pale and wobbly as junket – is *mahallebi*, a thin, rice-flour blancmange served with powdered sugar and rosewater. A seasonal favourite is *vişneli ekmek*: a sour cherry relation of Britain's summer pudding.

One of the joys of Middle Eastern cooking lies in recognizing the connections between dishes that are still commonly prepared in that part of the world and those that were once staples of Western European cuisines. A clear example is *tavuk göğsü*, a milky blancmange given its unique, slightly clingy texture by the addition of well-pounded chicken breast meat, as in medieval British recipes.

In the gloomy warren of white-tiled rooms that make up the main basement kitchen of Istanbul's Divan Hotel, head-chefs Hüseyin Özoğuz and Süleyman Özgen preside over a *brigade* that immediately seems interchangable with that of any grand hotel kitchen anywhere in the world. All the roles of the classical French kitchen are filled – *saucier*, pantryman, *pâtissier* and so on. The only chefs that might find themselves under-employed at London's Connaught or Paris's Crillon are the *dönerci* (kebab chef), *zeytin yağlıcı* (braiser of vegetables in olive oil) and Adnan Aslan, from a village near the bleak city of Sivas on the Anatolian plateau, whose surname means 'lion' and who devotes his time to preparing purely Turkish puddings.

Adnan learnt his trade at a *pasthane* (pastry shop) in Kızıltoprak, then served time at two others in the city before moving to the Divan in 1984. He lives with his wife, son and daughter in Üsküdar (Scutari) – the area of Istanbul on the Asian shore of the Bosphorus, where Florence Nightingale had her hospital – but returns as often as he can to see the rest of his family back in the village.

Visiting him at work is to watch an exacting craftsman. The simple preparation of sour-cherry bread gets as much attention as the laborious techniques required for the four other recipes shown here – all classics of Turkish cuisine.

These are basically thickened gels served cold. The variety is in the use of different thickeners, flavourings and ingredients affecting texture. *Keşkül* is milk thickened with almonds; *aşure* is a rose-scented suspension of boiled grains, pulses, nuts and fruit in a water-based gel thickened with boiled and mashed wheat; *fırın sütlaç* is a milk pudding thickened with rice and cornflour, made smooth and fragrant with mastic gum, and baked with beaten egg yolks to form a golden crust. But Adnan's pride is *tavuk göğsü* and the *kazan dibi* versions – rolls of chicken breast pudding burnt to a deep golden brown on the outside, adding the flavour of bitter caramel to the rich, creamy blancmange.

No clue to the Divan Oteli's reputation should be drawn from the fact that the exotica of Istanbul's transvestite population choose the street corner outside from which to pout at late-night kerb-crawlers. But, sitting safely behind a low hedge of shrubs on the open-air terrace of the hotel's *pasthane*, indulging in an enormous portion of the diabolical speciality 'Rokoko' ice-cream cake with chocolate sauce, one is a spectator at the most glamorous, and least idealogically sound, free show in the city.

Cumhürriyet Caddesi (Republic Street), which runs past this side of the hotel, is the nearest thing Istanbul has to a Parisian boulevard. It starts in the centre of the commercial part of the city at Taksim – Istanbul's Piccadilly Circus – then runs as a fast dual carriageway down past cosmopolitan restaurants, airline offices and the Turkish radio broadcasting headquarters, before forking toward the city's two most sophisticated areas of furniture shops and clothes boutiques. Old Stamboul, of the famous dome-and-minaret skyline, is a couple of miles (and centuries) away on the other side of the Golden Horn.

The Divan is the only Turkish-owned hotel to compete with the large international chains in the area around Taksim. It is a comparatively low, modern building – self-effacing beside the angular battleship-grey concrete high-rise of the Sheraton, the mammoth shoe-box Hilton and the fading sixties bulk of the Etap Marmara (formerly the Inter-Continental before a long and debilitating strike over staff pay and conditions).

Each of these hotels is well-used, for different reasons, by monied Istanbul residents with no reason ever to stay at them:

Adnan Aslan (right) preparing Chicken Breast Pudding

the Sheraton for wedding receptions, the Hilton for afternoon tea and its pool, the Etap for its top-floor night-club. But the Divan is perhaps closest to their affections. Its attractions include an informal pub with good buffet offering the likes of grilled bonito, steamed aubergine rissoles, club sandwiches and sour cherry pudding to a relaxed crowd of well-heeled young professionals and tourists. And then there is the restaurant, which offers some of the most elegant interpretations of Turkish dishes in the country. The main dining room, with its satiny dark-wood panelling, is on the first floor of the hotel. Immaculately starched linen cloths, dinner-jacketed staff and a still-life of seasonal fruits, vegetables and flowers at the entrance suggest, rightly, its seriousness of purpose, though its size, its extreme rectangularity and the low ceilings all keep the customer aware that he or she is in a modern hotel.

At lunchtime most of the non-resident customers are besuited businessmen. In the evening too, although by then there is an admixture of smart couples in darker suits and glittery dresses, well-to-do families, local hot-shot moneymen and international travelling salesmen. If conversation flags, you can pass an entertaining minute or two guessing who is the client and who the host.

On the menu, alongside passable internationalist compromises such as 'kanelloni romana' 'şatobrian sos bearnez' and 'pesmelba', there are fine local dishes executed with rare skill and delicacy.

An excellent meal might begin with silky, unctuous *imam bayıldı* (cold aubergine braised in olive oil), then go on to rich, savory *kuzu hünkarbeğendi* (thick lamb stew on a bed of smoky

The main dining room at the Divan has an air of traditional, formal elegance and serious purpose, despite the hotel's unmistakably modern architecture.

Turkish delight (lokum) and sugared almonds. The distinctive quality of the Divan's fistikli lokum is the high proportion of nuts in the mixture.

Adnan Aslan (right) and head chef Hüseyin Özoğuz stand beside a display of Divan puddings. These include Apples Poached in Syrup and Cold Baked Rice Pudding (front centre).

Traditional sweetmeats

aubergine purée) or a spicy grilled lamb dish such as *Urfa kebabı*. Some dishes come smothered in fresh tomato sauce and thick yogurt on a bed of hot, unleavened bread in a lidded, oriental tinned-copper bowl. Then come the puddings, to me the high point. (If you want to try the puddings by themselves, a limited range is sometimes available in the pub and pastry shop.)

If you asked any *Istanbullu* to wax lyrical about the Divan, they would soon come round to the pastry shop. At these tables – both inside and out – a cross-section of rich Istanbul society, from young bloods in Lacoste tee-shirts to ancient women from the last remaining Ottoman families in furs and too much 'Joy de Jean Patou', come to toy with baklava or ice-cream cakes or buy tarts, pastries and gâteaux to take away.

Gradual expansion over the thirty years since the hotel's

foundation means that the Divan's Turkish pastries are now sold not only in this spacious marble shop attached to the hotel, but also at specialist pâtisseries in three other fashionable areas of Istanbul – Moda, Erenköy and Bebek – as well as on Büyükada, the biggest of the Prince's Islands in the Sea of Marmara, during the summer season. Further afield, there are Divan pâtisseries in Ankara, Turkey's capital, and in Amman, Jordan, and Boca Raton, Florida.

The ice-cream factory, bakery and vast complex of kitchens supplying pastries, *lokum* (Turkish delight), chocolates and other sweetmeats for all these outlets is at Sütlüce – an industrial area at the top end of the newly sanitized Golden Horn. Production has recently been mechanized, boosting *lokum* output from forty tons a year to 180, but most of the technology is still charmingly low-grade.

The *lokum*, made just from sugar, water and cornstarch, is

Here the company shows an out-of-the-ordinary commitment to quality. The necessarily high-gluten flour (for a firmer, more elastic dough) is brought up from the areas fringing the fiery plains of Upper Mesopotamia, centred around the sublime cities of Urfa, Mardin and black-walled Diyarbakır. It is in this area of Turkey's southeast that the best *baklava* was traditionally produced – especially in the city of Gaziantep, which is surrounded by pistachio groves. So it is to this area that the Divan sends its pastry chefs to learn their craft. The secret of light, juicy *baklava* is in the thinnest possible leaves of *yufka* (phyllo pastry), brushed with the sweetest butter, baked at a high enough temperature to brown and crisp the top while allowing all the lower leaves to cook through more gently, and drenched with sweet but not cloying sugar syrup at exactly the right temperature.

This is not a process that Turks often attempt at home. Even the simplest syrupy pastries such as *kadayıf* (which looks like shredded wheat) are left to the professionals. A housewife shops for these things as her French counterpart would for apple tarts and *petits pains au chocolat*.

Baklava is cut into rectangular, lozenge or tapering 'carrot' shapes, and can be filled before baking with, for example, sweetened cream (when it is called *kaymaklı*); ground pistachios (*fıstıklı*); chopped walnuts (*cevizli*); or, more rarely, puréed chestnuts (*kestaneli*). Attempts to segment the market have led to the development of *baklavas* flavoured with orange and cocoa powder, but these have not proved popular.

Other traditional pastries made on the same principle as *baklava* – thin leaves of buttered *yufka* baked until crisp then soaked in sugar syrup (unlike Greeks, Turks hardly ever use honey in these syrupy pastries) – include *söbiyet* (rolled crescent shapes like tiny croissants), *bülbül yuvası* (literally 'nightingale nests' – little round pastry cushions filled with choppd nuts), and *dürüm* (slices of a thin sausage-shaped pastry, baked flat with a generous stuffing of pistachios and cream). All these delicacies tend to be eaten more with glasses of black tea between meals than as a dessert course.

mixed by an electrically driven paddle in five kettles heated by steam jackets, each kettle holdng 125 kilos. Flavourings – rose water, citrus oils or whole shelled pistachios – are added for the last two or three minutes, then the mixture is poured into wooden trays dredged with cornstarch and icing sugar, where it sits to set and mature for seventy-two hours.

The distinctive quality of Divan *fıstıklı* (pistachio) *lokum* is the high proportion of nuts in the mixture. In another attempt to stand out from the crowd, the Divan cuts its *lokum* into smaller cubes than its rivals, originally on marble slabs with a simple system of rotating knives, but now with a Greek machine brought over from Athens. But for all this, it is not the *lokum* that has made Divan's name – Haci Bekir, established more than a hundred years ago, is still the city's (and therefore perhaps the world's) best producer. The Divan's fame, rather, springs from its Turkish pastries – *baklava* and its cousins.

The Turks come from nomadic tribes that inhabited the steppes of Central Asia until not much longer than a thousand years ago. Forced by the Chinese ever further east and west, distantly-related groups of these tribes finally found permanent homes in what are present-day Japan, Finland, Hungary and Turkey. Whether or not they brought much of culinary interest with them, each of these groups of peoples seems quickly to have absorbed the native culinary practices of its new home, based around indigenous raw materials.

But, having absorbed them, the ways of cooking they inherited seem to develop very slowly in their hands – perhaps because they are all basically domestic rather than restaurant cuisines. Innovation is certainly not the hallmark of the Hungarian or Japanese kitchens. Neither is it of Turkish cuisine. The skill of the Turkish chef lies in perfecting traditional dishes, and in this respect the cooks in the Divan's factory and Adnan Aslan – in his own small field – are masters.

Cold Baked Rice Pudding

Fırın Sütlaç

Cold Baked Rice Pudding

1 litre (1¾ pints) full-cream milk
250 g (9 oz) sugar
125 g (4½ oz) cooked weight of short-grain rice
½ teaspoon ground crystals of mastic resin (from Greek, Turkish or Cypriot shops)
50 g (1¾ oz) cornflour
2 egg yolks, beaten

Preheat the oven to 220°C/425°F/Gas 7. Bring the milk to the boil in a large saucepan. Stir in the sugar and rice, and then – little by little – the mastic. The pan should still be steaming hot, but should not come back to the boil after these ingredients are added. Take the pan off the heat.

Mix the cornflour with sufficient water to form a thin paste. Whisk this with the egg yolks, then whisk into the hot milk, stirring (over a low flame if necessary) until the mixture thickens.

Pour into individual ovenproof bowls and let the mixture cool to blood temperature. Arrange the bowls in a deep oven tray, pour a little cold water into the tray, then pack ice cubes around the bowls. This is to prevent the mixture boiling while the crust browns.

Place the tray toward the top of the preheated oven for half an hour or so, until the top is dark golden brown. Chill the puddings before serving.

FOR SIX PEOPLE

Aşure

Noah's Pudding

250 g (9 oz) whole grains of wheat
75 g (3 oz) dry chickpeas
75 g (3 oz) dry white haricot beans
50 g (1¾ oz) dried figs
50 g (1¾ oz) dried apricots
50 g (1¾ oz) chopped hazelnuts
50 g (1¾ oz) seedless raisins
750 g (1¾ lb) sugar
2 teaspoons rosewater

Garnish
50 g (2 oz) pine kernels
50 g (2 oz) quartered walnuts
25 g (1 oz) currants
2 tablespoons fresh pomegranate seeds

Soak the wheat, chickpeas and white beans overnight, well covered with cold water, in separate bowls. Drain each and discard the soaking water.

In a large pan, boil the soaked wheat in 2 litres (3½ pints) of fresh water for 3 hours. Leave the wheat in the water that remains. Boil the chickpeas and beans separately until tender. Drain and reserve the liquid. Peel the chickpeas.

Coarsley chop the figs and apricots, reserving 6 thin, neat slices of fig for garnish. Put the chopped figs and apricots to soften in a little water.

Purée half the cooked wheat with enough of the cooking liquid to lubricate the process in a liquidizer or food processor. Strain back into the pan containing the rest of the wheat. Add the chickpeas, white beans, hazelnuts, raisins and the drained, chopped figs and apricots.

Stir in the sugar and bring slowly to the boil. Keep at a lively simmer for 20 minutes, adding more of the reserved liquid if the mixture seems to be getting gluey. Add the rosewater 5 minutes before the end.

Pour the mixture into individual glass dessert bowls. Let it cool a while before decorating with the slices of fig, whole pine kernels, walnut quarters, currants and pomegranate seeds. Serve cold.

Note: this dish may be too sweet for some tastes. If so, reduce the quantity of sugar to 350–500 g (¾–1¼ lb).

FOR SIX PEOPLE

Keşkül

Almond Pudding

2 egg yolks
1 litre (1¾ pints) full-cream milk
250 g (9 oz) sugar
50 g (1¾ oz) grated blanched almonds
50 g (1¾ oz) cornflour
desiccated coconut
ground (unsalted) pistachio nuts

Beat the yolks with a tumbler full of the milk. Bring the rest of the milk to the boil, then pour in the sugar. Cook together for a few minutes. Turn down the flame and pour in the beaten yolk mixture and the grated almonds. Continue to simmer very gently, without boiling, for about 5 minutes. Take off the heat.

Mix the cornflour to a thin paste with a little water, then pour into the steaming hot milk and almond mixture. Stir until it thickens, returning to a low flame briefly if necessary.

Let the mixture cool to blood heat before pouring into separate dessert bowls. Decorate with the coconut and pistachios. Eat cold.

FOR SIX PEOPLE

Almond Pudding

Noah's Pudding

217

Visneli Ekmek Tatlısı

Sour Cherry Bread

half a large square loaf of white bread
500 g (1¼ lb) fresh sour cherries (Morello)
225 g (8 oz) sugar
6–7 tablespoons water
crème Chantilly (sweetened whipped
double cream)
chopped, toasted almonds

Slice off and discard the crusts from the half loaf. Cut the bread into 12 equal, fairly thick, rectangular slices. Remove and discard the stones from the cherries (you should be left with at least 375 g (13 oz) of stoned cherries).

Put the cherries and sugar together in a large pan to rest for half an hour or so. Stir in the water, bring slowly to the boil, then cook at a lively simmer until syrupy – about 15–20 minutes.

Arrange the thick slices of bread in a large shallow baking tray. Toast in a moderate oven (160°C/325°F/Gas 3) for about an hour, until crisp all the way through and a light sandy colour.

Pour the cherries in hot syrup over the hot bread. Put the tray aside to cool.

To serve, arrange two slices of the bread on each dessert plate, with some of the cherries and a spoon of extra syrup. Pipe with crème Chantilly and sprinkle with chopped toasted almonds.

FOR SIX PEOPLE

Tavuk Göğsü

Chicken Breast Pudding

200 g (7 oz) long-grain rice, dry weight
half of 1 chicken breast portion (i.e. quarter of
a hen's total breast meat), off the bone, skinned
and trimmed of all fat
1 litre (1¾ pints) Channel Island milk
(buffalo would be more authentic, if you
could get it)
250 g (9 oz) sugar
powdered cinnamon

First make the *sübye* (thickening mixture). Rinse and pick over the rice. Soak it in cold water overnight. Drain the rice, reserving the water, then liquidize a little at a time in a blender with as little of the soaking water as is necessary to lubricate the process. You should be left with a thick, chalky milk with something of the texture of a cornflour-and-water paste. Be sure to keep the *sübye* cold until you use it: if it becomes warm, it will thicken.

Boil the chicken breast in plenty of water for an hour. Let it cool fully in the water (speed the cooling process by putting the pan in iced water). Drain the cold breast and discard the water. Pick the breast into small bundles of filaments, then rub each bundle hard between moistened palms. Collect the well-rubbed bundles in a small bowl containing a little fresh water, where they should separate further – gradually opening out rather like Japanese paper flowers.

Bring the milk and sugar slowly to the boil together in a large pan – the mixture should not boil until the sugar is completely dissolved. An extra pair of hands is useful now to stir the mixture continuously as you slowly add the *sübye*. When it is all added, tip in the fluffed-up chicken breast meat. Continue boiling gently for 45 minutes, stirring continuously. This process is wearing and tedious but absolutely essential to achieve an authentically silky-textured result.

For the simplest version of Chicken Breast Pudding, pour the mixture into individual serving bowls to cool. Sprinkle with cinnamon and serve cold. For a more sophisticated version – *Kazan Dibi Tavuk Göğsü (Pan-bottom Chicken Breast Pudding)* – pour the mixture at this point into a flat shallow flameproof baking tray, just big enough to take it to a depth of about 1 cm (⅓ inch). Starting with one corner, hold the tin over a medium-hot gas-flame, sweeping the area from time to time with a spatula. The spatula should not scrape the very bottom of the pan, just keep the mixture on top moving. The mixture will begin to catch and burn on the bottom. Let it do this, continuing to sweep across the top of the skin as it forms with the spatula, until the bottom is caramelized to as dark a shade of golden brown as you find appetizing.

Move the pan over the flame to continue the process on another patch until you have burnt the whole to an even shade. Be careful not to let any of the bottom blacken. When you are satisfied with the caramelized bottom, smooth the surface of the chicken-breast mixture with the spatula and put the pan to cool. When it is quite cold, cut the mixture into squares, then – using a relatively inflexible, sharp, flat, wide spatula (a clean wallpaper stripper is ideal) – scrape each square intact from the bottom of the pan. Roll each square up, caramelized side out. For extra succulence, the Divan's version of this pudding has a strip of plain, set, uncaramelized *tavuk göğsü* mixture laid down the middle of the unburnt surface of each square of *kazan dibi* before it is rolled. Serve cold.

FOR SIX PEOPLE

Sour Cherry Bread

Chicken Breast Pudding

Boiled chicken breasts

Shredding the cooked meat

Adding the meat to the milk mixture

Testing the final texture

Caramelizing the pan

Kazan dibi – the golden result

INDEX

Index

The recipes have been edited slightly for the home cook, but are otherwise authentic, although some require, for instance, two ovens at different temperatures and several pairs of hands. These are included because this book is about professional kitchens and the processes by which first-class food is produced are of interest to any serious cook or eater-out. All the dishes were photographed in the restaurant of origin and some of the garnishes photographed are seasonal and may vary slightly from the printed recipe. The imaginative home cook need not treat the presentation as sacred. The principles and the intrinsic quality of the dish, yes; the last shred of decorative radish, no. Use what you have to hand and, above all, your imagination. All the recipes are written for a specific number of people – few in some cases, more where the dish is based on a large ingredient or is time-consuming to prepare — but most of the photographs show a single plated serving with a 'restaurant finish'. Most dishes could be as well served to several people from a communal dish, with a minimum of decoration.

Both metric and imperial measures are given. As almost all the recipes were originally written in metric measures, these should be used wherever possible. Conversion, however flexibly employed, as in this book, can never be completely satisfactory.

RESTAURANT DETAILS

Note: it is necessary to book well in advance, especially if you want accommodation, and always in high season. The details given below are correct at time of going to press, but please check opening days and dates with a current restaurant guide. (For international dialling codes, consult an international directory.)

FRANCE

Michel Guérard
Les Prés d'Eugénie
Eugénie-les-Bains
40320 Geaune
(Landes)   Tel: 58 51 19 01
                            Telex: 540470
                            Fax: 58 51 13 59

Closed 11 December–5 February inclusive

35 apartments

Marc Meneau
L'Espérance
89450 Saint Pere Sous Vézelay
(Yonne)   Tel: 86 33 20 45
                            Telex: 800005
                            Fax: 86 33 26 15

Closed Tuesday lunch and dinner and Wednesday lunch only; January

21 rooms and suites

Dominique Nahmias
Restaurant d'Olympe
8 rue Nicolas Charlet
75015 Paris   Tel: 4734 86 08

Closed Saturday lunch, Sunday lunch and Monday all day; 1–24 August and 22 December–4 January inclusive

Roger Vergé
Le Moulin de Mougins
Quartier Notre-Dame-de-Vie
424 chemin de Moulin
06252 Mougins
(Alpes-Maritimes)   Tel: 93 75 78 24
                            Telex: 970732

Closed Thursday lunch and Monday all day except for dinner 15 July–31 August; 29 January–20 March inclusive

5 rooms and suites

GERMANY

Dieter Müller
Schweizer Stuben
Geiselbrunnweg 11
Wertheim-Bettingen
6980 Wertheim
Baden-Württemberg   Tel: 093 49 3070
                            Telex: 689123

Closed Monday all day and Tuesday lunch; 1–28 January inclusive

Eckart Witzigmann
Restaurant Aubergine
Maximiliansplatz 5
8000 München 2
Bavaria   Tel: 89 59 81 71/72

Closed Sunday all day and Monday all day; 4–24 August inclusive; Christmas Day and New Year's Day

GREAT BRITAIN

Raymond Blanc
Le Manoir aux Quat' Saisons
Great Milton
Oxfordshire
OX9 7PD   Tel: 08446 8881/2/3
                            Telex: 837552

Closed Sunday evening to Tuesday lunch; 24 December–21 January inclusive

7 rooms and 3 suites

John Burton-Race
L'Ortolan
The Old Vicarage
Church Lane
Shinfield
Near Reading
Berkshire RG2 9BY   Tel: 0734 883783

Closed last week February–first week March and last week August–first week September

Anton Mosimann
Mosimann's
11b West Halkin Street
London SW1X 8JL   Tel: 01 235 9625
                            Fax: 01 245 6354

(Members only; private rooms available)

David Wilson
The Peat Inn
Peat Inn
Cupar
Fife KY15 5LH   Tel: 033484 206

Closed Sunday all day and Monday all day; 2 weeks in January, 2 weeks in November

8 suites

HUNGARY

Imre Spielberger
The Café-Restaurant
New York-Hungaria
Lenin krt. 9–11
Budapest VII   Tel: 223 849
                            Telex: 224 987

IRELAND

Myrtle Allen
Ballymaloe House
Shanagarry
Near Midleton
Co. Cork   Tel: 021 6152531
                            Telex: 75208

Closed 24–26 December inclusive

29 rooms and 5 suites

ITALY

Annie Feoldé
Ristorante Enoteca Pinchiorri
via Ghibellina 87
50122 Firenze
(Toscana)   Tel: 055 242777
                            Fax: 55 24 49 83

Closed Sunday all day and Monday lunch August; Christmas

Gianluigi Morini and Valentino Marcattilii
Ristorante San Domenico
via Gaspare Sacchi 1
Imola
40026 Bologna
(Emilia-Romagna)   Tel: 0542 29000

Closed Monday all day

SPAIN

Victoria Roque
Restaurante Azulete
Via Augusta 281
08017 Barcelona   Tel: 3 203594

Pedro Subijana
Restaurante El Bodegon
Pinar 15
28006 Madrid   Tel: 262 31 37/262 88 44

Closed Saturday midday and Sunday; festivals and August

Pedro Subijana cooks on Wednesdays only

Pedro Subijana
Restaurante Akelaŕe
Igueldo
San Sebastián   Tel: 21 20 52/21 40 86

Closed Sunday night and Monday all day; 1–15 June and all December

SWITZERLAND

André Jaeger
Rheinhotel Fischerzunft
Rheinquai 8
Schaffhausen   Tel: 053 25 32 81
                            Telex: 897162
                            Fax: 053 24 32 85

Closed 3 weeks in February

12 rooms

TURKEY

Adnan Aslan
Divan Otel
Cumhuriyet Caddesi
Şişli
Istanbul   Tel: 1 1314 100
                            Telex: 22402